C000173765

A guide to the Pilgrims' Way
and North Downs Way

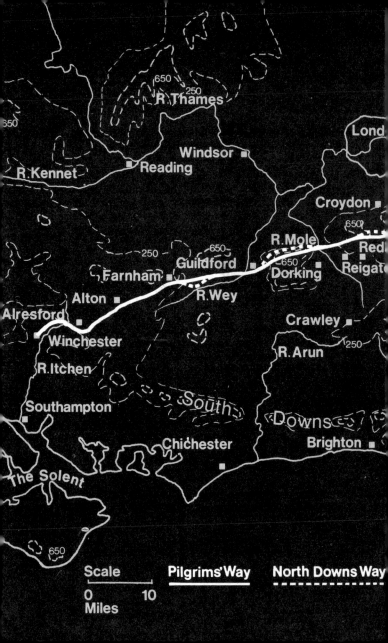

a guide to the
Pilgrims' Way
and North Downs Way

Christopher John Wright

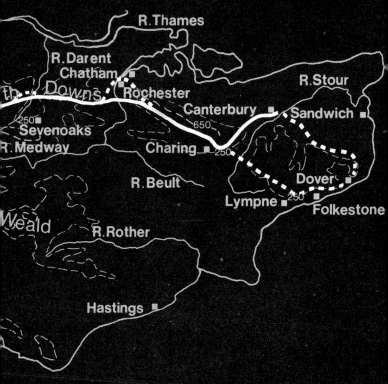

R.Thames

R.Darent
Chatham

th . Downs   Rochester

250
Sevenoaks

R.Medway

Charing

R.Beult

R.Stour

Canterbury   Sandwich
650

250

Dover
Lympne   250
Folkestone

Weald

R.Rother

Hastings

Constable

First published in Great Britain 1971
by Constable & Company Ltd
3 The Lanchesters
162 Fulham Road
London W6 9ER
© 1971 by Christopher John Wright
Second edition 1977
3rd edition 1981
Reprinted 1985
4th edition 1993
ISBN 0 09 4722307
Set in Palatino 9 pt by
CentraCet Ltd, Cambridge
Printed in Great Britain at
The Bath Press, Avon

Other Constable guides by the same author:
A guide to the Pennine Way
A guide to Offa's Dyke Path
A guide to the Pembrokeshire Coast Path

and by Cicerone Press
The Westmorland Heritage Walk

Contents

Illustrations

Acknowledgements

The author would like to thank the open-air organizations, fellow travellers, innkeepers, rectors and churchwardens and many others for their often unwitting help and guidance given whilst preparing this book, and for their valued criticism and support.

He would also like to thank Messrs Constable & Company Ltd, the publishers of Hilaire Belloc's *The Old Road* and Robert Goodsall's *Pilgrimage to Canterbury – A Progress through Kent* for the valued permission to use material therefrom, particularly on those matters concerning the history and the characteristics of the route, as outlined in the preliminary chapters.

The interior views of Winchester Cathedral and of Canterbury Cathedral are reproduced by kind permission of Pitkins Pictorials Ltd and A. W. Kerr Esq respectively.

Introduction

Beyond the fringe of the sprawling suburbs of London's metropolis are many wild, unspoiled acres of pine and heather, fertile valleys and rich woodlands, but perhaps the best-known feature is the long chalk ridge of the North Downs, crossing the middle of the country from west to east, from Salisbury Plain to the Channel Coast.

The escarpment of the North Downs was from the earliest times an important link between the prehistoric settlements in Wiltshire and the Continent. Stretching in a great arc around the northern edge of the Weald, the North Downs provided an almost continuous passageway for traffic. A trackway was made along the lower slopes of the escarpment when neither the Downs above, exposed to the elements, nor the vale below, with heavy clay soil and thick woods, were suitable for cross-country travellers.

The track long popularly regarded and now known as the Pilgrims' Way represents a large part of this route, and can still be clearly traced as it wanders through the green countryside from Winchester to Canterbury. The first authoritative account of the Pilgrims' Way was Hilaire Belloc's *The Old Road* of 1904, by which time the 'pilgrim' myth and legend had become firmly established. Subsequent antiquaries and mapmakers extended the application of pilgrim traditions, and the name found a place on Ordnance Survey maps which has been retained ever since. Belloc in his work was at great pains to build up the pilgrim aspect of this route between Winchester and Canterbury, but there is neither sufficient evidence to confirm or disprove its use to any degree of certainty.

Thomas Becket, Chancellor of England, had been elected Archbishop of Canterbury in 1162 by command of Henry II. Because he had excommunicated the King's followers, Becket was murdered in his cathedral eight years later on 29 December 1170, an event which altered the course of history in England. Henry had good reason to regret his hasty words, 'Will no one rid me of this turbulent priest?' for the result was, ironically, the opposite of his intentions; the cause of friction between King and Archbishop had been Henry's determination to increase royal jurisdiction over the existing Laws and Courts of the Church, but this conflict was immediately resolved by the horror-stricken monarch yielding his ground.

The Shrine of Saint Thomas became a centre of medieval pilgrimage from all parts of Britain and Europe, and brought fame and prosperity to Canterbury. Because of the political history and other particular influences at that time, Winchester was one of the principal starting-points for the religious pilgrimage to Canterbury, and the general or popular conception of the ancient trackway thus became established.

The pilgrimages reached their height towards the end of the fourteenth century, the period when Geoffrey Chaucer wrote his *Canterbury Tales*, one of the earliest and best-loved poetic works in the English language. The pilgrims whose progress is related by Chaucer followed another ancient route, the Roman Watling Street, which runs from London through Rochester and Canterbury to Dover. That particular journey started from the 'Tabard' in Southwark and seemed to have occupied the five days between 16 and 20 April 1386, a company of 'wel nyne and twenty', each pledged to tell two tales to while away the time on the long road to Canterbury.

Although the route followed by Chaucer was perhaps the most popular, it does not mean that there was little or no traffic on the North Downs route at the same time. Probably it was used extensively in both directions, for the ancient trackway was the obvious direct link for through traffic from east to west. Even as late as the seventeenth century this terraceway continued to be a useful road for those travellers wishing to avoid paying turnpike tolls. There is general agreement that there was an ancient trackway, but, unlike the South Downs Ridgeway, it was in part a ridge track and in part a terrace track below the escarpment, just as the North Downs Way is today. The two routes – the Pilgrims' Way and the North Downs Way – coincide for much of their respective lengths.

Now, for much of its route, the Pilgrims' Way is forgotten by modern traffic. In places grassy track, at others metalled but quiet lanes, the Pilgrims' Way affords the cyclist and walker a chance to enjoy the countryside whilst following in the steps of history. There is a wealth of material to interest the traveller – prehistoric monuments, ancient castles and churches, ecclesiastical palaces and great houses, fascinating towns and beautiful villages. The features of natural beauty and the places of historic interest ensure an interesting tour for those who care for the past and for unspoiled countryside.

'Whan that Aprille with his shoures soote
The droughte of Marche hath perced to the roote, . . .
Than longen folk to goon on pilgrimages . . .
And specially, from every shires ende
Of Engelond, to Canterbury they wende,
The holy blisful martir for to seke
Than hem hath holpen, whan that they were seke.'

Brief history of the route

Six great ridges of high land radiate from the plateau of Salisbury Plain, and it is safe to assume that Avebury and Stonehenge drew the importance of their sites from this convergence: for these continuous high lands would present the first natural highways by which primitive people could gather from all parts of the island.

Radiating like the spokes of a wheel they are, clockwise:

1　The Cotswolds
2　The Berkshire Downs and Chilterns
3　The North Downs
4　The South Downs
5　The Dorset Downs
6　The Mendip Hills

From their heights even today will be seen the remains of woodland which made the valleys and the wealds originally far more difficult to traverse. By reason of greater dryness, ease of contours and height, the turf-covered ridges of chalk were an ideal original means of communication.

The North Downs had especial value in very early times, because Britain had similarities in religion, language and blood with the Continent. The passage westwards from the Straits of Dover to the centres of Hampshire and Wiltshire must have been by far the most important line of traffic in Britain, because:

i　The Straits of Dover are the natural entry into the country from the Continent.

ii　The Thames was the northern boundary of settled England until the coming of the Romans.

iii　The west of the island contained its principal supplies of minerals – tin, lead and iron.

iv　Southern England had the best cultivated land, the best climate and was in close touch with the civilization of the

Continent. Before the Industrial Revolution the centre of gravity of England lay south of the Thames.

The ridge of the North Downs is cut by five rivers – the Stour, Medway, Darent, Mole and Wey; it has moderately steep slopes to the south, is dry and chalky, bare of trees and not often indented by coombes or projecting spurs. The clean-cut embankment of chalk stretches for miles, along which man could hardly deviate, and led from the coast to Farnham. No definite ridge continues west of Farnham, but high rolling downs give good enough going along a watershed which avoided the crossing of rivers.

But if the ancient trackways led from the Straits of Dover to Stonehenge and beyond to Cornwall, why did Winchester come to absorb the traffic of the west and become the political centre of southern England, and why did Canterbury, an inland town, become the goal of this long journey?

The prevalent winds and tidal conditions of the Straits of Dover necessitated a multiplicity of harbours for the crossing from France. Persons embarking from Boulogne, Ambleteuse, Sangatte or Calais might at any time land at one of several points along the Kentish coast – Winchelsea, Rye, Lympne (Portus Lemanis), Dover, Richborough (Rutupiae), Ramsgate or Reculvers (Regulbium). These several points created Canterbury – an inland town for trade and defence, a point of concentration to the interior from the coast, and the town was established near to the tide, but without the loss of fresh water.

Caesar landed at Deal, but had to take the fort at Canterbury, and Augustine fixed the origins of Christianity in England here although he landed at Richborough. Thus Canterbury became the great nucleus of English worship and the origin, under Rome, of English discipline and unity in the faith for nearly 700 years. At last, influencing as much as influenced by the event, the murder of its great Archbishop in the later twelfth century lent it, for the next 300 years, a position unique in Europe. Canterbury during those 300 years was almost a sacred city.

As Canterbury was made by the peculiarity of the Straits and the confusing complexity of meeting tides, so Winchester was made by the peculiar conditions of the Channel. The Normandy peninsula, jutting towards the Isle of Wight, produced a crossing second only to the Straits. Although almost three times wider than the Straits, it has:

i   Protection for the estuaries of the Seine, Solent and Southampton Water.

ii   High hills inland as landmarks for navigation – St Catherine's Hill, 830 ft/253 m, and Barfleur Hill, 510 ft/155 m.

iii   Refuges at Yarmouth, Newton, Cowes, and Ryde on the Isle of Wight, and Lymington, Beaulieu, Hamble, Portsmouth, Porchester, Langstone and Chichester on the mainland.

The submerged valley of Southampton Water continues inland to the valley of the Itchen, and the town of Winchester serves these Channel ports as Canterbury serves the Kent ports. The site of Winchester was central, it held the key to the only good middle passage the Channel afforded, and it was destined to become a capital.

A road must therefore have set out from Winchester to join the old east-west road from Stonehenge to Dover, and it would have led directly northwards towards Newbury. Later attempts were made at a short cut, to the east, and the Roman road to Silchester may have taken as its base some British track passing through Basingstoke. This was later superseded by a more direct route even further to the east, along the valleys of the Itchen and Wey, to join the original track at Farnham.

The old road then had Winchester for a new origin and Canterbury as a new goal. The neglected western end from Stonehenge to Farnham came to be called 'The Harrow Way' (from Hoar, or Old, Way); it fell into disuse and is now hardly to be recognized at all. Likewise the section of the Downs from the Stour to Folkestone became superseded, with the importance of Canterbury.

As Winchester began to assert itself as the centre of southern England – of open, cultivated, rich and populated

England – the road grew in importance, the main artery between the west and the Straits. Thus Canterbury and Winchester, having so much in common, grew up over 700 years as the centres of English life – Winchester as a capital, and Canterbury as a ruler of religion.

The Romans in this frontier province set up their capital at York, but London, Winchester and Canterbury were also great centres. One was the king's town, the other the primate's; the political and ecclesiastical capitals of the country. In the Dark Ages Winchester had its St Swithin and in the Middle Ages Canterbury, with the murder of Becket, put out the light of Winchester and carried on the tradition of a shrine for continued pilgrimage.

Doubtless the road would have vanished completely had it not been for one general and three particular influences, which, between them, have preserved a portion of it sufficient to serve as a basis for the exploration of the remainder:

1   Unlike the rest of the Roman empire, the British trackways survived and were not killed by the Roman roads. The political history of Britain at this period generally preserved antiquity.
2   The great pilgrimage to the shrine of St Thomas at Canterbury arose immediately after his murder in 1170. Helped by the Crusades between 1065 and 1292 to liberate the Holy Land from the Turks, the orders and appeals of a united church began to circulate throughout Christendom, men travelled and England became united. Henry II was perhaps the last king who thought of Winchester as his chief town; it was decaying and London more and more was becoming the capital of England. The roads from London to Southampton, Canterbury and the Channel ports would grow in importance, and the old road would decay. There was less traffic between west and east – the metals of Devon and Cornwall had lost their economic position and the iron of the Sussex Weald had taken their place. Winchester began to decline in importance. Then came the murder of Thomas Becket which brought to a head the quarrel between the Soul and the State. All the west

suddenly began to stream to Canterbury, and Becket's tomb became, after Rome, the chief shrine of Christendom. St Thomas was murdered on the 29 December 1170, and for 50 years his feast had been kept on that day, but on the jubilee 7 July became the new and more convenient date upon which Canterbury was most sought. But the habit of such a journey had now grown so general that every season saw a pilgrimage. The pilgrims were compelled to take the old road because of its peculiar association of antiquity and religion, and the pilgrimage thus saved the road. But the pilgrims did not always follow the ancient way step by step. A prehistoric ford was lost in favour of a bridge or ferry, and sometimes the path was left to visit some notable shrine.

3   The establishment of the turnpike system in the eighteenth century perpetuated the use of the old road, as the tolls chargeable upon these new and firm roads furnished a very powerful motive for drovers and pack riders to use an alternative route where such charges would not fall upon them. The Hog's Back summit road, for example, was a turnpike, but the old track lower down on the south side of the hill linking Seale and Puttenham was once more used as a way between Farnham and Guildford.

4   The existence of the chalk was a most important influence. It was never cultivated and therefore invited the wayfarer who was not permitted to trespass on tilled land, and a visible track was soon worn down by the feet and vehicles of travellers. There are many chalk pits on the hills, and almost certainly their presence has been one of the reasons for the road's survival in later centuries. The chalk, as well as the resulting lime when it was burnt, had to be transported, and the old road provided the obvious east-west route. Some are of great age, and nature, exerting her inexorable power, has clothed them in a mantle of greenery so that they are barely noticed. These chalk pits generally lie on the left-hand side of the route when proceeding east, because the Downs form the northern protection of the old road, and the quarry floors are at the same level as the trackway.

A general survey

The route of the Pilgrims' Way between Winchester and Canterbury is some 120 miles/192 km long, and the route of the North Downs Way between Farnham and Folkestone is 123 miles/209 km long, or via Canterbury to Dover 130 miles/ 217 km.

These two routes between them follow the entire length of the North Downs in Surrey and Kent for much of their respective distances – 28 miles/44 km at the western end from Winchester to Farnham belong to the Pilgrims' Way, and about 22 miles/35 km at the eastern end between Wye and Folkestone belong to the North Downs Way: apart from the diversion of the NDW to cross the Medway, these two routes cover substantially the same ground for the distance in between.

A branch of the NDW leads off from near Wye and the River Stour, first following the PW to Canterbury, and then to Dover and back along the cliffs to Folkestone. This loop is a concession to the PW, and although it doesn't follow the North Downs it takes in some orchard country typical of the 'Garden of England' and is only slightly longer than the main route from Wye to Folkestone.

The NDW was the second of the great chalk ridgeways to be made into a long-distance footpath, and it shares many of the characteristics of the South Downs Way and of the Ridgeway Path, although it is longer than both of these routes. It has the same short, springy turf and smoothly rounded hillsides, and a soil basically of chalk; but the hills have rather less downland because of the layer of clay with flints that covers the chalk and gives rise to heavy tree growth.

The Downs are cut by a number of river valleys, all flowing northward – the Wey, the Mole, the Darent, the Medway and the Stour. These rivers rise in the Weald, and the fact that they cut through the chalk and are not deflected by it suggests that the valleys were formed at a time when the Weald was at a much higher level.

For a greater part of its length the North Downs gives superb views southwards over the Weald of Kent and Sussex. The scarp falls away directly to the pasture land and villages in the gault clay and greensand, the greensand forming a secondary ridge where there is much heathland and natural conifer growth. Beyond this stretches the clay of the High Weald itself, with the South Downs visible in the far distance. On the Downs the deciduous woodland is heavy and varied, and in addition to beech, oak and ash there is much juniper, yew, whitebeam, and box.

The whole length of the North Downs has been designated as the Kent & Surrey Area of Outstanding Natural Beauty. There are large areas of land owned by the National Trust at Ranmore Common, Box Hill, Colley Hill, and Reigate Hill for public access, and many other places, such as Newlands Corner, have been acquired by the county councils as access land and laid out with car parks and picnic areas, because of the popularity of the North Downs as a recreation area for those people who come in large numbers by car to walk, picnic or simply to enjoy the view.

Winchester to the River Wey

The Pilgrims' Way starts outside the W door of Winchester Cathedral and runs northwards through the town to the banks of the River Itchen, a famous trout stream, which it follows upstream to Alresford by footpaths and minor lanes. From Alresford to Farnham the route follows some minor lanes, but for the most part it follows the line of the A31 main road to Alton and down the valley of the infant River Wey, running out of Hampshire and into Surrey just to the West of Farnham.

The North Downs Way starts near Farnham railway station, and a way leads up the Wey valley, then crosses the river and rises to higher ground just N of Crooksbury Hill, S of the

Pilgrims' Way. Continuing eastwards, the NDW crosses heathland below the ridge of the Hog's Back, a thin ridge of chalk just wide enough to carry the busy A31: here the North Downs are at their slenderest. The NDW passes through pines and firs, passing close to, and S of, the village of Seale, and enters Puttenham by way of Puttenham Common. The PW follows the A31 out of Farnham as far as Runfold, then follows a minor road through Seale parallel to the NDW, and both routes join at Puttenham. From here to St Martha's church the two routes are coincident, passing N of Compton and under the Guildford Bypass, skirting the N side of Losely House, with views of the park on the one hand and Guildford Cathedral and University on the other. At the Guildford-Godalming road, on a sandy height overlooking the River Wey Navigation, are the remains of St Catherine's Chapel, the siting of which inevitably suggests that it was built there for the use of the pilgrims.

The River Wey was crossed by a ferry, once operated for pilgrims: it is no longer in use. The river is now crossed by a new footbridge, but one may make a detour into Guildford.

Guildford to the River Mole

East of St Catherine's the PW/NDW runs first along the N slopes of the wooded Chantries ridge and then straight over St Martha's Hill with its church placed squarely on the top. E of St Martha's, the NDW makes an abrupt climb of Albury Downs to the A25 at Newlands Corner. It then runs along the escarpment of the North Downs at a general height of well over 600 ft/180 m, overlooking the Tillingbourne valley, the A25, and the villages of Albury, Shere, Gomshall and Abinger Hammer. The ridge is heavily wooded, planted predominantly with conifers, and the path along the forestry rides and tracks gives few distant views. After Netley Heath, however, the path crosses Hackhurst Downs where there is thinner growth of mixed deciduous woodland and bushes, with better views; and it follows the edge round White Downs to Ranmore Common.

The PW meanwhile drops down from St Martha's to the villages of Albury and Shere in the valley of the Tilling Bourne. Between Shere and Dorking the line of the PW can be seen but not followed, so the path takes a line up to Hackhurst Downs to follow the NDW to Ranmore Common. The Mole valley opens out in front of you with Box Hill ahead and Dorking below: this break in the hills made by the Mole was used by the Romans to take Stane Street to London. The routes burrow under the busy A24 road N of Dorking, to reach the Mole at the foot of Box Hill.

Box Hill to the Surrey/Kent boundary

Our routes cross the River Mole, either by the famous stepping-stones or by the footbridge a little way downstream if these are covered. The path climbs Box Hill, passing through a thick cover of whitebeam, yews, and junipers, as well as oak, beech, and box on the escarpment, well above the line of the PW. The NDW continues along the upper edge of the Downs to Betchworth Hill, above the great scars made by the chalk pits and lime-works, and then joins the PW at Pebble Combe, where the path follows the line of the Downs round the valley. The two routes are coincident along the Buckland, Juniper, Colley, and Reigate Hills, and continue so for several miles. This section, generally below the woods, provides some of the pleasantest views in Surrey, the prospect extending across the Weald ridge of Ashdown Forest as far, on a clear day, as the South Downs, where Chanctonbury Ring may be picked out.

Behind these hills runs the South Orbital Road M25, and we pass over this just W of the A23 road after having crossed the Reigate road by the bridle-bridge and passed through Gatton Park.

The way out of Merstham is above the large quarries, avoiding the great multi-level interchange of the M23/M25 and up to White Hill, where it joins the route of the NDW again. The two routes pass over Gravelly Hill together, and run past Fosterdown Iron Age Fort to the busy A22 Eastbourne Road

N of Godstone, which is crossed by a footbridge. For the remaining stretch to the county boundary at road B2024, the NDW takes the line of the PW some way down the scarp slope, because the crest of the Downs is followed by a road and there is a large quarry and lime-works at Oxted, and plantations at Limpsfield. The line of the PW across Titsey Park cannot be followed, and a sunken lane takes us up from the plantation to Botley Hill, where the North Downs reach their highest point at 882 ft/270 m, though the thick woods deny us views over the fertile Vale of Holmesdale. The B269 is followed downhill to Titsey Church, on the line of the PW, and a minor road is followed for several miles, taking the PW out of Surrey and into Kent. The NDW follows a higher line through the woods, across the B2024 to Tatsfield church and the county boundary.

County Boundary to the Medway
From the county boundary the PW follows minor roads at the foot of the hills to Chevening Park, but has to make a detour round the N side of the park before reaching the Sevenoaks bypass. The NDW on the other hand follows the best course it can on the mid-slopes of the hills above, descending to Dunton Green and across the bypass and on to Otford in the Darent valley. Otford is a busy village which contains the remains of a palace of the Archbishop of Canterbury, near the site of a Roman villa, while Lullingstone Roman villa, down the valley near Eynesford, may also be visited.

From Otford to Wrotham, the PW follows a metalled road through Kemsing to St Clere, so the NDW avoids this, takes a steep climb up the nose of the Downs, and makes the best of an irregular course through fields and woods, then descends quickly to St Clere to take advantage of a green lane continuation of the PW at the lower level, which it follows to the A20 at Wrotham.

At Wrotham there is no special crossing over the busy and difficult A20, but this is best done at the large roundabout above the village. It then follows a continuation of the metalled PW again. After a short way along this road, the NDW strikes up through the woods to run almost parallel to the A227 for 2 miles/4 km to the 'Vigo' Inn, soon dropping down to join the PW above Trottiscliffe.

Just below our route is the megalithic tomb of the Coldrum Stones, a burial chamber of unhewn stones, once covered with a mound. This Neolithic barrow, and others in the area, are matched by a similar monument on the other side of the valley, Kit's Coty, and by the Countless Stones, all formed from sarsen stones, or sandstone boulders, which were no doubt found scattered near the sites. Their siting has been adduced as evidence that early man did in fact make a detour some way down the Medway valley instead of venturing across the wide plain upstream, and that the crossing-place was probably at Snodland.

The NDW however follows the gentle curve of the Downs northwards beyond Whitehorse Wood and Holly Hill, along the escarpment of the wide Medway valley. The old tracks that we follow are tree-lined or pass through woodland of beech, hornbeam, and yew. The views extend across the river to the distant horizon, across an intricate landscape of woods, fields and orchards. The NDW would have crossed the river just slightly downstream of Snodland, if the ferry at Halling had still been in operation, but the M2 Medway Motorway bridge with its pedestrian crossing provided a suitable alternative without entering the urban area of Rochester.

The Medway to the Stour

The PW crosses the Medway near Burnham and follows a road to the prehistoric sites of Kit's Coty and the Countless Stones. The NDW on the other hand, having crossed the Medway bridge, crosses Wouldham Downs and Burford Downs to Bluebell Hill, where it descends the hill beside the busy A229 to Kit's Coty, and then follows the PW to the White Horse Stone. An alternative would be to cross the A229 to Aylesford Common and pass beneath the radio masts to Westfield Wood, because here the NDW leaves the PW to follow a higher, but parallel, course above Boxley to the A249 at Detling.

Between Detling and Hollingbourne the PW follows metalled lanes through Thurnham and Broad Street, but the NDW runs at a higher level.

Both Ways join at Hollingbourne and they follow a rough track all the way to Charing and Boughton Lees in the Great Stour valley, a distance of about 12 miles/19 km, only about 2 miles/3 km of which are on metalled roads – the longest stretch where both routes are coincident. Parallel to this route runs Watling Street, now the busy A20, passing through Harrietsham, Lenham and Charing – charming villages with medieval churches, old inns, manor houses, and cottages of brick and timber, set in a landscape of woods, orchards, hopfields, parkland, and farms.

It is at Boughton Lees that the two routes divide. The NDW route continues across the Stour valley to Wye and then climbs the Downs to follow what is probably the most open section of the route past Folkestone and along the coast to Dover. The 'Canterbury Loop' keeps to the line of the PW down the valley to Chilham and on through orchards to Canterbury. Here the PW ends, but the NDW Alternative passes through more orchards and the E Kent coalfield, and then follows the line of a Roman road due S to Dover.

We shall follow the main NDW from the Stour to the sea, and then return to complete the PW and make the Canterbury Loop.

The Stour to the Sea

From the Great Stour valley the main NDW route picks up the line of the Downs again and follows it to Folkestone. A track runs south-eastwards from Boughton Lees through fields and orchards and across an old bridge over the river into the little town of Wye, where the University of London has an agricultural college and farm. The path climbs up to the Downs, past Hastingleigh and proceeds along the crest as far as is possible. The clear-cut character of the path as a ridge route tends to be spasmodic, and there is a short descent beyond Brabourne to Stowting, a village which lies in an embayment of the hills so that it is surrounded on three sides by the lowish hills.

Maps mark a route below the hills in the vicinity of Brabourne and Postling as the PW, but there is no substance to justify the credibility of such a claim in this part of Kent.

From Stowting, the scarp continues to be fragmented but the path keeps to the principle of following the high ground and avoiding numerous small roads. At Etchinghill the Downs project forward to one of the highest points in this stretch at Brockman's Bushes, and the route passes behind these hills to traverse and climb an attractive coombe, and to join the final section of ridge which runs into Folkestone. For most of the way the path runs close to the road on the crest of the ridge, and it takes us over Cheriton Hill, Cherry Garden Hill, Castle Hill, and Round Hill, where we can look over Folkestone to the sea. After crossing the main road A260 on the outskirts of the town near Sugarloaf Hill, the path follows Cretway Down along a road to the 'Valiant Sailor' on the A20.

The path continues along the cliff-tops to Dover, first above The Warren, an area where the chalk has slid over the under-lying slippery clay and forms one of the great classical land-slips of the country. At the far end of The Warren you become more conscious of the new A20 which services the Channel Tunnel. There is then a clear and breezy walk over the turf of Shakespeare Cliff, where the path finishes overlooking the port of Dover spread out below.

The Canterbury Loop
At Boughton Aluph, just before Wye, at a point overlooking the Stour valley, the Canterbury Loop Alternative branches off on a sudden turn NE to follow the PW, to ascend to Soakham Downs and into the great forest of Challock, where there is a clear track between the trees. The path curves around the N side of Godmersham Park and then skirts the eastern boundary of Chilham Park to enter Chilham village.

From Chilham, the Way passes mainly through orchard

country by Chartham Hatch and the earthworks of Bigbury Fort, to Harbledown and Canterbury. The NDW stops on the outskirts of the city, but the PW continues right up to the door of the cathedral.

The NDW starts again on the E side of Canterbury on the Sandwich road, leaving the A257 near the prison, to stride a SE course parallel to the A2 towards Dover. It passes through more orchards to Patrixbourne, and over Barham Downs, close to the A2 overlooking the Nail Bourne and with fine views to the NW. The path runs parallel to the A2 for 3 miles/ 5 km then bends away E into Womenswold.

Ahead are the Kent Colliery areas at Eyethrone and Betteshanger, but the path avoids these by bending S to Shepherdswold, then turning E and NE through Waldershare Park where there are fine beeches, limes, and chestnuts. A mile beyond the park, after the crossing of the A256, the path makes a sharp turn at Ashley, to join the Roman road which ran between Dover and Richborough (N of Sandwich) where the Romans under Claudius landed in AD 43. The path's final few miles are a straight run, due S, and mostly over flattish land, into Dover.

Route finding

The Pilgrims' Way

The route of the Pilgrims' Way from Winchester to Canterbury is a distance of about 120 miles/192 km, a journey of some 8–11 days. Finding the route is not always easy, even with the help of the modern Ordnance Survey 'Landranger' maps. The old route has been lost in many places and it is often difficult or impossible to locate it; it was not paved nor was it embanked. It has often disappeared from the clay, always from marshy soil, and only on the chalk has it preserved its unmistakable outline.

Modern highways and road improvements, and new intensive farming methods, are together altering the face of the land faster than at any time since the war. The route has been obliterated in several places, and in others its line is purely conjectural, so that even eminent archaeologists differ in choosing the possible alternatives.

Just over 80 miles/128 km of the total length of the route are certain and fixed – i.e., two-thirds of the distance – but there are no great unbroken stretches between the lengths of existing road. No gap between the known lengths is greater than 7 miles/11 km, and some lengths of the road stretch 10, 13 and even 15 miles (16, 21 and 24 km) without a break. Between the lengths of known road it is reasonably easy to conjecture the 'probable' line of the remainder of the route.

The route has several principal characteristics:

1 The road never turns a sharp corner save to avoid a precipitous cliff face or sudden bend in a river. It is not always straight like a Roman road, but it is always direct.

2 The road always keeps to the southern slope where it clings to the hills, and to the northern bank (i.e. southern slope) of a stream. The slope which faces S is drier. There are four exceptions to this, but no stretch is longer than

a mile/1.6 km in length:
Gatton, Arthur's Seat, Godmersham, and Weston Wood.

In the case of the first three an excellent reason can at once be discovered: the road goes just N of the crest in order to avoid the long jutting-out spur with its re-entrant curve. This is because the re-entrant curve would be worse going, wetter, than even the short excursion to the N of the crest. In the fourth case there is no satisfactory explanation; the one true exception to the rule.

3   The road does not climb higher than it needs to. It flanks the ridge in several places, save for the obvious reasons:

a)   To avoid too steep a slope for comfort.

b)   To avoid the ins and outs presented by a number of projecting ridges – as at Colley Hill, Bletchingley, and Boughton Aluph. Once on a ridge the road will continue, especially if advantage can be taken of a descending spur – as after Godmersham Park down to Chilham. The road would probably gain the slope and run along about 50–100 ft/15–30 m above the valley floor because of

i)   A better view of the way ahead;

ii)   a better drained clay slope where the land would be drier than the clay of the lower levels;

iii) being above the margin of cultivation.

4   Wherever the road goes right up to the site of a church, it passes upon the S side of that site. (On its route the Way passes right up against 13 existing or ruined churches – Kings Worthy, Itchen Stoke, Bishops Sutton, Seale, Puttenham, St Martha's, Shere, Merstham, Titsey, Snodland, Burham, Boughton Aluph, and Chilham. In the case of eight of these, it passes right up against the S porch, and in two (Bishops Sutton and Seale) it misses them by a few yards. St Martha's stands on the line exactly, whilst the route at Shere and Albury is doubtful.)

The road commonly goes N of a village and should, therefore, commonly go N of all churches. Indeed, it does pass many churches to the N, but it always leaves them to one side – as at Chevening, Lenham, Charing and the rest. It never goes close to their sites.

This rule is important when one considers the spot in which a church stands or has stood, and where, at the same time, the track is doubtful and has to be determined.

5   In crossing a river valley, the road makes invariably for the point where spurs of dry ground and rising ground come closest upon either side and leave the narrowest gap of marshy land between. Primitive man would keep to a ford, seek shallow water, seek gravel rather than clay, pass as high up the river as possible, and keep to the general alignment of the track as much as possible.

The crossing of the Itchen, Wey, Mole and Darent give a clue to the important crossing of the Medway.

6   Where a hill must be taken, it is taken straight and by the shortest way to the summit, unless the road is too steep for easy going.

7   The road seeks the saddle of a watershed, if it be high, when passing from one valley to another.

Ivan D Margary, in his *Roman Ways in the Weald*, sums up these characteristics as follows:

'The prehistoric route followed the main escarpment of the North Downs as closely as possible. In doing so it is in part a ridgeway, but it is also, for long distances, to be found as a terraceway near the foot of the steep escarpment, and, in some parts, both forms occur as alternative ways. The reasons for this are quite practical. Unlike the main ridge of the South Downs with its hard-turfed greenway right along the crest, the surface soil of the North Downs frequently takes the geological form known as "clay-with-flints" overlaying the chalk. This sticky covering may make the going difficult in wet weather, especially just upon the flat crest of the ridge where the ridgeway would normally run. Again, the escarpment is sometimes complicated by re-entrant coombes and ridges which make it awkward for a direct track to maintain its position invariably upon or below the crest. Common sense indicated the best route, and this is why we find the Way now upon the ridge and now as a terrace below.'

The North Downs Way

Because much of the PW has now become a busy road unsuitable for long-distance walkers, the NDW was designed primarily as a scenic walking route, chosen to follow a physical rather than a historical feature. The pilgrims preferred to keep to a middle line, above the forests of the clay vale but below the exposed hilltops, although the NDW follows those parts of the PW where the prehistoric route has no hard surface and is not used by traffic.

A long-distance footpath along the North Downs was first suggested by the Ramblers' Association in its evidence to the wartime Scott Committee on 'Land Utilisation in Rural Areas'. It first received official recognition when the Hobhouse Committee on National Parks was set up to examine the need for national parks in this country. Hobhouse set up a special committee to examine public access in the countryside and public rights of way, and its report, published in 1947, recommended a number of 'long-distance routes', most of which were later adopted. The proposal then was for a path from Salisbury Plain to Winchester and along the Pilgrims' Way to Canterbury, and for a continuation of a Ridgeway Path from Lyme Regis to Cambridge, with a South Downs spur running from Winchester to Eastbourne. These grand plans have only been partially brought to fruition. After discussions with the Hampshire, Surrey, and Kent County Councils, the Countryside Commission submitted proposals for a North Downs Way from Farnham in Surrey, for 142 miles/227 km, to Folkestone and on to Dover on the Kent coast, including an alternative route following the Pilgrims' Way from near Wye to Canterbury and then on to Dover.

On 16 July 1969 the Minister of Housing and Local Government announced his approval of the scheme, since when the Surrey and Kent County Councils have been working to make the route available. Some 36 miles/58 km of new rights of way were needed in 1969, and a section of 43 miles/69 km – including the 'Canterbury Loop' – was declared open by Kent County Council in 1972.

The North Downs Way was officially opened as Britain's eighth national long-distance footpath on 30 September 1978 by Dr Donald Coggan, Archbishop of Canterbury, in a ceremony on Broad Downs near Wye. However, the approved route is still incomplete, as at Hognore Farm, E of Wrotham, new rights of way have still not been established.

Route finding in general

It is hoped that this guide gives useful and detailed assistance in clearly defining the routes of the Pilgrims' Way and the North Downs Way on the map, though more waymarking for the PW is required on the ground. Kent County Council is alone among the three counties through which the route of the PW runs – Hampshire, Surrey and Kent – in having erected occasional signposts, but unfortunately these are in places where they are really least needed and hardly ever where they would be most appreciated. The signposts are marked with a scallop shell, associated in particular with St James of Compostella and the symbol of pilgrimage in general.

In Surrey, the NDW signposts are wooden and sited well above ground, whereas in Kent extensive use has been made of small concrete signstones which are fixed at ground level, and consequently are sometimes obscured by vegetation. These are now gradually being replaced with metal finger-posts. Throughout, the Countryside Commission's stylized acorn-symbol for a long-distance footpath is used to mark the NDW.

Be sure to follow the official waymarked routes, and do not attempt to walk across stretches of private land. An indication of the route is given on the maps and in the text.

The modern pilgrim should be a dedicated footpath preservationist, and should carry pruning saw, shears, and wire cutter, to deal suitably with natural and man-made obstructions across his route. In high summer nettles, thistles, brambles, hawthorn, blackthorn and barbed wires are painful in their multitude. Modern farming policies have encouraged the use of portable, single-strand electric fences that can appear literally overnight and may be moved a few weeks later. Even the familiar line of a hedgerow can soon disappear.

Although the PW and the NDW have been specially surveyed for this book, such new and perennial hazards cannot be charted. Fortunately, their occurrence need rarely spoil the day's pleasure. Although these are not strenuous paths where special walking equipment is necessary, it is nevertheless advisable to wear comfortable footwear and take adequate windproof and waterproof clothing.

In general the PW is a public highway, a byway open to all traffic (BOAT), road used as a public path (RUPP), bridleway or footpath over which rights of way exist, but in places there is no public right of way, even where the route is distinctly clear. The NDW follows rights of way throughout its length. It is designed to take walkers away from roads and traffic as much as possible, but there are a few places where such contact is unavoidable. Although both the PW and the NDW are routes primarily for walkers, some quite lengthy sections are bridleways which can also be used by horse-riders and cyclists, and some parts are BOATs or RUPPs which may be lawfully used by motorised traffic. Byways are usually signposted and waymarked in red, bridleways in blue and footpaths in yellow.

The modern pilgrim and long-distance-footpath walker will require the following Ordnance Survey 1:50,000 'Landranger' maps:

178 The Thames Estuary
179 Canterbury & East Kent
185 Winchester & Basingstoke (Pilgrims' Way only)
186 Aldershot & Guildford
187 Dorking & Reigate & Crawley
188 Maidstone & The Weald of Kent
189 Ashford & Romney Marsh (North Downs Way only)
(Sheet 178 only covers about 5 miles/8 km of path not covered on another sheet.)

Ordnance Survey 'Pathfinder' maps at a scale of 1:25,000 will be better for most districts.

The maps in this book are at a scale of approximately a half inch to one mile. The route of the PW is marked by a broken line, whilst the route of the NDW is marked by a dot-and-dash line. The route of the PW, where it is not followed by a right of way, is marked by a dotted line. Where the routes of the PW and NDW run together the route is marked —|—|—.

Travelling for pleasure is best during the months of April, May or June, when the hotels, hostels, and inns are less full and the roads not so congested. At these times the countryside is at its best; lovely stretches of remote and unspoiled track through deeply wooded shades and between growing hedgerows and banks bedecked with wild flowers. The North Downs are highly cultivated and heavily wooded, so that nowhere can one walk for long unhindered by plough and wire. Although every year the farmer ploughs yet higher up their flanks, the Downs remain largely covered with thin, springy turf, sympathetic to walk upon. One may walk for miles without meeting a soul, unless it be some equally robust modern pilgrim, and from a hundred vantage-points may see some of the most breathtaking views in southern England.

Transport facilities

When planning a tour of either the Pilgrims' Way or the North Downs Way, ramblers often wish to know what transport is available to enable them to complete their programme in the time available.

As both Winchester and Dover and all points between are within easy travelling distance of the centre of London, the modern pilgrim could easily set out from the city in the morning and return to his home in the evening, having completed a 10–15 mile section of the journey during the day. By using a combination of rail and bus services, the walker may return to the route each day, and save money and time in searching for over-night accommodation by sleeping in his own bed at night. Because the routes are so easily accessible at reasonable cost by public transport, this feature will enable the route to be walked during days off and at weekends, summer or winter, by those who cannot afford a week or ten days off their annual holiday.

Motor Bus Services
There are five principal motor bus companies operating in parts of the North Downs country:

1 Thames Valley & Aldershot   Serves North-East
  Omnibus Co Ltd   Hants and West Surrey
  Thorn Walk
  Reading RG1 7AX

2 Maidstone & District   Serves North and
  Motor Services Ltd   West Kent areas
  Station Road West
  Canterbury
  Kent CT2 8AL

3 East Kent Road Car Co Ltd   Serves East Kent
   (same address as Maidstone
   and District)

4 London Country Bus   Serves London and
   Services Ltd   the Home Counties
   Bell Street
   Reigate
   Surrey RH2 7LE

5 National Travel   as above
   Victoria Coach Station
   Buckingham Palace Road
   London SW1W 9TP

London Country Bus Services Ltd, associated with the National Bus Company, serves London and the Home Counties with express and country bus services:

a) Green Line Coaches are limited-stop buses and provide luxury express travel to Guildford, Dorking, Reigate, Redhill, Oxted, Westerham, Sevenoaks and Wrotham.

b) Country Buses operate on all the above radial routes, but in a more leisurely manner, and connect with other satellite towns and rural villages. They are integrated with the red Central Buses which cover all main roads in central and suburban London.

Green Rover tickets may be used any day of the week for one day's unlimited travel on green Country Bus routes, but not Green Line Coach routes. Buy them from Country Bus conductors.

Golden Rover tickets may be used any day of the week for one day's unlimited travel on any London Country Bus or Green Line Coach. Buy them from the bus or coach.

Timetables of local Road and Rail services, and other London Transport publications, may be obtainable from London Transport, Publicity Manager, Griffith House, 280 Old Marylebone Road, London NW1.

Long-distance, limited-stop coach services are operated daily by Alder Valley, East Kent, Maidstone & District, Royal Blue, and Southdown from Victoria Coach Station, Buckingham Palace Road, London SW1. Since the de-regulation of bus services in October 1986 a number of new bus companies have started up (and collapsed!) and there is now wide competition on most links between major towns. Particulars of these and other services are given in the *ABC Coach and Bus Guide* issued in April and October, which is obtainable from many bookstalls, or direct from the compilers, Thomas Skinner & Co. (Publishers) Ltd, 30 Finsbury Square, London EC2.

An information sheet, giving details of the transport operations, the frequencies and the level of the service they provide, is available from the Ramblers' Association, 1–4 Crawford Mews, York Street, London, W1H 1PT.

Rail services

Train services operate from the London stations of Victoria, Charing Cross, Cannon Street and London Bridge to (from west to east) Southampton, Portsmouth, Worthing, Brighton, Hastings and Dover to get you to Winchester, Alton, Bentley, Farnham, Guildford, Box Hill, Merstham, Oxted, Folkestone and Dover.

The Reading – Guildford – Redhill – Gatwick line runs through Shalford, Chilworth, Gomshall, Dorking, Betchworth, Reigate, Redhill and Godstone, while the line from Victoria across north-east Kent connects with Otford, Kemsing, the Medway villages, Rochester, Hollingbourne, Harrietsham, Lenham, Charing, Wye, Chilham and Canterbury.

British Railway's Network Southeast issue timetables of their summer and winter passenger services in the region, and details may be obtained from:

The Divisional Manager (South Western Division),
British Railways Southern Region,
Travel Facilities, Room 401,
Waterloo Station,
London SE1.

The following types of tickets are available:

a) Day Excursion tickets are issued from the London terminal and suburban stations to the coastal resorts and other towns.

b) Runabout Rover tickets are available for unlimited travel in six areas of Southern Region for seven days between mid-March and early October. Unfortunately none of these areas conveniently extends over the North Downs area. However, a Southern Railrover ticket is issued from March to October for seven days' unlimited travel in the whole of Southern Region.

c) Special Ramblers' Excursion trains are run on alternate Sundays throughout the year. They start from one or the other of the London termini, and call at certain suburban stations in parts of the south-east counties, thus enabling walkers to reach interesting and out-of-the-way country at reasonable cost.

Leaflets giving particulars of these services and other concessions – cheap day returns, party travel, family travel, etc – may be obtained from the above address or any railway station. ABC publish a monthly rail guide of train services throughout Britain.

A code for the countryside

The Countryside Commission have prepared the Country Code as a guide to visitors, some of whom are perhaps unaccustomed to country ways. Please remember to observe the following standards of good manners when you go to enjoy the beauties and the pleasures of the garden that is Britain's countryside.

1 Guard against all risks of fire
Don't drop lighted matches or cigarette ends, particularly near crops, plantations, woods, heaths, and hay ricks. A fire, once started, is difficult to put out.

2 Fasten all gates
Animals can do great damage to crops and themselves if they stray. They may be injured by traffic or be the cause of accidents.

3 Keep dogs under proper control
Animals are easily frightened by strange dogs, so do not let them disturb cattle, hens, or sheep; keep your dog on its lead when near other animals or walking along the road.

4 Keep to the paths across farm land
Avoid damaging crops in any way. Corn, grass and hay that have been trampled flat are difficult to harvest. Do not trespass.

5 Avoid damaging fences, hedges and walls
Where a man can go, an animal will follow, and damage to crops will result. Use gates and stiles where they are provided.

6 Do not leave litter
Take your litter home, including bottles and tins. All litter is not only unsightly but dangerous. Broken glass, opened tins, and plastic bags can very easily harm livestock and damage farm machinery.

7 Safeguard water supplies

A stream, brook or well may be the only water supply for a farmer and his animals. Water is precious in the country. Do not pollute it in any way.

8 Protect wild life, plants and trees

Never dig up plants and flowers, carve on trees, and please do not take birds' eggs. Wild flowers, birds, and trees give more pleasure to more people if left alone.

9 Go carefully on country roads

Blind corners, hump-back bridges, slow-moving farm vehicles and herds of cattle are all hazards for the motorist, cyclist, and walker. Careless car parking may block the entrance to fields or farmyards.

10 Respect the life of the countryside

Enjoy the countryside, but do not hinder the work of the countryman. Roads and paths run through the farmers' land, and animals, machinery, and buildings are the raw materials from which he earns his living. You, the public, are on trust. Be considerate.

Where to stay

In the twenty years since this Guide was first published the author has received a number of requests to recommend places to stay. Whilst it would be invidious to offer individual bed and breakfast accommodation addresses it is appreciated that knowledge of accommodation guides would be helpful.

Accommodation lists are available from:

English Tourist Board, 4 Grosvenor Gardens, London SW1 ODU. Tel. 071-731-3400. Ask for the 'Where to Stay in South East England' brochure.

Tourist Information Centres (TICs) in towns along the route also provide accommodation reservation facilities, usually free.

The Ramblers' Association, 1–5 Wandsworth Road, London SW8 2LJ. Tel. 071-582-6878. Their Yearbook and Accommodation Guide is available from bookstalls or from the RA.

The Youth Hostels Association, Trevelyan House, 8 St Stephen's Hill, St Albans, Hertfordshire, AL1 2DY. The YHA provides accommodation for members. There are six hostels on the route: at Winchester, Tanners Hatch, Kemsing, Canterbury and two at Dover. Their Handbook and Accommodation Guide is available from bookstalls or from the YHA.

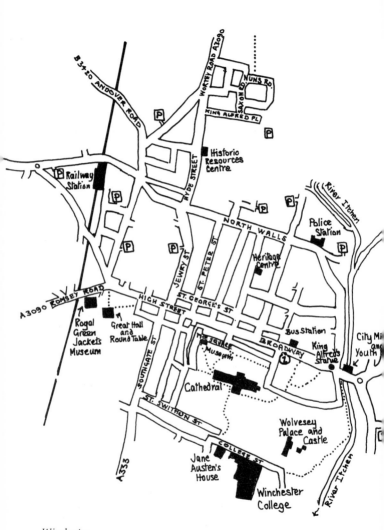

Winchester

Part One: River Itchen to River Wey

1 Winchester

Winchester, once the capital of England, lies within a fold of the Hampshire Downs and at an important crossing of the River Itchen. Easily accessible by road and rail from both London and the Midlands, Winchester is a city well worth exploring before we commence our modern pilgrimage.

Brief history

There was some settlement on the site of Winchester in the first century BC. During the Roman occupation the city, called Venta Belgarum, was the commercial and administrative centre for a tribal area covering a large part of what is now Hampshire, and at least five roads met here.

The Romans came about AD 44 and built great walls to enclose 138 acres/55.8 ha of land, defended by ditches and the river. It is unusual in plan in that the main streets do not divide the city into four equal quarters. The crossing of these streets is close to the western wall, probably to avoid an exit upon the marshy lands beside the Itchen, which flowed against the eastern wall. The Romans constructed five great roads, radiating to Silchester, Marlborough, Old Sarum, Southampton and Porchester. What remains of the Roman town is now 8–12 ft/2.4–3.6 m down, and excavations have brought to light traces of the street-grid and of several buildings.

Winchester became the capital of Wessex under the Saxon Cerdic in c.519. A castle was built on the high ground in the SW part of the fortified Roman area. There were then six gates into the city, but only two now remain – the West Gate at the top of High Street and the King's Gate to the south. Bishop Birinus came to Winchester in 635 and in 643 converted King

Cenwealh to Christianity; a church was set up and this became the bishop's seat in 674, and was known as the Old Minster. The Bishop St Swithun (852–62) was buried outside the W door of this cathedral 'where the rains of heaven might fall upon him'.

After the Norman Conquest, William made Winchester his capital and the city became very prosperous. St Giles' Fair, granted by William Rufus to Bishop Walkelin for the building of the Cathedral, became the most famous in England, and was attended by merchants from all over Europe.

The city seems to have reached its zenith in the twelfth century. It was a battleground for seven weeks in 1141 and a great part of it was destroyed by fire. The city also suffered severely at the hands of Simon de Montfort the Younger in 1265, and was later devastated by the Black Death, 1348–51, which killed one third of England's population of 3 million.

During the Civil War the City suffered much from its loyalty to Charles I, and its ancient castle, founded by William the Conqueror, was destroyed in 1645. Charles II intended to make Winchester a royal residence once again, and he began building a palace in 1683. It was unfinished at the time of his death in 1685 and became a barracks.

In the later half of the eighteenth century, many of Winchester's historical buildings were removed. Most of the City Walls, together with the N, S, and E Gates were pulled down, and many of the ancient features of the city disappeared.

The nineteenth century saw Winchester develop into a residential and educational centre and a place of pilgrimage for lovers of antiquity.

Winchester Cathedral

The Cathedral Church of the Holy Trinity, St Peter, St Paul, and St Swithun lies in a hollow and there are no dramatic distant views of it. It is only in the grassy Close that one

King Alfred's statue, Winchester

realizes its size, but the splendid interior belies its somewhat austere external appearance.

The Saxon cathedral was rebuilt under the Norman Bishop Walkelin in 1079, and was completed 14 years later on 8 April 1093. Walkelin's masterpiece consisted of a nave, W front and central tower, flanked by two transepts, with aisles, crypt, choir and range of cloisters. The church thus rebuilt was the longest in western Europe, its nave being second only in length to St Peter's in Rome. The overall length of the great cathedral is 556 ft/169 m. The height of the nave vaulting is only 78 ft/23.7 m but its width at the transept's crossing is 231 ft/70.4 m. The height of the tower is 140 ft/42.6 m, and the building is largely of stone from the Isle of Wight.

On 15 July 1093 the relics of St Swithun were transferred from the old to the new building. Heaven's disapproval of the moving of the saint's body from its original modest resting place was shown by continuous rain for forty days, and the saint's name has been associated in popular memory ever since with the fickleness of the English summer climate.

Bishop Godfrey de Lucy (1189–1204) began a reconstruction of the eastern part in 1202 by building a retro-choir and the Lady Chapel. St Swithun's shrine was moved from the SE aisle of the nave to a more fitting place in the retro-choir, as it had already begun to attract great numbers of pilgrims. The shrine was destroyed and its treasures confiscated at the Dissolution in 1539, but a new shrine has been erected on its site.

A total remodelling of the nave was begun by Bishop William Edington (1346–66) by the W front, and continued by the transformation of the Norman nave into Early Perpendicular style by Bishop William of Wykeham (1366–1404). This tremendous undertaking resulted in one of the glories of Winchester, and completed the major construction works. Later additions were directed towards the elaboration of the interior – the Lady Chapel was remodelled by Bishop Cour-

Winchester Cathedral. The Nave, looking east

tenay (1486–92) and Bishop Langton (1493–1501), and the Chancel by Bishop Fox (1501–28). The beautiful chantry chapels are the various works of Bishops Edington, Wykeham, Beaufort, Waynflete, Langton, and Fox.

Excavations made in 1957 and 1961 have located the Old and New Saxon Minsters and aim at their complete restoration. The Old Minster lies immediately N of the present nave, at a slight angle, so that the W end of the Minster is partly below the W end of the Cathedral. The New Minster was built in 903 and lies N of, and parallel to, the Old Minster, in places as little as 3 ft/1 m away. It was abandoned for a new site in 1110. In the late ninth century Alfred and his wife founded the Nun's Minster, but this has not been precisely located, although it is within the same monastic enclosure as the Old and New Minsters.

As the burial and coronation churches of many of the kings of Wessex and of England, these Minsters formed an ecclesiastical group without parallel in this country. The Bishopric is still one of the most important in the country, and carries with it the prelacy of the Order of the Garter.

Other places of interest

The castle was built by William the Conqueror and was the birthplace of Henry III and Arthur, son of Henry VII. In it Henry VIII entertained the Emperor Charles V in 1522, who inspected the Round Table of King Arthur.

The Round Table is not older than the time of Henry III and was repainted by Henry VIII for Emperor Charles V's visit. It is 18 ft/5.4 m in diameter and painted in the Tudor colours of green and white. In the centre is a Tudor rose, surmounted by King Arthur, and it bears the names of 24 of his knights around the edge. It has been suggested that the Round Table may have been the chief tribunal or superior court of justice.

The Great Hall, built between 1222 and 1236, is all that remains of the castle after the Civil War in 1644–5. It was the

Winchester Cathedral. The Choir, looking east

seat of Parliament for centuries, and here was held the famous trial of Sir Walter Raleigh in 1603 for conspiracy against Charles I. It is one of the finest medieval halls in England. (Open daily 1000–1700, except in winter, and weekends between 1000–1600).

The historic Peninsula Barracks in Romsey Road is the home of The Royal Green Jackets Museum. It contains a collection of military history from 1702 to the present day and claims to be, probably rightly, the finest regimental museum in the country. Amongst its models of battle layouts is a diorama of the Battle of Waterloo, measuring 6.7 m/22 ft by 3.35 m/11 ft and containing 22,000 model soldiers and horses, complete with sound and light effects. The museum also contains the collections of The Royal Hussars, The Light Infantry, The Royal Hampshires and The Gurkhas. The museum was opened by the Colonel-in-Chief of the Regiment, HM Queen Elizabeth II in December 1989. (Open daily throughout the year except for the two weeks over Christmas and New Year. Mondays – Saturdays, 1000–1700, Sundays 1200–1600).

Winchester College was founded in 1382 by William of Wykeham (of 'Manners makyth man' fame), and is the oldest of the major public schools in England. The College was begun in 1387 and opened in 1394 to educate clergy in canon and civil law, and as an adjunct to Wykeham's New College in Oxford, founded 1379.

Wolvesey Castle, the palace of the medieval bishops of Winchester, was built by Bishop Henry de Blois (1129–71) in 1137. Here Queen Mary Tudor lodged before marrying Philip of Spain in the Cathedral in 1554, the last royal marriage in Winchester. The castle was levelled to the ground by the Parliamentarians in 1645. Only the chapel remains, and this adjoins the palace begun by Sir Christopher Wren for Bishop Morley in 1674. (The Palace grounds are open from 1 April–30 September between 1000–1300 and 1400–1800).

Winchester Cathedral. West front

Henry de Blois's Hospital of St Cross dates from about 1133. It is the oldest institution of its kind in the country and was founded for 'thirteen poor impotent men so reduced in strength as rarely or never to be able to raise themselves without the assistance of another'. In the porter's hatchway under the tower is provided a 'wayfarers' dole', of bread and beer to all comers – so long as the daily ration lasts. The hospital lies 2 miles/3.2 km S of the city centre and may be approached by the W bank of the River Itchen. It is unfortunately on the wrong side of the city to be visited by the modern pilgrim travelling up the valley towards Alresford.

The City Mill dates from 1743 and operated until the 1920s. In 1928 it was given to the National Trust and since 1931 it has been used as a youth hostel. (Open to the public 1 April–30 September, daily except Wednesdays, 1000–1700).

There are many other ancient buildings to see in Winchester, but within the centre of the city some old street frontages have disappeared and with them a number of interesting buildings. Yet much of the essential charm of Winchester remains, and an observant visitor must carry away with him the memory and atmosphere of a great cathedral and its small-scale street.

Not only is Winchester the start of the Pilgrims' Way but it is also the start of the extension to the South Downs Way to Eastbourne. It is also one end of The Clarendon Way to Salisbury and is on the King Alfred's Way from Portsmouth to Oxford linking places with associations with King Alfred.

The TIC is at The Guildhall, Broadway. Tel. (0962) 840500. Open daily throughout the year, 0930–1800 (but to 1700 on Sundays and winter days). Accommodation booking service. Enquire here about guided walks around the historic city centre.

Winchester to New Alresford

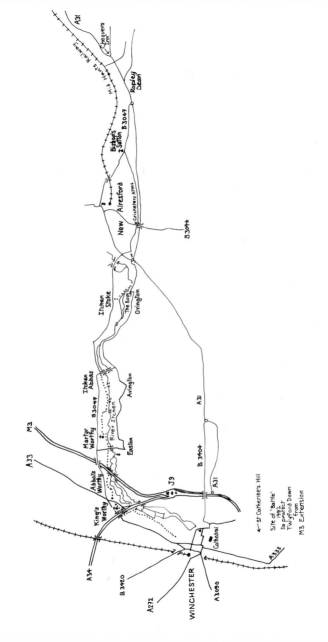

2 Winchester to Alton 19 miles/30 km

We begin our journey from the great W Door of Winchester
Cathedral and bear half-right along the paved path between
the avenue of trees to a road at The Square, passing the City
Museum (open Mondays–Saturdays, 1000–1700, Sundays
1400–1700) on our right just outside the cathedral precincts.
Cross over the road into the cul-de-sac street where stands St
Lawrence's, a church built upon the site of William the
Conqueror's Chapel Royal.

Pass under the Pentice archway to emerge at the High Street
by the beautiful High Cross, perhaps the finest Perpendicular
cross in England. The cross was erected about 1450 in the
reign of Henry VI, and restored in 1865. It has figures of St
John the Baptist (original), William of Wykeham (with staff
and books), King Alfred and a city mayor. High Street is a
picturesque and bustling thoroughfare on which all other
streets converge at right-angles, and as in Roman times is still
the spine of the town, though now partly pedestrianized and
bypassed by city-centre traffic.

Turn left along High Street. After 20 yds/18 m or so, you
come to Lloyds Bank, a building dating from 1711, formerly
the Guildhall, with its statue of Queen Anne and town clock,
both dating from 1713. The curfew bell is still rung from here
at 8pm each weekday. Here turn right along narrow St Peter's
Street to the crossing of St George's Street. On the left-hand
side is the site of the church of St Peter. It is one of the sites
of the many vanished parish churches of medieval
Winchester.

Continue ahead along St Peter's Street. On the right hand
is the Royal Hotel, once a Benedictine convent, and a little
way further on is Avebury House, a five-bay house built 1690,
with a very elegant Doric doorcase with Tuscan columns and
a fluted frieze. As we follow the street we also pass a former

High Cross, Winchester High Street

Methodist church and a Catholic church, soon to come to the junction with North Walls.

Turn left in North Walls to the traffic lights at the cross-roads. At this point stood the North Gate, but it was demolished in 1756 and only a plaque remains to mark its site. Here the pilgrims left the walled city and took the old road now followed by Hyde Street.

Continue past the site of the former Hyde Brewery (now a brewery distribution depot) and the Resources Centre of the Winchester Museums Service (Open Mondays–Thursdays, 0900–1630, Fridays 0900–1600), for a few hundred yards/metres to King Alfred Place. Turn right into this little street to the church of St Bartholomew, built 1185 for the tenants and servants of the Abbots of the Abbey of St Peter and St Grimbald. Hyde Abbey was a famous Benedictine monastery founded by Alfred and his son Edward, and the establishment was moved here in the reign of Henry I. The present remains of the abbey, which was destroyed in the Reformation of 1538, are the gateway to the Abbot's Lodgings, the mill stream and its bridges, and some fragments in St Bartholomew's church. King Alfred was buried in the abbey, but his bones were not disinterred as were others in the Reformation. His leaden coffin was dug up unopened in the building of the prison (now vanished) and sold in 1788 for £2.

Follow a path for a few yards/metres, with the church on your right, soon to reach Saxon Road. When this bends sharp left, turn slightly right and cross over a stream into Nun's Road, then immediately turn left, opposite a telephone call-box, along a footpath called Nun's Walk through a turnstile and so into open fields.

Winchester to Alresford 9 miles/14 km
This stream now on our left is one of several drainage channels in the Itchen valley, and we keep beside it for nearly 2 miles/3.2 km, the only stretch of proper footpath between Winchester and Farnham.

After a few hundred yards/metres cross a stile ahead and

keep straight on again along a clear track to a small-holding ahead opposite a thatched cottage. Here turn left over the stream by a bridge and immediately right again along a path, with weeping willows lining the bank of the stream on your right. After a while the path crosses the stream again beside a water pipe, then bears slightly right to a stile beside the main stream of the River Itchen.

Modern roadworks, being the continuation of the Winchester Bypass, have caused the diversion of the original footpath, but at this stile beside the river you can see the line of the old path striking half-left across the field. Climb the stile and turn sharp left with the new road on your right. Continue for a few hundred yards/metres, then turn right under the road by a new pedestrian subway. Pass under the arch ahead and then immediately turn left along a narrow path at the foot of the embankment and past an industrial trading estate on the site of Kingsworthy Foundry, where the path is called Nun's Walk. Where the driveway turns left continue straight on, with a line of trees on your right, coming soon into the graveyard on the S side of Kings Worthy Church.

This path from Winchester is probably the original track, variously known as the Monk's or the Nun's Walk, but there is an alternative along the line of the modern road A33 passing Headbourne Worthy. This main road is above the level of marshy land, avoids the crossing of any stream, and indicates the continuity of the Worthy villages as a string of similar sites of similar antiquity.

The track we have just followed, however, is shorter, and follows the edge of the chalk and just avoids the marshy alluvial soil of the valley. The Bourne stream from Headbourne Worthy has been diverted, embanked along the Monk's Walk, presumably for the purpose of giving power to the mill at Hyde Abbey and supplying that community with water. The Monastery presumably would have had its gates upon the oldest highway of its time: the Roman road also took the same line, straight from the N Gate of Winchester to Kings Worthy Church.

The Church of St Mary, Kings Worthy, is mostly thirteenth century, though it was over-restored in 1864. The polygonal vestry is perhaps the only feature one may remember in this church. After Kings Worthy the modern roads B3047 and A31 correspond with the ancient track for the next 16 miles/24.75 km to Alton, although there is a footpath through to Itchen Abbas which meanders on a lower level by the river.

Follow the B3047 for nearly 5 miles/8 km past the hamlets of Abbots Worthy, Martyr Worthy and Itchen Abbas to Itchen Stoke. The churches of St Swithin, Martyr Worthy, and St John Baptist, Itchen Abbas, lie just S of this road.

The Church of St John Baptist, Itchen Abbas, is a Neo-Norman style building built in 1867 on a cruciform plan. In the churchyard is an ancient yew tree and under its branches is the grave of one John Hughes, aged 26, hanged at Westminster on 19 March 1823, for horse-stealing. It is said that he was the last man to be hanged in England for that offence.

Charles Kingsley stayed at a pub in Itchen Abbas, the predecessor of the present 'Plough'. He fished here, and possibly got the idea for *The Water Babies* whilst doing so – his description of the stream fits the Itchen perfectly.

Two miles/3.2 km E of Itchen Abbas lies Itchen Stoke, where the Pilgrims' Way crossed the river. The valley of the Itchen here makes a sharp bend northwards round a low but rather difficult hill, and leads on to the Alresfords; and the modern London–Winchester road A31 follows this line. The old road crossed the river, crested Tichborne Down and joined the London road by the church at Bishops Sutton, 1 mile/1.6 km E of New Alresford.

'Stoke', as is usual in places by rivers, means an artificial causeway or crossing of the water, and here the river is shallow, the bottom firm, and the banks not too widely separated. Just above Itchen Stoke is the confluence of the Itchen, Alre and other streams, and as such a confluence is invariably marshy this could not have been avoided save by a long bend to the N, where no trace of a track exists. On the S of Itchen Stoke there is a steep dry bank on which to continue

The crossing of the River Itchen near Ovington

one's journey. An old church once stood by the river in such a position that the road to the ford passed just by its southern porch, but this interesting place disappeared in 1831.

It is true that an ancient trackway leaves Old Alresford to the NE, but this does not point direct to Farnham, the known junction of the short cut. Old Alresford is too far to the W and N of the track we have been following to be visited, save by an abrupt and inexplicable bend. New Alresford is nearer to this track, though not on it, but it was not in existence till the twelfth century, whereas a bishop's palace had stood for some centuries at Sutton close by, hence Bishops Sutton.

As has been and will be seen, a high but narrow watershed has to be crossed between Winchester and Farnham. To approach this watershed by the easiest route, avoiding marshy ground, one would cross the ford at Itchen Stoke and go straight across the hill to Bishops Sutton and then follow in a direct line to one's object. The hill S of Alresford afforded a view ahead, and a direct advance upon the ridge of the watershed could be planned eastwards under the advancing night.

Immediately opposite the Church of St Mary, Itchen Stoke, 1866, take the lane down to the river, signposted 'Footpath to Ovington', to a footbridge. Cross this and follow a beautiful footpath between the streams of the crystal-clear river to another footbridge which leads to the 'Bush' at Ovington, whose garden tends to fill with importunate ducklings.

Follow the road between streams and go uphill to cross the B3047 just N of the A31 roundabout. Take the A31 E and soon take a bridleway on the L to a T-junction of a minor road, then cross the River Itchen by a footbridge over a deep ford, past some watercress beds to reach the 'Cricketers Arms' at road B3046. New Alresford lies ¾ mile/1 km to the left, down the hill, and we will return to this point when we have visited the little town.

New Alresford

Alresford (pronounced *Awlsfd*, although others say *Arlsfd*) was once a prosperous country town with a flourishing trade, though now it is a large village depending on Winchester and Alton. It once seems to have been called Aldersford, the ford by the alders, and the river now called Arle or Alre is possibly an awkward corruption.

The town was founded and laid out by Bishop Godfrey de Lucy (1189–1204) in 1200 when he built a great dam across the River Itchen to form a reservoir of 200 acres/80 ha to make the

Church of St John Baptist, New Alresford

river navigable down to Southampton at all seasons. The reservoir has since shrunk, but it is still beautiful and large enough to attract a great many water birds.

The main street, Broad Street, runs N from the Winchester road and is the best village street in Hampshire. The broad street is lined with two rows of lime trees and flanked by rendered houses, making it agreeable without exception. One of the houses in Broad Street, No. 27, was the birthplace on 16 December 1787 of the novelist Mary Russell Mitford. She lived here until she was 10, when her winning of a £20,000

Napoleonic tombstones in churchyard of St John Baptist, New Alresford

lottery prize enabled her father to move the family to a new home in Reading. The great house by the church was built by one of our greatest naval heroes, Admiral Lord Rodney (1719–92), and he is credited with the building of most of the pubs in the village. There are a great many spaced out on opposite sides of the straight road, spaced, so it has been said, in order that the Admiral might 'tack' from one to the other and home again. He is buried in Old Alresford church.

The Church of St John Baptist, New Alresford, lies just to the S of the main junction of the streets. The flint church dates mostly from 1898, though the W tower is early fourteenth-century and has a seventeenth-century brick top. French names on five tombstones in the churchyard recall that French prisoners were quartered here in the Napoleonic wars. The church has specimens of cuneiform inscriptions on two ancient bricks – one from the Ziggurat at Ur of the Chaldees, dedicated to the Moon God Nannar, dating from c.2150 BC, and the other from Nebuchadnezzar's Palace at Babylon, dating from about 604–562 BC.

Go through the churchyard on a public path, past public toilets and the police station, to Ashford Station.

British Rail closed the line between Alton and Alresford in 1973 but in 1977 it was re-opened as a preserved railway, the Mid Hants Railway, or 'Watercress Line'. Steam-headed trains run on occasions – usually between mid-April to mid-September at weekends and Bank Holidays and most weekdays during July and August. The rail journey is a useful alternative to the busy main road and inconvenient footpaths. Details of the timetable are obtainable from The Railway Station, Alresford, Hants, SO24 9JG. Tel. (0962) 734200 or 733810 or a talking timetable on (0962) 734866.

Alresford to Alton 10 miles/16 km

From the 'Cricketers Arms' at road B3046 and with the A31 on your right, continue over Tichbourne Down and steeply down White Hill Lane to Bishops Sutton, a place so called because here was once a residence of the Bishops of Winchester.

The Norman Church of St Nicholas is built of flints, with a brick porch and weatherboarded bell-turret. There are two noteworthy Norman doorways, both with weird half-human birds' heads, and some Norman windows in the N and S walls of the wide nave.

The modern highway A31 corresponds to the old road as far as the 'Chequers Inn' at Ropley, following the lowest part of the valley. But here the valley curves N, and it might be presumed that the original way, making more directly for the saddle of the watershed, would gradually climb the southern hillside. By doing so it would have the dual advantages of taking a shorter cut and conquering at one stretch, and rapidly, the rise of 350 ft/106 m from the inn to the summit.

However, the old road does not follow the valley but takes a straight line upwards direct to the summit, and traces of the

Jane Austen's house, Chawton

old track can be seen in its early stages. The place-name
'Street' is a guide, as it is a word invariably found in connec-
tion with an ancient roadway – to the S of this line is Gilbert
Street and N of it is North Street. (Other examples are West
Street and Broad Street near Lenham, Dunn Street near
Eastwell, and the old name for Albury – Weston Street.)

Just after the Bighton-Ropley crossroad at Ropley Dean, a
few hundred yards/metres before the 'Chequers Inn', in a
field on the right is an embankment, perfectly straight, turning
slightly away from the main road and pointing directly
towards the saddle. It may continue through the garden of
'Chequers Inn' but in a few fields beyond it has entirely
disappeared and cannot be followed. It would have crossed
the Gilbert Street-North Street road just S of Manor Farm and
entered Brislands Lane, which takes the hill steeply and
continues straight to the saddle.

Brislands Lane runs wide and straight for 2 miles/3.2 km or
so, and after a crossroad continues at Blackberry Lane, passing
through an extraordinary collection of bungalows and wooden
cottages which have mushroomed upon either side. At the
summit, bend left to the thirteenth milestone on the London
road, A31, which has been climbing the valley below through
Four Marks. The line of the old road continues ahead through
a wood, but is lost among the houses built along Farringdon
Lane. Here one finally leaves the valley of the Itchen to join
that of the Wey.

At the point where the old road leaves the wood it is joined
by the London road which continues as far as Alton and to
just beyond Farnham, a distance of 14 miles/22.5 km. For
2 miles/3.2 km the road follows the bottom of the valley,
falling in that distance some 300 ft/91 m. It descends by the
easiest gradient, for had it taken to the hillside it would have
fallen at last upon Alton by way of a steep spur.

The valley road leads straight ahead, but after the roundabout of the Meon valley road (A32) it turns right to Chawton,
where Jane Austen lived for the last seven years of her life.

Jane Austen's house stands at the corner of the Winchester

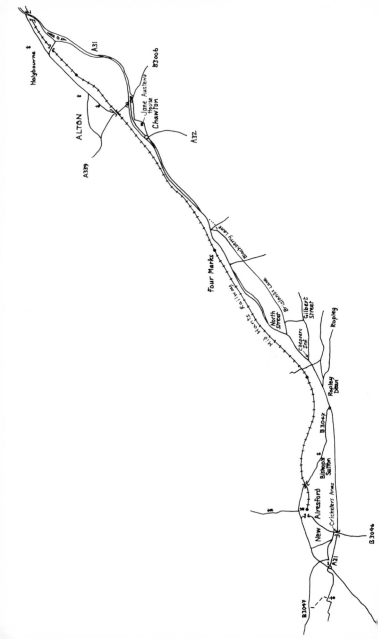

and Alton roads, A31 and A32, and is open to the public.
(Open April–October inclusive, daily 11.00–16.30; and
November–March inclusive, daily 10.00–16.30, but closed
Mondays and Tuesdays.) The modest, square, two-storeyed
red-brick house was her home from 1809 to 1817. Here she
revised *Sense and Sensibility* (1811) and *Pride and Prejudice* (1813)
and wrote *Mansfield Park* (1814), *Emma* (1816), *Northanger Abbey*
(1818) and *Persuasion* (1818). These later novels aroused great
enthusiasm and drew forth high praise from such men as
Lord Macaulay and Sir Walter Scott. The house is beautifully
cared-for by the Jane Austen Memorial Trust, and has many
treasures to delight her admirers: furniture, clothes, pictures,
and books (including an American first edition of her novels,
1832). Jane Austen lived her last days and died on 18 July 1817
in a house in College Street, Winchester, next to Winchester
College.

The old road did not pass through Chawton but would
have continued to enter Alton at its SW end, at the same point
by which an ancient road from Old Alresford via Medstead
entered the town.

However, the ground has lost all its original character
because the railway embankments have obliterated
everything.

At the roundabout at the end of the Alton Bypass A31, take
the road on the left. Pass under the railway arch and at the
end of the road turn right.

After ½ mile/0.8 km go past the large Alton Sports Centre
(on the R) and then (on the L) the Lord Mayor Treolar
Hospital, originally built for the wounded of the South African
War. In 1908 Sir William Purdie Treolar (1843–1923), Lord
Mayor of London in 1906–7, founded a hospital here for
London's crippled children. This foundation has since moved
to split sites at Holybourne and Upper Froyle as the Lord
Mayor Treolar College and the original building is now a
Regional Health Authority community hospital.

New Alresford to Alton

Cross road B3006 and go along Butts Road, A32, beside a green to enter the High Street at Alton.

Church of St Lawrence, Alton

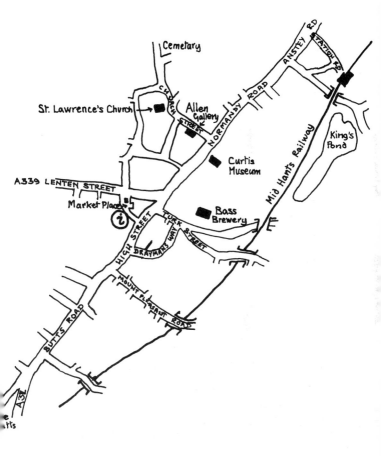

Cemetery

St. Lawrence's Church →

Allen Gallery

CHURCH STREET

NORMANDY ROAD

ANSTEY RD

STATION RD

Curtis Museum

King's Pond

Mid Hants Railway

A339 LENTEN STREET

Market Place

②

HIGH STREET

YORK STREET

DRAYMANS WAY

Bass Brewery

MOUNT PLEASANT ROAD

BUTTS ROAD

A31

rtis

Alton

3 Alton to Farnham 9 miles/14.5 km

Alton stands at the head of the Wey valley and is an ancient borough. In the eighteenth century there was a considerable industry in silks and woollen cloths, but these have now disappeared and brewing is the main business today. There are several sixteenth- and seventeenth-century houses camouflaged by modern fronts, some genuine ones, and picturesque old inns in the main street.

Winchester Road and All Saints Church, 1873, leads us into the High Street, where there is a Wesleyan Chapel of 1846 in the Italianate style, with arched windows. After a stretch Market Street leads off to the left to the small and attractive Market Place, with its renovated Town Hall, dated 1813. Leading off this is Amery Street which hides a small house where Edmund Spenser, the great Elizabethan poet, lived in 1590.

Market Street continues as Lenten Street and at No. 25 was born on 11 January 1746 the world-famous botanist William Curtis. Curtis founded the *Botanical Magazine*, and with his family, all of whom were interested in natural history, founded the Curtis Museum in 1855. This is housed in a building at the top of High Street and should be visited by everyone who has the chance. It contains a valuable collection of bygone agricultural implements, china, and Roman pottery, and old views of the town. (Open Tuesdays–Saturdays, 1000–1700, admission free).

Opposite the Curtis Museum runs Church Street and just round the corner is the Allen Gallery, the home of an outstanding collection of ceramics – pottery, porcelain and tiles dating from 1250 to the present day. (Open Tuesdays–Saturdays, 1000–1700, admission free). Church Street

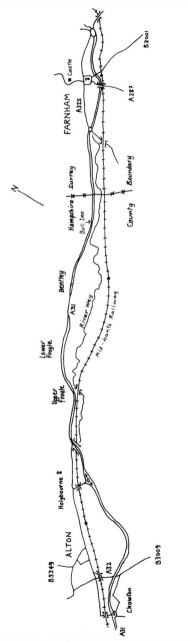

leads to the interesting parish Church of St Lawrence. It is one of the very rare churches which have two naves and two chancels. St Lawrence's is a Perpendicular town church built round an Early Norman crossing tower. This now stands in the S aisle, for in the fifteenth century a new nave and chancel were built N of the previous church. At the same time the former nave was rebuilt and alterations made to the chancel. The exterior of the church is fifteenth-century throughout, except for a Victorian broach spire.

In the Civil War the town was held by 80 Royalists under Colonel Richard Boles, but they had to retreat to the church under the heavy fire of the Roundheads. The great S door and walls show the scars of the fight, for deeply embedded in the timbers are still some of the actual bullets. A brass tablet on one of the pillars in the nave, a replica of the original in Winchester Cathedral, tells the story of Boles, who died serving the Royalists on 13 December 1641.

In the cemetery, some 200 m NE of the church, is the grave of 'Sweet Fanny Adams', an eight-year-old girl from Alton who was brutally murdered in 1867.

On the S side of the town is the vast Manor Park Brewery, producing 1.2 million barrels of national beers per annum. Group tours are conducted Mondays–Thursdays, but individuals can join tours on Tuesday afternoons. Enquire at the TIC.

The TIC is just off the Market Place at 7, Cross & Pillory Lane. Tel (0420) 88448. The TIC provide an accommodation booking service and free leaflets on The Hangars Way, a 17 mile/27 km route that starts at Alton and runs through Selbourne to Petersfield.

Return to the High Street and continue eastwards along Normandy Street, passing the stuccoed Congregational Chapel, 1835, then along Anstey Road leading out of town, past the Infirmary, 1793, with its mansard roof, and the Grammar School which was founded in 1638.

The pilgrims usually travelled by the main track through the valley, as this was the easiest and quickest way of reaching

Farnham, and it is now the main road. This stretch has several peculiarities:

1 It follows the River Wey for miles, not, as it followed the River Itchen, on a dry ledge above the stream, but right along the low land of the waterside. It is within easy reach of the water for men and animals, but avoids the low levels, thick cover and danger of floods. The nearness of the track to a river is not to be found in any other part of its course – be it Itchen, Mole, Darent, Medway or Stour.

2 In every other stretch of its length the old road passes along the edge of villages and farmed land, but here it forms the main street of Alton, Bentley, and Farnham.

3 There is the correspondence between the old road and the modern road for the whole of this considerable distance, a character which is unique. It so remained identical up to and beyond its point of junction with the older 'Harrow Way' at Farnham.

An explanation for this coincidence is that the hills which everywhere else afford so even a platform for the prehistoric road are here of a contour which forbids their use. Any road down this valley must have run upon this lowest line. There are deep coombes at Holybourne Down, two at Froyle, one at Bentley and another before Farnham. Any path attempting these hillsides would either have doubled its length by avoiding the hollows, or would have been a succession of steep ascents and descents had it remained direct. All the dry slopes which bound the valley to the N are a succession of steep and isolated projections, and the road is compelled to take to the valley floor.

As far as Froyle, 3 miles/4.8 km from Alton, the road never leaves the river by more than ¼ mile/400 m, but the valley here is dry, a narrow strip of gravel. For 2 miles/3.2 km after Froyle there is clay, but the road follows greensand. At the entry to Bentley village the clay is unavoidable, but after a mile of it the road takes advantage of a patch of gravel on the 300 ft/91 m contour as far as the 'Bull Inn', avoiding the marshy levels. Then to within 2 miles/3.2 km of Farnham the

Holybourne Church

road has to negotiate a good deal of clay, but it picks out a long irregular and narrow patch of gravel, and at the end of this, just E of the county boundary, it finds the narrow belt of sand again, which it keeps to all the way to Farnham on the low level without difficulty.

Though the valley is full of clay, the road avoids it with remarkable success, and the whole is an example of how a primitive track will avoid bad soil. The old road keeps throughout this passage to the sunny northern bank of the river, so that while it is compelled to keep to the bottom of the valley, it attempts at least to get the driest part of it.

Holybourne is a straggling continuation of Alton on the Farnham road, and we pass S of Froyle and Bentley – a real life 'Ambridge' which featured in a documentary radio series in 1991–2 – to leave Hampshire just 2 miles/3.2 km W of Farnham. At the roundabout at the junction of roads A31 and A325, bear left along A325 to enter Farnham at West Street.

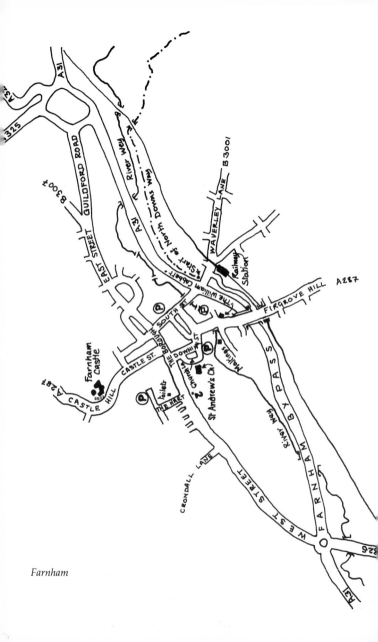

Farnham

4 Farnham to Guildford 11 miles/17.7 km

Farnham lies in a dip carved out by the River Wey, which flows S of the ridge to break through at Guildford on its way to the Thames. Being at the mouth of this valley, Farnham was a common meeting-place of travellers coming from all directions. It is at the junction of the old road and its still older predecessor from Salisbury Plain, and was always a place of importance – the meeting-place of roads from Salisbury Plain, the Channel, from London, and the Straits of Dover.

Farnham was the greatest market town in England for wheat, and had thriving hop fields, though it is now mainly a stockbroker suburb. It has many attractive Georgian buildings and is generally regarded as one of the best Georgian towns in England: two superb set-pieces are grouped in West Street and Castle Street, but there is a depressing amount of neo-Georgian throughout the rest of the town.

We will begin our exploration of the town as we enter at the west end along the long main street, here called West Street. Immediately we come upon the two show houses of Farnham, side by side on the south side of the street – No. 39, Sandford House, built 1757, and No. 38, Willmer House, built 1718. Both show the same sort of Baroque style, but the older Willmer House has one of the finest cut-brick façades in the country. The house is now the town's museum and includes personalia of William Cobbett, of *Rural Rides* fame. (Open Tuesdays–Saturdays, 1000–1700. Admission free).

Beyond, continuing towards the centre, is Vernon House, originally sixteenth-century but redone in 1727. It is now the public library and TIC. Tel 715109. (Open March–October, Mondays–Saturdays including Bank Holiday Mondays and November–February, Tuesdays–Saturdays, 1000–1300 and 1400–1730). Charles I stayed for a night here with Harry Vernon on 20 December 1648, on his way from Hurst Castle

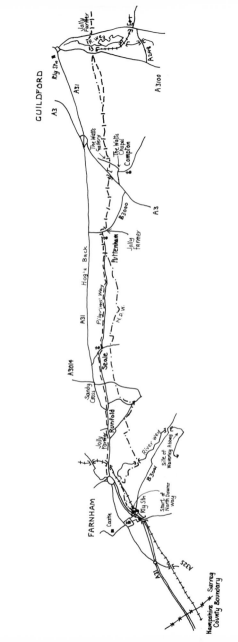

to London as a prisoner to his trial, and it was here that he met the Roundhead general Thomas Harris who was soon to sign his death warrant.

Opposite, on the N side, Nos. 88 to 94 are the best formal group in Farnham, all plain houses of 1760–80 except No. 94 which is a clever piece of twentieth-century building. This group shows eighteenth-century town housing as its very best; there is nothing so good as this further E. The *Surrey and Hants News* office is a converted eighteenth-century house and the 'Lion and Lamb', with close timbers and brick infilling, dates from 1537.

At the end of West Street, Downing Street runs off to the S and off this runs Middle and Lower Church Lane, leading to the Church of St Andrew, one of the largest in Surrey. The church has grown up from a Norman cross-shaped building, with a very long narrow nave and chancel and with wide aisles. It dates mostly from the early fifteenth century, but was so violently restored in 1855 that little but the medieval proportions remain. The best part is the impressive W tower with polygonal buttress, left unfinished at the Reformation but completed with a nineteenth-century top which looks like a fortress. About the church are many beautiful and interesting tributes to Farnham people – windows, stone inscriptions, brasses, and monuments; old, quaint, and fascinating. Cobbett was buried outside the N door of the church in 1835, beneath a marbled altar-tomb beside the simple stone slab to his father. A tablet with his portrait in relief is fixed on the S wall of the tower.

Leave the churchyard by its SE corner and go into Lower Church Lane, through the Waggon Yard car park to its SE corner, and cross the River Wey to The Maltings. The Maltings was originally a tannery but became a brewery in the 1850s and in 1969 was converted into a community centre.

Go into Red Lion Lane to Tanyard House, dating from 1500. Opposite in Bridge Square is the 'William Cobbett' public house, where William Cobbett was born in 1762.

A farmer's boy and soldier, William Cobbett became a publicist and reformer. He founded the *Political Register* in 1802 to publish political debates, which were printed by Luke Hansard, under whose name the reports are still printed today. Cobbett was gaoled in 1810 for two years for denouncing flogging in the army. After his release he became a Member of Parliament. When he died in 1835 he left in his writings a rich heritage of fine thoughts finely expressed. Of these, his *Rural Rides*, collected from his *Political Register*, are the most famous. They describe the English countryside and the sufferings of the exploited agricultural poor, the problems of home and farm, of estate and kingdom; and his work is a memorial to the death of old rural England. A column with the bust of Cobbett, standing in the riverside Gostrey Meadow, calls him the 'Champion of Democracy, master of English Prose and enemy of Cant in Public Affairs.'

Turn away from the William Cobbett, cross the River Wey by Longbridge and turn L with the traffic back up Downing Street to the West Street junction and turn right into the Borough, the narrow centre section of the main road. The National Westminster Bank has an Italianate front of 1860 and lies slap on the axis of Castle Street, the tallest building on this frontage and closing the view from the castle.

Castle Street, the former market place, runs N from the centre of Downing Street and sweeps up to the S side of the castle, which is seen above the trees, and then side-steps just at the last moment. Houses of 1750–1850 combine to make an impressive example of townscape, the group of Nos. 12 to 42 on the W side being particularly fine. On the L is a fine five-bay Georgian House of 1720, set back from the street, while beyond, on the E side, are the Windsor Almshouses, dating from 1619 and the only houses in Castle Street that have not been given a Georgian facelift. A notice declares they are for '8 poor, old, honest, impotent persons'!

Windsor Almshouses, Castle Street, Farnham

Farnham Castle

A flight of steps at the top of Castle Street called 'Blind Bishop's Steps' (seven flights of seven steps with seven paces between them) leads to the castle, which stands on the site where King Alfred's son, Edward, defeated the Danes in 893. The castle stands proudly on its hill, and those who climb to the top are rewarded with wide views of Farnham and the sweeping Downs.

The earliest structure was probably an earthen motte thrown up by Bishop Walkelin, and the castle remained the residence of the bishops of Winchester for 800 years until 1927. It was conveniently mid-way between Winchester and London.

The great shell-keep was built round the motte in 1138 by Bishop Henry de Blois (1129–71) and he also built the triangular bailey, in which is the bishop's residence. The group of domestic buildings adjoining this central core date from the same period, but they have been much transformed as the castle grew in significance down the centuries. The red brick parts of the castle visible from the town were built in 1470 and made it one of the finest brick buildings in England, as well as one of the best examples of a domestic castle in the country. The locally hand-made bricks were erected by Flemish masons.

To this episcopal palace came the greatest churchmen in the land. Here lived William of Wykeham, builder of Winchester; William of Waynflete, Lord Chancellor and founder of Magdalen College; Cardinal Beaufort, who saw Joan of Arc burned in the market place of Rouen; and Cardinal Wolsey with his master Henry VIII. They were followed by Mary I, who was entertained here by Bishop Gardiner on her way to marry Philip of Spain at Winchester in 1554; here Elizabeth I delivered her famous warning to the Duke of Norfolk (then planning to marry Mary, Queen of Scots) to beware on what pillow he laid his head. There are also recorded visits to the

The Keep, Farnham Castle

castle by James I, George III, and by Queen Victoria.

The castle keep is under the guardianship of the Department of the Environment (English Heritage). (Open daily April–September, 1000–1300 and 1400–1800. Free tape recorded commentary). The domestic parts of the castle were for 30 years up to 1956 the residence of the Bishops of Guildford but today they are the home of an organisation briefing people for official visits overseas. (Open every Wednesday, 1400–1600, for guided tours).

Church of St Lawrence, Seale

Farnham to Seale 4 miles/6.4 km

Farnham was the common meeting-place of travellers coming from all directions and it was from here that all the western tracks proceeded to the Straits of Dover, or rather Canterbury, the rallying-point of the several Kentish ports.

There were three ways to Guildford. Those in a hurry sped along the chalk ridge of the Hog's Back, but the great majority followed the lower track, below the ridge, on a straight line through Seale and Puttenham to St Catherine's Ferry on the River Wey. Many would follow this second route as far as Puttenham and then make the diversion to Compton, to rejoin the main route at St Catherine's.

The Pilgrims' Way

From the centre of Farnham continue along The Borough and East Street for nearly 1 mile/1.6 km, passing a good many old houses but nothing of real interest. Bear right along Guildford Road and continue ahead to the huge roundabout at the intersection of A31 with the Farnham Bypass. Continue ahead on the same line, E, on the A31 and cross over the railway.

At this point just outside the town the road begins to rise; an indication that it is about to take to the flank of the hills, a position which it holds uninterruptedly (save for the four short gaps occasioned by four river valleys) until just before Canterbury.

The rise continues gradually until the 'Jolly Farmer' at Runfold and the fork at Whiteways. Here the main road bends sharply left to take in the ridge of the Hog's Back, while the old road continues ahead, 200 ft/60 m below, on the side of the hill to Seale. As you enter the village bear right and reach the church.

Seale church of St Lawrence stands on a little mound and the track passed S of it, not right against its porch, but as near as it could. The church was built at the expense of Waverley in the period of enthusiasm that followed the first pilgrimages, just after 1200. The timber porch is 600 years old and is perhaps the most impressive thing left in the church since its

Victorian 'restoration', though there are interesting and tragic memorials, and one of the six bells in the tower was made 300 years ago.

(The PW continues on page 88.)

The North Downs Way

The North Downs Way starts at Farnham on the S side of the A31, just E of the traffic lights near the railway station. Follow a rough lane alongside the River Wey and parallel to the A31, and at 'The Kiln' pass under the railway, following the edge of a wood to reach a road. You soon turn E and cross the River Wey to reach Moor Park.

Moor Park was built about 1630 and was bought and altered in 1684 by Sir William Temple, the diplomat. The only part of Temple's work which survives is the sober Wren-style loggia and doorway of the main entrance, with Temple's arms painted on a cast-iron cartouche. The original walls are encased in stucco. It is a shame that the gardens have disappeared into a wilderness of weeds and blocked-up lakes in the fields below the house, because Temple built them to exemplify the ideas set out in his essay 'Of Gardens' – ideas which were really little removed from the then current Anglo-Dutch formal practice. Temple brought the Chinese word 'sharawaggi' into the language, meaning an informal pictur-esque landscape, but from surviving prints it does not seem that he attempted anything on that scale. He did, however, try for more informal picturesque gardening than the French practice then common. Moor Park is now a college for adult Christian education.

Jonathan Swift, aged 22, came to Moor Park in 1689 to act as secretary to Sir William Temple and as tutor to Temple's sister, the 8-year-old Esther Johnson, the famous 'Stella' to whom he wrote his *Journal*. Swift was waiting to be appointed to a church in Ireland, which he hoped Temple would secure for him, but, disappointed in the extent of Temple's patron-age, Swift went to Ireland of his own accord in 1694. Never-theless, his connections with Temple continued, and Swift

Waverley Abbey

returned to Moor Park in 1696, where he wrote his satires *The Battle of the Books* and *The Tale of a Tub*, which were published together in 1704. When Temple died in 1699, Swift returned to Ireland and later became Dean of St Patrick's Cathedral in Dublin. Stella, now a beautiful 18-year-old, inherited Temple's property in Ireland, and went there in 1701; tradition has it that Swift secretly married her in 1716. Stella died in 1728, aged 47, and was buried in the cathedral. Swift was 78 when he died, 17 years later, and he was buried by her side.

A little way downstream from Moor Park is the site of Waverley Abbey, the very first Cistercian house in England, founded in 1132 by the Bishop of Winchester, William Giffard, with monks from Anmone in Normandy. (The second English Cistercian house was Tintern, founded in 1131, on a similar style; and the abbeys of Rievaulx and Fountains both followed in 1132.) Waverley was completed by about 1160, its plan expressing perfectly the extreme austerity of the Cistercian order. It has a long un-aisled nave, a short, square-ended presbytery, short transepts, each having one chapel. The width across the transepts is 150 ft/45 m and the nave is 300 ft/91 m long. The Cistercians rebuilt the abbey between 1203–1278, but none of the church now survives. The only things left, besides heaps of masonry, are a few fragments of the monastic buildings. (Open 15 March–15 October Weekdays 0930–1830, Sundays 1400–1830 and 16 October–14 March Weekdays 0930–1600, Sundays 1400–1600. Admission free).

The house now called Waverley Abbey is admirably composed in the landscape when viewed from near the abbey. The present structure was built c.1770, and supersedes one built here c.1725 for Aislabie, the Chancellor of the Exchequer who was disgraced by the South Sea Bubble in 1720. The house gave Sir Walter Scott the inspiration for his 'Waverley' novels. It is now a Christian training centre.

Returning to Moor Park College, we follow the line of the NDW uphill in a generally NE direction (in line with the bridge over the River Wey) for about 1 mile/1.6 km, to reach a minor road. We cross this to reach another minor road and follow it SE in the direction of The Sands for about ½ mile/ 800 m. Here we turn N up the road by the golf-clubhouse to Binton Cottage, and then round the N side of the golf-course, across another minor road, gradually turning E towards Seale on a line about ½ mile/800 m S of the Pilgrims' Way.

(The NDW continues on page 89.)

Seale to Puttenham 2 miles/3.2km

The Pilgrims' Way
Just to the S of the church, by the war memorial, the road bends left along the flank of a hill, passing East End Farm, a group of buildings round a fine sixteenth-century timbered house with striking chimneys. In another mile/1.6 km we

come to Shoelands, a Tudor house with parts dating from 1616. Its name has been connected with 'schooling', or almsgiving, from 'shoolers' or beggars who preyed on pious pilgrims.

(The PW continues on page 90, in Puttenham.)

The North Downs Way

The NDW leaves Seale on the S side of the village through and alongside woods about ½ mile/800m S of the PW, and reaches a drive at the entrance of the Hampton Estate. The house is not very interesting – a small picturesque villa of 1798, altered out of all recognition about 60 years later – but the park is quite untouched, a superb piece of Repton-style gardening, which Pevsner thinks is probably the best in Surrey. The NDW (a RUPP) crosses the slopes of Puttenham Common, from where there are good views of the Hampton Park. When the path forks, keep straight ahead, eventually coming out on a lane – Lascombe Lane – which takes us down to the edge of Puttenham village, where we join the PW at a road junction beside a telephone box.

(The NDW continues on page 91, with the PW.)

Puttenham village consists of one long street in a pretty

The old and new A3 cross the Pilgrims' Way near Compton

situation just S of the Hog's Back, fortunately not yet the nine-storey-high village with poultry farm and vitamin factory of *Brave New World*. It lies on the exact dividing line between chalk and sandstone, so the cottages use both, with a lot of brickwork also. Just before the church is reached is Greys Home Farm, with a good set of weatherboarded barns including a range of four oasthouses, a rarity in the country, now converted into dwellings.

Just before entering the centre of the village from the W, the PW turns a sharp corner, so much against its nature that there must be an explanation for it. The present road goes round to the N of the church, outside a high wall, which therefore forbids any passage. It turns sharp round a corner and proceeds due S along road B3000 to the 'Jolly Farmer' inn. The old road has been lost in the village and it is probable that it passed south of the church direct to the 'Jolly Farmer'. The road through the village, the S porch of the church and the front of the inn are all in the same alignment, and short of any physical obstacle, there is no reason but private property, and property long established and defined, to give rise to such an unnatural and sudden right-angled turn in the road: a ninteenth-century occupant of Puttenham Priory caused the old road to be re-routed because it passed in front of his windows!

The medieval details of the Church of St John Baptist merge into a clumsy restoration of 1861, but the inside still keeps plastered walls and a pleasant village appearance. The fifteenth-century tower patched with red brick lost its spire in a fire 200 years ago, and we enter the church through the unusually decorated S porch dating from 1170. The oddest thing about the nave arcade columns is that their bases rise from bay to bay as if the floor had originally been kept at an incline. The four-bay N arcade has windows of 1160 and there are other renewed twelfth-century features. The chancel is very attractive with its modern oak panelling and carvings, and has mainly Perpendicular windows. There is a 20-in/50cm high brass on the chancel floor of Edward Cranford, rector of the church c.1400–31, and a charge is made to take a rubbing. In the N aisle is a memorial to Esther Bellasis, who married Captain George Bellasis of the East India Company: he killed a man in a duel and was transported to Botany Bay; poor Esther died of a broken heart in 1805.

To the S of the church stands Puttenham Priory, a handsome provincial Palladian house of 1762. The main front looks W, and is faced with golden stucco in a very good imitation of stone. The picturesque Tudor building among trees just E of the church is the Rectory.

From the road junction at the top of the street beside the church bear right to the 'Jolly Farmer'. We have now come 34 miles/55km from Winchester, and except for the first 2 miles/3.2km the route has followed principally a busy highway and other metalled roads. At this point, however, now we have gained the chalk ridge, we leave the main roads behind and continue our journey along pleasant tracks and footpaths.

Puttenham to Compton 2 miles/3.2km
From the 'Jolly Farmer' the road B3000 continues S to the village of Compton before turning eastwards towards the Wey, and pious pilgrims probably travelled this route to visit Compton church. We must also visit Compton, but we will first follow the main track over Puttenham Heath before making the short diversion to the village.

Between the villages of Puttenham and Compton, the PW and the NDW follow the same course, and do so for 4 miles/6.4km, until just short of Littleton Cross (see page 96.)

Directly opposite the 'Jolly Farmer' take the left-hand rough track passing Pilgrims' Way Cottage on your right beside the golf-clubhouse (bridleway). The track runs clearly at the left edge of the heath beside a hedge and you keep straight on along it, keeping the golf-course on your right. When the gravelly track bears left, keep right along a sandy track, and at the next fork keep left, i.e. straight ahead. Pass beyond a modern bungalow and a few cottages, and when the golf-course ends on the right, pass between thick saplings to a broad crossing-track (bridleway).

This broad dirt track comes in from the left from Monk-shatch and continues S to the A3 at the junction with B3000. The old road disappears at this crossing, but 350 yds/320m ahead a slightly sunken way reappears. Cross the Monkshatch track to a path opposite running along the foot of a wooded slope known as Hurt Hill, and after 750 yds/685 m join the track from the farm we have just passed. Pass under the new A3 on a metalled road, then through a brick-built arch under the old A3 – the bridge was designed by the distinguished architect Sir Edwin Lutyens and is topped by two prominent wooden crosses to indicate to motorists the crossing of the Pilgrims' Way. Continue to a road, passing on the left hand the driveway up to Limnerslease.

Limnerslease was the home of the great artist of the late Victorian era, George Frederic Watts, OM, RA (1817–1904). He came to Compton in 1866 from Kensington, London and built Limnerslease in 1891. He had decorated the Houses of Parliament and some of his portraits and pictures hang in The National Gallery and The Tate Gallery. From Limnerslease, the Watts Gallery is just up the road to the left. It stands behind the building which formerly housed the Potters' Art Guild, founded by Mrs G. F. Watts in 1903, and contains hundreds of his great paintings, sculptures and sketches. (Open free to the public daily except Thursdays, 1 April–30 September, 1400–1800, 1 October–31 March 1400–1600, and on Saturday mornings 1100–1300. There is also a tea shop, open seven days a week, 1030–1730).

We must make the short detour to see the church at nearby Compton, for it is believed to have been visited by many pilgrims on their way eastwards. It has a unique upper sanctuary which is thought to have contained important relics.

Halfway along the road to Compton we come to a cemetery with the Watts Mortuary Chapel, one of the most curious and one of the least-known ecclesiastical edifices in the country. Mrs Watts designed this terracotta burial chapel in 1896 for

The Watts Mortuary Chapel, Compton

her husband, and it was built in local materials by local men and plastered by trained villagers who worked in the pottery which she had founded.

Inside and out it is covered with scores of mystic symbols. The outside is a mixture of Italian Romanesque motifs and heavy Victorian symbolism. A great frieze runs round the outside walls and shows on the east face Hope, next Truth, then Love and finally Light. Angel faces look down inside the triple arch of the doorway, which has a wrought-iron cross copied from a gravestone at Iona.

The remarkable interior was designed in 1901 and is pure Art Nouveau – a very startling and effective room with angels and cherubs and heavy colours of gold, red, and green. The silver roots of the Tree of Life decorate the walls below and in the roof is the Circle of Eternity. On the walls are four great groups of angels, all carrying three pairs of symbols; on entering the doorway these are, clockwise: Day and Night, Flow and Ebb, Growth and Decay; next Life and Death, Good and Evil, Labour and Rest; then Joy and Sorrow, Spirit and Flesh, Real and Ideal; and finally Freedom and Limit, Union and Conflict, Stability and Change. The walls are also covered with mystical work in ruby plaster and gilded: there are over 100 medallions and winged cherubs. There is a picture by Watts painted to express the idea of the All-Pervading, with suns and rolling systems in the lap of a great enfolding figure encompassed by the hands of Love. Watts is not buried in this chapel but in the 'cloister', also designed by Mrs Watts, at the top of the cemetery, which is also worth exploring for other Art Nouveau memorials.

One-quarter of a mile/400m further down the road we come to the Church of St Nicholas, Compton, on the N side of the village. It is mainly a Norman church with great round pillars and timber roof, but it has a Saxon tower, impressively plain, unbuttressed, and with simple rectangular openings.

The fame of Compton church is in its remarkable chancel, quite unlike any other church in England. It is one of the smallest but has a two-storey sanctuary, and no one has yet been able to give a reason for it.

The first Norman chancel arch was built about 1080 and then 100 years later when the style was changing into English the remarkable upper storey was added. Two arches, one set back inside the other, rest on round columns bedded in circular bases on square plinths, and carry the upper sanctuary; the columns are entirely of chalk, with beautifully carved capitals which lead the eye up to the inside of the arches, where the coating of the Norman plaster is cut into a unique decoration.

The two-storey sanctuary is enclosed by a little chancel screen with nine simple arches cut out of one piece of oak or chestnut, one of the earliest and sole surviving examples of Norman church woodwork in the country. The little stone

Interior of the Watts Mortuary Chapel, Compton

chamber which leads up the steps to the upper storey was once the home of a hermit.

When the interest of the chancel and its sanctuaries are exhausted there are many other splendid works to investigate in the church. Compton, with its Church of St Nicholas and Watts Chapel and Gallery, must be one of the most interesting places we visit along the line of the PW/NDW.

Compton to Guildford 3 miles/4.8km
The two routes from Compton continue as a public bridleway, passing immediately S of the Watts Gallery. It is a pretty, sunken, tree-lined path that lives up to its name of Sandy Lane. After 1½ miles/2.4km, just after a break in the woods on the S side, opposite Conduit Farm, the NDW takes a higher line, on a track (footpath) to Piccards Farm, to reach the main road A3100; while the PW takes a lower line (bridleway) to reach a road at a sharp corner, known as Littleton Cross, and then follows this road, past the police headquarters, to join the PW at 'The Ship' on the A3100.

Just S of the routes, and seen from the gap in the trees near Conduit Farm, is the impressive N front of Loseley House, the best Elizabethan house surviving in Surrey. It was built in 1562 for Sir William Moore, one of the Queen's counsellors, with the main range in Burgate stone, with whitened clunch dressings looted from Waverley Abbey (near Farnham) which had recently been dissolved by Henry VIII. It has attractive asymmetrical elevations, but a wing added by Sir George Moore (d.1632) was pulled down in the nineteenth century. Sir George's daughter ran away from here to her secret marriage with John Donne, the poet and divine. The house is still occupied by Sir William's descendants, and is open to the public in summer. (Open June–September, Wednesdays–Saturdays, 1400–1700).

Just S of the point where the two routes meet the main A3100 Guildford road is St Catherine's Chapel, standing on a

The Pilgrims' Way, Sandy Lane, Compton

St Catherine's Chapel, Shalford

curious platform on the crest of the hill just to the S of Ferry Lane, which takes our routes down to the River Wey. It is believed that there was a chapel here 700 years ago, but the ruins of the walls we see are early fourteenth century. It has been suggested that the large number of doors was necessary to allow pilgrims to file past some holy relic. Nobly have they stood the storms of time, but the feeble iron railings hardly prevent vandals from advancing its destruction.

St Catherine's had the right to hold a fair, which was timed for the return of pilgrims from the July festival of the Translation of St Thomas in Canterbury. It became so popular that it later moved to nearby Shalford, where it occupied 57 ha/140 acres. John Bunyan had lived on Shalford Common for some time and the fair may have given him the idea for *Vanity Fair* and the nearby marshy ground by the river was perhaps the Slough of Despond.

Although it appears obvious from the map, the exact spot at which the River Wey is crossed is not easily determined, but the PW appears on the other side, half a mile/800m away, by the north-west corner of Chantries Wood.

There is a precipitous face towards the river and the summit of St Catherine's Hill is isolated and commands views up and down the valley. It would have been a site sacred to a primitive tribe, and such men would have chosen a ford over the river than a ferry, and the ford exists. It has given its name, 'the shallow ford', to the village of Shalford, which grew up near it, with the church standing close by. So it would appear that the PW would pass over the crest of St Catherine's, come down to the S and cross to Shalford; but from Shalford to Chantries Wood no track is apparent, and no passage could be made to Shalford except by a detour much sharper than the old road executes in any other part of its course.

However, a sunken way of great antiquity leads directly from St Catherine's Hill down to the river. It follows the only practicable descent of the bank, at its foot was a ferry, and beyond a path crosses a field, crosses the main road A281 and leads immediately and without any diversion to the corner of Chantries Wood. Perhaps the passage at Shalford was used first, and soon replaced by the ferry a little way downstream.

From 'The Ship', Ferry Lane crosses the London-Portsmouth railway in a deep cutting and then drops steeply down to the River Wey. After having crossed the railway, notice Pilgrim Cottage on the left, with a mosaic of St Christopher, the patron saint of travellers, on the chimney stack.

St Catherine's Ferry used to operate during the summer season, at weekends, and at other times, but it no longer does so. At last, after many years, a footbridge has been built over the River Wey at this point to give access to the route ahead. There had been difficulties about the abutments of the bridge in the sandy, tree-clad slopes above the river, about not interfering with passage along the towpath, and respecting the privacy of adjoining cottages, but the bridge has finally been erected.

If you need accommodation in Guildford, or wish to take a walk around the town, then it is a pleasant walk alongside the river into the town. Alternatively, cross the bridge and go across the meadows and playing fields to just S of a block of toilets, telephone and bus stop on the A281, ½ mile/800m S of the 'Jolly Farmer'.

(Note that we have passed three pubs between Farnham and Guildford called the 'Jolly Farmer'. I can't imagine many farmers in these towns, never mind jolly ones. Perhaps they sold their land to the breweries for pubs to be built on them!)

Part Two: River Wey to River Mole

5 Guildford to Dorking 12 miles/19km

Guildford

Guildford is an interesting and ancient town with an old castle and a modern cathedral. The town developed in this gap in the North Downs in Saxon times. Its name 'The Golden Ford' is of Saxon origin, and the town had a Royal Mint in late Saxon times. The tower of St Mary's Church is an excellent example of late-Saxon architecture, and is the town's oldest building.

As the wool trade died out in the seventeenth century Guildford became important when the River Wey was dredged, straightened and canalised in 1653 so that barges could sail up to the town from London. The growing port of Portsmouth was then only a days ride away over land.

The steep, cobbled High Street was declared by Dickens to be the most beautiful in the kingdom: although spoilt by plate-glass shopfronts, part of its glory has been restored by the removal of modern traffic congestion and the introduction of a partial pedestrian precinct. In and around this street cluster all Guildford's ancient places, the centrepiece of attraction being the quaint sixteenth-century Tudor Guildhall with seventeenth-century front and its magnificent overhanging seventeenth-century clock. The case is original and was made in 1683, but modern works have replaced the original works made in 1560. Notice the nice ironwork and also the buttresses upholding the little balcony, carved like ships' figureheads.

There are several places to see and visit in Guildford – the Tudor Royal Free Grammar School founded by Edward VI in 1553 at the top of High Street; the Jacobean gatehouse of the Abbot's Hospital, founded as an almshouse in 1619 by George Abbot, Archbishop of Canterbury; the Norman castle keep

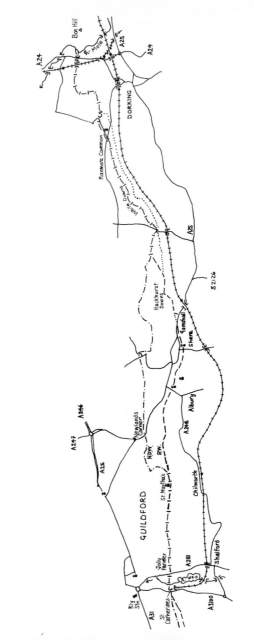

built by Henry II; and the Yvonne Arnaud Theatre, 1965, beside the river. The Rev C. L. Dodgson, better known as Lewis Carroll, died in the house called The Chestnuts below the castle in 1898, and is buried in Guildford cemetery.

One must not fail also to visit the massive Cathedral of the Holy Spirit dominating Stag Hill to the W of the town. It is a long way to walk, by way of Farnham Road, turning first right up Guildford Park Road to Stag Hill, and is perhaps best reached by taking the bus.

Travellers will come to this impressive building in a hundred or a thousand years' time, just as we now come from Winchester to Canterbury. The cathedral is built in the shape of a cross to Sir Edward Maufe's design, and from end to end measures 365ft/111m. It is 70ft/21m high and 40ft/12m wide, and the top of the tower is 180ft/55m above the ground.

The main vaulting is of concrete, sprayed with asbestos plaster to prevent echoes, and externally faced with rose-red coloured brickwork. You will have to decide for yourself whether you approve of this neo-gothic compromise, but it is the proportions of mass, volume, space, and line rather than elaboration and the repetition of ornament, that make this cathedral so imposing. The foundation stone was laid by the Archbishop of Canterbury on 22 July 1936, and rests on stones brought from the fabric of both Canterbury and Winchester Cathedrals. The cathedral was completed and consecrated in 1962.

Guildford to St Martha's 2 miles/3.2km
Leave Guildford on the A281 and follow it southwards beyond the 'Jolly Farmer' for a further ½ mile/800m, to the point where a grassy path comes across the meadows of Shalford Park to the public toilets. E of the main road take Pilgrims' Way Road, which after a few hundred yards/metres bends left into Echo Pit Road. Here a private drive forks right, signposted to Chantries and St Martha's, a bridleway all the way.

Guildford to Ranmore Common

Guildford

Bear left at whitewashed Chantry Cottage and enter the fringe of Chantries Wood, passing soon South Warren Farm on the left. Continue on the track through the wood, then fenced between fields, shortly to emerge at the road by Tyting Farm. Where the track bends there is a rustic seat and two notice-boards, and we take a path continuing in a forward direction to emerge at Half Penny Lane, a few hundred yards/ metres S of Tyting Farm.

At this road turn left for a short distance, and at the '30 mph' signs take a narrow path on your right leading up to the open heath, used as a car park for those visiting St Martha's. Keep the close-boarded fence on your right, and when this ends keep straight on up the hill. (The bridleway contours round the S flank of the hill while the public footpath goes over the top, passing N of the church). The old road is just discernible as a sunken way through the pines, but as it nears the summit it disappears, only to reappear some 20yards/18m or so at the beginning of the descent on the other side.

On the isolated summit of this high ridge stands the famous little church known as St Martha's on the Hill. It was originally, rather inconveniently, the parish church of Chilworth, a hamlet of modern bungalows in the valley below where, from Elizabeth I's reign until the eighteenth century, banknotes and gunpowder were made: 'two of the most damnable inventions' of man, according to Cobbett.

St Martha's stands 573ft/175m above sea-level with a glorious view over the wooded Surrey countryside. It stands at a place where, almost certainly, heathen worship was practised by the Early Bronze Age people who lived on this hill, and it is thought also to mark the place of massacre of early Christian martyrs. Some say the church is dedicated to St Martha because she – Mary Magdalene's sister – actually visited this spot when, in company with Lazarus and St Joseph of Arimathea, she visited Britain. There is no other church in England dedicated to St Martha.

The church is constructed of Burgate ironstone with sandstone dressings; materials from the hill on which it stands –

an isolated summit of ironstone surrounded by sandstone of a geological fault. The church was in ruins until it was rebuilt in 1850 in the impressive Norman style on its original cruci-form foundations and with a low central tower. It contains a minimum of carved detail, but has a window in the S wall of the chancel dedicated to St Thomas Martyr and bearing the Arms of Canterbury.

St Martha's stirs the imagination, yet there is only a brief outline of its history on record. It became one of the pos-sessions of Newark Priory, a few miles/km away, before Magna Carta. When Edward I and his queen were away in the Holy Land, candles were lit here for their little son Henry lying ill in Guildford Castle. In the reign of Edward IV, Bishop Waynflete of Winchester granted Forty Days' Indulgence to any penitent who made a pilgrimage here or gave money for the upkeep of the church. In his document, dated 20 May 1463, the church is called 'the chapel dedicated to Saint Martha the Virgin and all the Holy Martyrs commonly called Martirhill'.

After the monasteries were dissolved St Martha's came into the hands of the squire of Chilworth Manor, and it gradually fell into ruin as the generations came and went. Roofless and neglected, but with services still being held in the chancel, it had become a sorry sight until it was rebuilt in 1848–50. The church is open all Bank Holidays and every afternoon except Monday during the period April 1–October 1, and services are held every Sunday.

At St Martha's the Pilgrims' Way and the North Downs Way part company and they rejoin at Hackhurst Downs.

The North Downs Way – St Martha's to Hackhurst Downs via Newlands Corner 5 miles/8km
We leave St Martha's by a gate in the churchyard wall at the E end, passing along the sandy ridge, which soon begins to descend sharply. After passing through trees to a small

The Angel Hotel yard, Guildford

clearing 50yds/45m before an old wartime pill-box, fork left to go down to Guildford Lane at a corner at Ramshackle Cottage. The route turns left, then immediately right, on a path parallel with the road northwards, past Whitelane Cottage, to a bend in the road. On reaching some concrete steps, cross the road and turn E up into the woods. Take a right fork almost immediately, then left up and out on to grassland, where another fork left takes the path to the edge of the woods. Keep to the well-defined path which follows the S edge of the woods, and, where it ends, cross to the car park, picnic area, toilets, visitor and countryside centre and refreshment facilities at Newlands Corner.

Newlands Corner gives one of the finest views of Southern England. The South Downs act as a backcloth with Chanctonbury Ring in the distance, and close by are the greensand hills of St Martha's, Hascombe, Hindhead and Blackdown. The viewpoint is named after Abraham Newland, a signatory of the banknotes made at Chilworth.

Cross the busy A25 at a dangerous corner and take a bridleway opposite at a barrier signposted 'Open Space – Newlands Corner'. Just E of the main road here is a fine bowl barrow, 60 ft/18m in diameter and 4–5ft/1.5m high. It appears to have been opened, but with no recorded results.

There now follows 1½ miles/2.4km of trackway and drove-road due E, eventually passing through the car park at West Hangar and on to the Shere-East Clandon road, called Staple Lane. Cross the road to the path opposite, and on reaching another road – Combe Lane, the Shere-East/West Horsley road – turn due S to Hollister Farm. At the farm turn E again to enter woods at a gate, continuing on a path for another 1½ miles/2.4km, ignoring other tracks coming in from left or right. There is a confusing variety of tracks at Gravehill Gate on Netley Heath, above the Colekitchen Coombe, but you keep straight on to a point where the track forms a circle. Here you leave the drove-road to cross the open slopes of

The Keep, Guildford Castle

The Pilgrims' Way on the ascent to St Martha's

Hackhurst Downs. Turn S down a wide path, and after 200 yds/180m fork E to maintain height on the vast open space of the downs. The cross-track coming up from the S brings the Pilgrims' Way route up to the Downs.

(The NDW continues on page 119, with the PW.)

The Pilgrims' Way – St Martha's to Hackhurst Downs via Shere 5 miles/8km

We leave St Martha's by a gate in the churchyard wall at the eastern end and pass by a clump of pines. At the foot of these trees can be seen the sunken trackway again, fenced on the right hand side by measures to control erosion.

An old wartime pill-box marks the start of The Downs Link, a footpath created in 1984 linking the NDW with the SDW,

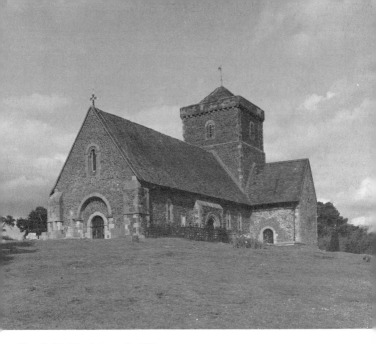

Chapel of St Martha's on the Hill

largely along the line of the old railway tracks from Guildford to Horsham. The pill-box stands on the line of the sunken way at the fringe of the trees, and the depression of the old track can be followed to a prominent yew tree, then to the Albury-Guildford road called Guildford Lane. We will come to see several of these wartime defensive structures in the new few miles/km, but whether by coincidence or design they all seem to be sited on the line of the PW, and they therefore help to define the route we must follow.

Go along the bridleway between fences on the opposite side of Guildford Lane to a corner of a wood. Continue along the top edge of the next field, with the wood on your right, down to a hedged lane which serves Newbarn Farm. Pass through the gateway immediately opposite and bear slightly right uphill across the field to a wicket gate at the corner of a wood. Pass through this into the wood, and with the wood on your right and the field over the hedge on your left, drop down to Water Lane leading N from Albury up to Newlands Corner.

Here arises a difficulty unique in the whole course of the Way. The trail for once goes to the damp and northward side of a hill, upon which stands Weston Wood. Turn left up Water Lane for 20 yds/18m, then right past two pairs of semi-detached houses along a grassy lane (bridleway), sunken between hedges, to pass N of Weston Wood.

One hundred yards/metres or so past a little cottage, by a prominent chestnut tree on the left, bear half-right along a sunken track, with a row of beech trees on your right, to emerge at the corner of the wood in a clearing. Albury sand pit lies concealed in the trees on the right and the track on the left leads to the main road A25.

Cross the track to the sand pit on a footpath and climb a stile ahead, bearing right round the edge of the wood to another stile, then bear left beside a barbed-wire fence to a stile at the main road A248, just S of its junction with A25.

Just to the N of this road junction is the famous Silent Pool, reputed to be haunted by a beautiful maiden named Emma who was drowned in the pool many centuries ago. If you come on a moonlight night you may see her bathing, and if you keep still and quiet you may hear her shriek as she disappears below the surface of the still waters. The Silent Pool was made famous by Martin Tupper's romance, *Stephen Langton*. She was bathing naked when surprised by 'wicked' Prince John and wading deeper and deeper to hide her embarrassment she got out of her depth and drowned.

Albury lies just S of the Way in the gentle Tillingbourne valley, a picturesque estate village of the 1800s. The village was bodily transplanted from its old site in the Park in the early nineteenth century to this location ½ mile/800m west-wards, the site of a hamlet then called Weston Street. Pretty cottages cluster around in the Romanesque church of St Peter and St Paul, built of brick with a tall tower topped by a pyramid roof in 1842 in a style by William McIntosh Brooks that would hardly be out of place on the Italian Lakes.

To the E of the village and the main road A248 is Albury Park which had a very interesting history as it passed through successive wealthy hands in the eighteenth and nineteenth centuries.

The original house was Tudor, half-timbered, but was almost entirely rebuilt for the Duke of Norfolk in 1653 to the design of George Evelyn. The house was accidentally burnt down in 1697 and was rebuilt c.1700.

In 1784 the property was bought by a Captain Finch, a very wealthy man who had captured a rich Spanish ship in the Spanish War of 1779. When he died in 1794 the estate was bought by Samuel Thornton who was Governor of the Bank of England for fifty-three years (1780–1833). Thornton commissioned Sir John Soane to alter the house c.1800, but in 1811 the estate was sold to Charles Wall, who lived there for eight years. In their thirty-five years of ownership of the estate these three owners closed the roads, annexed land and harassed the villagers, causing most of them to leave and to be resettled at Weston Street.

Henry Drummond, politician and banker, bought the estate in 1819 and the house was finally completed and depressingly remodelled for him by the ageing Augustus Pugin in 1846–52. Architecturally it now has little to offer except an 'unconvincing Tudor style, with brick dressings to the windows, battlements and gables, and a set of 68 ornate brick chimneys culled from every imaginable Tudor source, each one different.' (Nairn and Pevsner).

The house was, for many years until her death in 1965, the home of the Dowager Duchess of Northumberland. It stood empty for four years until 1969 when purchased by the Country Houses Association, a non-profit-making organisation dedicated to preserving country houses for the nation and to providing housing for retired and semi-retired people. Conversion work was completed in 1971 and provides 40 private apartments. The park is open to the public for access to the old church, and the house grounds and its reception rooms by Soane are open to the public. (House and grounds open 1 May–30 September, Wednesdays and Thursdays, 1400–1700).

Historically the main interest in Albury is the landscaped park, laid out by diarist John Evelyn and George Evelyn for the Duke of Norfolk between 1655–58, chiefly in two parallel terraces 400m long along the side of the hill N of the house and below the ridge carrying the PW. A grotto was excavated under the main terrace and a tunnel, 146m/160 yards long, which still exists, was driven right through the hill to Silverwood Cottages.

The old church of St Peter and Paul in the park near the house can just be recognised from the PW by its shingled fifteenth-century dome to the tower peeping through the trees. The church has a Saxon foundation with Norman plan of nave, tower and chancel. A S transept was added in 1290 and decorated in 1839 by Augustus Pugin in red, blue and gold as a chapel for Henry Drummond. There is a fine brass of a knight in full armour: the Latin inscription says 'Here lies John Weston, Knight, who died 23rd day of November anno domini 1440 on whose soul may God have mercy.' The Weston family held the manor of Weston and Albury from about 1200. William Oughtred (c1573–1660), mathematician and tutor to Christopher Wren, was rector here from 1610 for fifty years to his death. He invented the multiplication sign (x).

The church was disused from 1842. (Open 1 April–31 October daily, 1000–1700). Drummond had become a member of the Catholic Apostolic Church and his faith could not allow him to permit this church to remain in use whilst on his property: the village population had anyway moved to Weston Street so he employed William McIntosh Brooks to design and build a new church for the new parish priest in Weston Street.

Brooks also designed for Drummond, at a cost of £16,000 in 1840, the Catholic Apostolic Church or Irvingite Church for

The Pilgrims' Way on St Martha's Hill

his founder-friend Edward Irving. The church lies just S of the PW beside the main road, a spectacular and surprising sight among the trees. Irving had created a great sensation in London by his preachings and prophecies, and was later tried for heresy. The interior has some handsome woodcarving by a local man, the best of which is the very beautiful altar made of cedar wood brought from the Holy Land. The church is no longer used for services and is not open for viewing.

Cross the road A248 and take the track opposite (footpath) past the caretaker's cottage, over a stile and straight ahead through a field to a field gate and stile at the edge of a wood. Here the PW reaches a prominent ridge, from which one may gain occasional glimpses of Albury House through the trees.

When you enter the wood take the higher, left-hand foot-path to the crest of the ridge where some tree felling has taken place. Keep to the right along the ridge, descending to the edge of the wood at an iron kissing-gate. Pass through the field to another similar gate straight ahead, and drop down to a metalled lane. Cross this and take a footpath directly opposite, which soon leads to a road. Turn right in this, crossing over the Tilling Bourne ford by a footbridge, then bear left into the village of Shere.

Shere is a pretty little village, often claimed as Surrey's most beautiful, and has drawn many an artist to paint the quaint-ness of its narrow picturesque streets and colourwashed cottages. The old grey Church of St James adds much to the delight of the scene and is found at the end of a funnel of cottages forming Church Square on the S side of the Tilling Bourne stream.

The church has an early Norman central tower topped by a big shingled broach spire dating from about 1275. There are two fine doorways: the S having a Norman arch richly carved with chevrons and foliage, and with several mass-clocks scratched below it. The W doorway is thirteenth-century and beautifully moulded, framing a big studded door of 1626. There are several beautiful windows containing fragments of fourteenth-century glass, and the best remains show the symbols of the Evangelists: Matthew's angel, Mark's lion, Luke's bull and John's eagle. The E window of 1902 is an effective mosaic of colour, particularly when seen from a distance. There are several fifteenth-century brasses, four in the S aisle and two in the chancel. Also in the S aisle is a case displaying woodwind instruments used in the minstrel gallery during the early nineteenth century.

The PW may have passed beside the southern porch of the church, and if it did it would have to cross the Tilling Bourne again; this double crossing of the stream may be accounted for by the presence of a shrine and of a settlement in the

Church of St James, Shere

oldest times. If the road bridge be taken as an indication of the original place where the stream was recrossed, however, then the track would have left the church on the right, and would have turned round to become the present Dorking Road leading to A25.

A map on display in the village shows the PW leaving Shere church by a path leading to the SW corner of Gomshall, then just E of the railway bridge over A25, having crossed the Tilling Bourne and Gomshall Marsh. It is then shown making a right-angled left turn up Beggars Lane, under the railway again, and on to Hackhurst Downs. This right-angled turn has been made for no possible reason and this line cannot but be a confusion with the old drove-road to London.

From Shere the track must have crossed the high road A25 at a point nearly opposite Netley House, and by a slow climb made for the flank of the Downs and the chalk, and followed this line until it reaches Chilham, some 65 miles/104km away.

Beyond the grounds of Netley House just before you enter Gomshall take a road on the left (Colekitchen Lane) sign-posted 'No Through Road for Motor Vehicles' and after a few hundred yards/metres take a signposted footpath on the right. The old road is lost here, but it must have turned gradually eastwards to cross the mouth of Colekitchen Coombe, which here runs into the hills, and have reached in this fashion the 400ft/122m contour at the corner of Hackhurst Downs near a pill-box, on the edge of National Trust property. Our footpath goes directly NE up through a block of NT property on Hackhurst Downs, but another route, parallel to it and only 100m away, is a RUPP called Beggars Lane and seems to confirm an ancient right of way.

From this point the line of the PW can be followed for miles without undue difficulty. Its platform is nearly always distinct, and the line is marked by yew trees, though the platform is cut here and there by later roads. Box Hill attracts and holds the eye as one looks eastwards, a hill prominent in the landscape of the Downs.

Three hundred yards/274m beyond the pill-box the bridleway crosses Beggars Lane, which comes up from under the railway arch at Gomshall. Although at this point the PW can be seen continuing straight along the 450ft/137m contour above a wood, as an overgrown, sunken pathway, its route cannot be followed. An old chalk quarry guarded by a wartime pill-box above Hackhurst Farm lies on the route of the PW, whose barely discernible line lies just above the field hedge-rows, and emerges by another chalk pit as a distinctly sunken track at the apex of a hairpin of the road which leads up steeply over the Downs to Effingham. From Beggars Lane, therefore, we have to climb up to Hackhurst Downs to join the NDW just before reaching a junction of six paths at Blind Oak Gate.

Hackhurst Downs to Ranmore Common 3 miles/4.8km

From Hackhurst Downs the routes of both the PW and the NDW are coincident as far as the Surrey-Kent border at Titsey, a distance of 22 miles/35km, or almost so: in several places where the PW can be seen it cannot be followed.

From the open downs, veer E on a curved grass track which first skirts and then enters the woods. As it does so the path meets a bridleway coming in from Blind Oak Gate. This track trends gradually downhill, then into trees again on a well trodden path. The bridleway turns away L and the footpath continues, passing some five pill-boxes shortly before meeting a road at a point just above the apex of a hairpin bend. This road leads up over the Downs to Effingham: it is steep and dangerous for motorists, and walkers should be careful.

Go uphill for 150yds/137m then turn E on a path, parallel to the road at first, then trending E, at about the 600ft/182m contour, to a clearing on White Downs, where Ranmore Church and Box Hill become visible. The path contours round the thickly wooded coombe of Pickett's Hole, passing a pill-box, overlooking a disused rifle-range near Coomb Farm. After about 1 mile/1.6km at this level, you enter a field – a National Trust picnic area and car park – and leave by an enclosed path, emerging on the Dorking-Effingham road near 'The Old Post Office' of Ranmore Common.

Ranmore Common is a village with a long green with a few houses around it. The southern edge of the green gives views over Holmesdale and the greensand hills to Leith Hill, and glimpses of the wider Weald to the SE.

The spire of St Bartholomew's, atop a strong, central, octagonal tower, is a landmark for miles. The church was built by Sir George Gilbert Scott in 1850 for Lord Ashcombe, son of Thomas Cubitt, builder of the family fortunes. Born in 1788, Cubitt built large parts of London, including Belgrave Square and one front of Buckingham Palace. He died in 1855, leaving £1m. The church is faced entirely in cobbles (i.e. round flints) and has a portrait of Ashcombe and his tomb in the church-yard. There are also frescoes in memory of his grandsons – Henry, Alick and William Cubitt – three young men who died in foreign fields.

Immediately NE of the church are the schools and former rectory, also presumably by Scott. The school is quite a clever piece of asymmetrical design.

In the eighteenth century the Denbies estate was owned by John Tyres, the eccentric who laid out the Vauxhall Gardens in Kennington, London. In contrast he laid out the gardens here to represent death: a temple covered with sad texts, pedestals topped by human skulls and a clock that struck every minute to remind people of approaching death. Denbies was a swagger Italianate house, designed and built by Thomas Cubitt for himself in 1849. It was demolished in 1954: only the stables remain. The 245 acre/100ha grounds now belong to the National Trust.

Ranmore Common to Dorking 2 miles/3.2km
It is doubtful if the track of the PW passed over Ranmore Common. Undoubtedly a prehistoric track led over the heath, passing the church and Denbies Farm, but it was a branch track leading to the Thames. The PW trackway is quite noticeable on the hillside below Ranmore Common, a delight-

White Downs

Ranmore Church

The North Downs from the slopes of Box Hill, looking west

ful semi-metalled track, becoming a metalled drive at about
the 400ft/120m contour, running for 2 miles/3.2km to a lodge
on the Ranmore Road just W of the Dorking Lime Works.
Presumably the old road followed the spur of the Downs
down the shoulder of the hill to the River Mole, but the actual
line is lost in the ploughed land of the valley.

The NDW leaves Ranmore Common by following the West Humble road past the church, and when it takes a sharp turn N you turn right on a drive signposted 'Bridlepath to Dorking'. After 100yds/91m, bear E on a stony track, the old coach road to Denbies, turning round the corner of the Downs into the Mole valley. Go straight over a cross-track and past a track coming up from Bradley Farm, then, 25yds/23m on, fork right and go down a tree-lined track to the Dorking-Leatherhead road, A24, where a subway takes you under the main road.

The line of the PW reappears on the lower slopes of Box Hill across the river, but we must leave the exploration of the next section for the following day after we have seen Dorking, an old market town situated on the River Mole where it breaks through the Downs.

Dorking

Dorking is an excellent centre for walking, and was at one time noted for its edible snails. The town obtained the grant of a weekly market in the reign of Edward I, and today its ancient inns, winding High Street, raised causeway and bow-fronted shops give a strong feeling of its original character. The spire of St Martin's, which is clearly seen from Ranmore Common and Box Hill, is a memorial to Bishop Samuel Wilberforce who was killed by a fall from his horse whilst riding near Abinger Hammer in 1873. He was known as Soapy Sam because he was always getting into hot water.

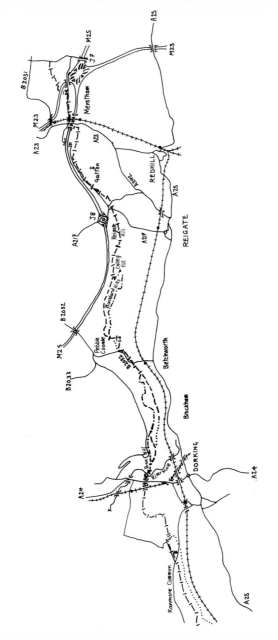

Part Three: River Mole to River Darent

6 Dorking to Merstham 9 miles/14.4km

It has been argued that the PW crossed the Mole at Burford Bridge, 2 miles/3.2km N of Dorking. Burford suggests a river crossing, and possibly pilgrims may have crossed the Mole over stepping-stones and contoured round the western flank of Box Hill, but this route would have taken early travellers far out of their way – a diversion of 3 miles/4.8km rather than a direct 1½ miles/2.4km between the two known points on either side of the Dorking Gap.

The name Burford suggests a ford, but the Mole is unlike other streams south of the Thames in that it 'swallows' and 'burrows' underground, and at any one of these 'swallows' the river could quite easily be crossed. It was reported in 1700 that an improbable experiment took place when a duck was sent down a swallow-hole to reappear downstream with all its feathers plucked out. Perhaps no other stream in England has attracted so many poets. Spenser wrote of it in his *Faerie Queene* as

Mole, that like a nousling mole doth make
His way still underground, till Thames he overtake.

Milton called it 'sullen Mole, that runneth underneath', and Pope, in his *Windsor Forest* mentions the 'sullen Mole, that hides his diving flood'.

Whenever, in crossing a valley, the old road diverges from its general alignment, it does so either to avoid bad soil or to find a ford. It always chooses a place where some spur of high land leads down to the river and corresponds to a dry rise

The crossing of the River Mole below Box Hill

immediately opposite upon the other bank, but at Burford, on the western side, there is quite a little plain which must have been marshy. Burford Bridge was in fact built in connection with the Stane Street Roman Road which runs N–S through the Dorking Gap.

Box Hill

Many people will wish to continue along the ridge over Box Hill, and those doing so will find it best to take the wide chalky footpath just N of the Burford Bridge Hotel. The hotel, formerly known as the 'Fox and Hounds', was where Nelson bade farewell to Lady Hamilton before Trafalgar, and here also stayed Keats and Stevenson. It is said that Keats found his inspirations for the last 500 lines of *Endymion* on Box Hill, and in a letter to a friend he tells how he went up the hill by moonlight and came down with some of these lines in his thoughts. Keats stayed here for two weeks in November–December 1817 and consistently wrote about 80 lines a day to finish *Endymion*; and Stevenson wrote part of *The New Arabian Nights* when he stayed here in 1878.

Box Hill is the best-known beauty spot in Surrey, with the NT pay and display car parks, tourist centre and cafe. More than 900 acres/364ha are held by the National Trust, and every day in summer trippers from London and all the country around flock to the top of the hill for its famous view. It is not one of the most extensive of views, but from its 590ft/180m summit we can look down and across the Weald and wide expanses of countryside. Far beyond the blue-green haze are Ashdown Forest and the South Downs, while nearer at hand are the greensand hills and the landmark of Leith Hill, 956ft/294m high; and at our feet the Mickleham valley with the shining River Mole winding its way to the Thames.

The hill is densely wooded not only with box trees from which it gets its name – some of the finest in England – but also with juniper and yew, and in spring and summer the whitebeams show finely among their deeper green and that of oaks and beeches.

Dorking to Pebble Coombe 3 miles/4.8km

From Denbies on Ranmore Common, then, it is probable that
the old road went E down the spur past the chalk pits to the
valley, crossed the railway just N of Pixham Mill. It would
then ascend the hill before it to that spot where it distinctly
reappears on the 300ft/91m contour line just W of the lane
leadng up to Boxhurst and the crest of the hills from the
Reigate Road, A25.

The PW cannot be followed until the Betchworth Quarry is
reached, so from the subway under the A24, ¼ mile/400m N
of the junction of B2038, we must take a driveway which leads
down to some stepping-stones across the Mole. (These step-
ping stones mark the start of the 322km/200 mile London
Countryside walk, which makes a complete circuit of London.
It follows 29km/18 miles of the NDW route from Hackhurst
Downs above Gomshall to Tandridge Hill near Oxted). If the
river is in flood it can be crossed by a footbridge about 300yds/
274m downstream. A path rises and falls as it crosses the
lower slopes of Box Hill among the trees, but it follows just
above the level of cultivation and soon reaches Boxhurst. The
NDW strikes uphill, to the open top, and round to the famous
viewpoint. Turn L to the NT tea rooms, tourist centre and
toilets. The monument is to Leopold Solomons who gave Box
Hill to the NT in 1914.

From the viewpoint the NDW continues E on the gravel
path, and when this develops into a grass track, bears half-
left across the open Downs to enter the trees. Follow the well-
worn path ahead to cross a broad, and then a narrow, track,
both of which come up from Boxhurst, to near Upper Boxhill
Farm. Cross a ditch and a sunken path, and after 100yds/91m,
fork left. Keep to this path for about 300yds/274m through
Dukes Plantation, then climb some steps to reach a wide track.
When this makes a hairpin bend back to Boxhurst, go straight
ahead down some more steps to Brockham Hills. At a bridleway coming up from Brockham, turn left to contour round

Pages 128/129: *The North Downs from below White Downs, looking east*

Ranmore Church

Box Hill

Buckland Hills

the coombe, skirting above the old Brockham chalk pits and along the edge of a caravan site. At the far corner is a memorial to a racehorse, Quick.

The NDW was originally planned to continue eastwards at the same level, about 650ft/198m, contouring above the Betchworth chalk pits on the Betchworth Hills to reach the B2032 in Pebblecoombe after 1 mile/1.6km but rights of way for this stretch could not be negotiated. The NDW path leads down to the newer quarry seen ahead. The winding path takes you through trees to the remains of a viaduct, where you turn right and the path widens to veer left round the bowl of the quarry. The path crests a slight incline, passes through trees, and over a red-brick bridge. This path is also the PW, which has followed the lower level from Boxhurst. The path now crosses a wide track, and runs out to a rough lane, past a row of cottages, bearing right, and down to the B2023, ¼ mile/400m N of Betchworth station.

The PW is very distinct between Boxhurst and Betchworth, a terraced track lined by yew trees along the bottom edge of the woods, but 'officially' the trackway cannot be followed until a public footpath follows its route E of the bridleway which comes up from Brockham, and the track can be taken for 1 mile/1.6km to the B2023, making a slight diversion where the Betchworth Pit forms an impasse across the route. On the way you pass the Brockham chalk pits and old lime-workings: an interesting time can be spent looking at the old kilns – a massive brick-built, twelve-bay structure, now sadly overgrown.

The chalk hills between the Mole and the Medway have had many bites taken out of them by man, and many of them have cut into and destroyed the old road. The chalk would have furnished the flints which were the first tools and weapons of primitive man, but it is now necessary for the building of roads and the making of lime for soil dressing. As the old road was originally the only track along these hills, it was necessarily the base of every chalk pit that was dug. Later, when valley roads were developed and the old road was no longer continually used, it was profitable to sink the pits deeper, below the level of the old road, as far as the point where the chalk comes to mix with the sand or clay of the lower strata. As the old road became more and more neglected the obligation of protecting it was forgotten, and the commercial exploitation of the chalk pits destroyed the road at these several points. The pits therefore afford a guide to the line of the old road in the few cases where it is lost.

The Pilgrims' Way – Pebble Coombe to Colley Hill
2 miles/3.2km

The old road crosses straight across the mouth of Pebble Coombe, and assumes a character of some perplexity. The escarpment of the hills here is very steep, so steep that it could not support a terraced road without such engineering works as primitive man would have been incapable of performing, and this steep scarp slope continues for some 4 miles/6.4km to Quarry Hill above Reigate.

If the road could not be supported upon the bank of the escarpment, and yet desired – as it always must – to escape the damp land of the lower levels, it was bound to seek the crest. Nowhere hitherto has the road attempted the summits of the hills, but here it is going to keep to them as long as the steepness of the escarpment lasts.

It is possible that the Pilgrims' Way passed over the spur of Brockham Hill before reaching the Pebble Coombe road at height 353ft/107m, but if it did its line cannot be traced or followed. Climb the busy B2032 Pebblehill Road (fortunately there is a footway) for ½ mile/800m to a point just three or four houses after a series of bends in the road where a footpath turns off E to the site of Bridlecombe Bungalow. A line of yews can be seen in the woodland up to the left above the field, indicating the climb of the old road across the hillside from height 535ft/163m to a height of 600ft/183m along the ridge.

At the end of this path turn left on a bridleway up to the crest of Lady Hill and at the top cross over a bridlepath in a steep-sided cutting coming up from Underhill Farm. Do not descend, but turn right between yews along the 600ft/183m contour on the ridge. When the wood ends follow a barbed-wire fence between two fields to another wood ahead, and follow the path round the S side of this with another field on your right.

The gables and chimneys of a large whitewashed house, Mount Hill, are now in sight, and we soon pass this on our right hand. Cross the drive to this house to a footpath opposite along the crest of the Buckland Hills. The path becomes very muddy under laurel bushes, and emerges at the gates of Juniper Hill on the edge of the famous Walton Heath Golf Course. That the route along these hills was an important trackway is shown by a coal post, near the entrance to Juniper

The Pilgrims' Way between Boxhurst and Betchworth

Place, set up by the City of London to extract a toll on incoming coal. Here bear left, then after a few yards turn right, to the north of Swiss Cottage. Note the sunken way on the right of the bridleway, which leads us out to the open grass slopes of Colley Hill at the corner of Margery Wood.

(The PW continues lower on this page.)

The North Downs Way – Pebble Coombe to Colley Hill
2 miles/3.2km
From the B2032, the NDW follows the same line as the PW as far as Bridlecombe Bungalow, and takes the path N to the wooded hills. When reaching the woods, instead of taking the path which strikes uphill, bear right following under the line of pylons, passing the entrance to an old quarry. The path contours round at the foot of the hills, just above the level of cultivation, occasionally through woods but mostly on pleasant grassy slopes. Having turned the flanks of Juniper Hill, the path reaches a broad track, Clifton's Lane, a bridleway, which doubles back to take you up to the top of Juniper Hill. Here you join the PW, and a wide path through trees takes you out on to the grassy slopes of Colley Hill.

Colley Hill to Reigate Hill 1 mile/1.6km
The old trackway following the crest of the Buckland Hills, Colley Hill and Reigate Hill is much overgrown, shaded from the sun by the mass of old yews, and less well drained on this flat top of the summit than it is on the hillside where it usually hangs. However, it is still there to be seen, broad and sunken and parallel to the present bridleway/NDW, running for 2 miles/3.2km to Reigate Hill.

Since the opening of the NDW the Surrey C.C. has much improved the bridleway, but it misses the views so it is best to come out on to the widthe widswept slopes of Colley Hill, a magnificent stretch of open ground with wonderful views over to Reigate and Gatwick Airport far below. The sunken way can be clearly seen to the N of the bridleway in the fringes of Margery Wood. The path continues past an ugly brick water tower (1911) to a small temple-like building, known as The Horseshoe, at the far end of the open Downs. This is your objective by whichever path you choose to traverse the grassy slopes, and when you reach it you can see your exit off Reigate Hill. The temple was given to the people of Reigate in 1909 and had its roof decorated with blue tiles and design of the sun and planets. It originally contained a drinking fountain, but this was out of use for many years and has now been converted to a viewpoint indicator with seats. A drinking water tap has been provided nearby.

A good track leads E of Reigate Hill through a wood, passing a vague area of unidentifiable military property on the right and a concrete water tower and a steel radio mast on the left. These masts, buildings, bunkers and chain links are an eyesore when seen close at hand, yet to do them justice these towerscape installations do not seriously mar the thickly wooded skyline.

The boundary to the military property is marked by a stone 'WD ↑ No13' on its E face, and on its N face 'War Department Boundary is the Northern Edge of Pilgrims' Way'. The track leads past a few houses and WD post No. 14 similarly inscribed, then drops down to the A217 Reigate Road. A footbridge carries the PW over a deep cutting at the summit of the London Road, to a place where a car park, toilets and snack bar have been provided at a viewpoint overlooking the Weald.

Reigate

Down to the right lies Reigate, an ancient town which has become a popular residential and commuting area. The town has been imagined to take its name from the old road, but it lies too far below in the valley to be connected with its passage. Pilgrims must have come down to this point to sleep, as they came down to many other places along the route. So common a halting-place was Reigate in the Middle Ages that

Water tower on Colley Hill

at the centre of the town, where the town hall now stands, there was a chapel of St Thomas from perhaps the thirteenth century to the Reformation.

Reigate Hill to Merstham 3 miles/4.8km
The line of the PW coincides with Gatton Way, a minor road running E of Reigate Hill, as far as Tower Lodge, the northern entrance to Gatton Park. Here the way enters a wood N of the

Above: *The Horseshoe on Reigate Hill*

Right: *The Town Hall and House, Gatton Park*

Hall, and is marked by a terrace and an avenue of trees pointing towards the East Lodge. The Way cannot be followed through the Park, but a public footpath passes close to it through the grounds: this is the route taken by the NDW.

From the A217 bear left along the road, past the car park, toilets, and refreshment hut, across a road ascending from the R (Wray Lane) and enter the National Trust woods opposite. After 20yds/18m, take the right fork and keep to the main path through Great Buck Wood for over ½ mile/800m, to where you come out to a driveway near the Tower Lodge. Turn right on a private road (but a RUPP) and enter the grounds of Gatton Park.

Gatton Park is a 558-acre/226ha estate with an Italianate house built by Lord Monson in 1830 and a church, though the former was burnt down in 1934 to be replaced by a new house which is now the Royal Alexandra and Albert School for Orphans, founded in 1864. The Park was laid out by Lancelot Brown in 1762. The Hall was entirely rebuilt in 1936 by Sir Edwin Cooper in poor Classical Revival style, but it incorporates the impressive portico of 10 Corinthian columns of 1891, rescued from the previous house.

Gatton was created a borough in 1450 and was conferred on Henry VI's steward in order to persuade him to vote for Henry's marriage with Margaret of Anjou. The 'rotten borough' returned two members to Parliament until it was swept away by the Reform Act of 1832. What makes Gatton unique is the urbane irony of the eighteenth-century owners, who played a very English political joke when they solemnly erected the Town Hall in 1765 and set up an inscription deploring the death of the borough in mock-romantic style.

The Town Hall is an open Doric temple sheltered by chestnuts on a knoll in the Park, quite close to the church and Hall, having six iron columns and a pedimented roof, under which 'elections' (or, more accurately, nominations) for the rotten borough were solemnly held. In front of it a huge urn stands on a plinth, each face of which has a line from the following inscription:-

Church of St Andrew, Gatton Park

Stat ductis Sortibus Urna
Salus populi Suprema Lex Esto
Comitum Gattoniense MDCCLXV
H M Dolus Malus Aberto

which translated means:

When the lots have been drawn, the urn remains
Let the well-being of the people be the supreme law
The place of assembly of Gatton 1745
Let evil deception be absent.

The urn was erected by the lord of the manor in grief for the passing of the Reform Act of 1832 which abolished Gatton's privileges. Political cynicism could hardly have gone further than this, but there may at the same time have been an element of genuine, if hyper-sensitive, melancholy behind it, the exact spirit of which pervades Gray's famous *Elegy* (written in 1751) and Goldsmith's *Deserted Village* (1770).

The little fifteenth-century Church of St Andrew's is a mainly Renaissance structure and contains old treasures from all over Europe. Pevsner says that 'most counties have one church which has become an involuntary museum from the attentions of someone who went on the Grand Tour with an acquisitive eye,' and that St Andrew's is Surrey's example. The church was lavishly decorated in 1830 by the fifth Lord Monson, who had built the original house, and looks more like a choir of a cathedral than the interior of a village church. Elaborate stalls from a Benedictine monastery in Ghent, Belgium, face into the nave, and many have misericords carved with faces. Looking down on them from a height is a rich pulpit, dating from about 1530, which, with the carved panels in the altar, is probably Flemish. There are carved doors from Rouen and altar rails from Tongres, and the windows have sixteenth-century Flemish glass from a church near Louvain. All round the nave are delicate traceried panels, leading up to a beautiful English Gothic screen beneath the gallery at the western end. The W window shows the arms of Henry VII. The N transept is the Monson family chapel, a perfect example of the English nobleman's wish to worship in comfort. It has a fire-place, panelled overmantel, padded benches and comfortable chairs. It is a sumptuous private chapel, one of the best in the country. This N transept chapel was once connected to the house by a covered way: it is a shame that it has gone, as it was quite a rarity. Keys for the church may be obtained from Whitehall House, Rocky Lane, outside the North Lodge gate.

From the white gate by the thatched North Lodge, both the PW and the NDW follow a road for a short distance, then S of Whitehall Farm along a track past a nursery garden. When this ends at a kissing-gate, continue on a footpath which goes gently down the ridge of the falling crest, over two stiles, to follow a wire fence and a series of stiles. At the point where the path trends SE, it leaves the line of the old road, which passes through the grounds and S of The Glade House at the top of Quality Street to just S of Merstham church. This line cannot be followed, so we just take the footpath skirting a sports ground, coming out at Home Farm at a corner of A27 at the S end of Quality Street. Here turn left to the end of Quality Street and take a path on the right-hand side beside The Forge to cross the M25 South Orbital motorway by a new footbridge and to emerge at Merstham church.

Merstham

In medieval days the quarries at Merstham were famous for their sandstone, for it was used in 1259 for the King's palace at Westminster Abbey, and a century later for Windsor Castle. It was used for old St Paul's and old London Bridge and many other public buildings. Like many quarry villages, Merstham has little architectural evidence of its own product, except the church and the unexpectedly pretty Quality Street.

Quality Street was so named because the leading actors Seymour Hicks and Ellaline Terriss in Barrie's *Quality Street* were living here at that time, in an ensemble 1600–1700 buildings of stone, brick, timber and tile-hanging with trim front gardens. In complete contrast to this bit of the original village is a depressing estate out in the 'green belt', a malignant growth dating from the 1950s, to the E of the main road and railways and next to the M23/M25 junction. The faults of this, and other, dull housing estates could, perhaps, be overlooked if they were not so uniformly bad in their architecture. The sheer monotony of it all is depressing in the extreme.

The Church of St Katherine's was built on the wealth of the stone quarries in 1220 to the N of the village on the slope of the Downs. It has two fifteenth-century chapels with some original glass, while at the top of the tower arch is a carved heraldic stone which came from the old London Bridge. The lych-gate is said to be made from the oak timbers of an old mill which was pulled down when the railways came this way.

Another railway memory lingers in the empty cutting with a little bridge beside the 'Jolliffe Arms' on the Brighton Road to the N of the church. It is a relic of the first public railway in England, the Surrey Iron Railway, operated with horses from 1805 to 1838. It was used chiefly to carry the stone and lime from Merstham to Wandsworth for Thames shipment.

Church of St Katherine, Merstham

Merstham to Gravelly Hill 3 miles/4.8km

White Hill, Quarry Hangers and Gravelly Hill lie to the E of Merstham, forming an extremely steep escarpment, and it would be obvious that the old road would be forced to take to the crest. The hills have a number of steep ridges with spurs and intervening hollows, and these would have made it impossible for men and animals to go at a level half-way up the hillside. The old road, then, would have to gain the crest of these Downs before their steepness had developed.

The pilgrims in the Middle Ages probably went straight up the hill from Merstham by an existing track to the ridge. It would climb the hill at a slant, keeping to the chalk till it should reach the summit at some point where the clay had stopped and the slope below had begun to be steep.

E of Merstham church the old road is lost among the confusion of the road A23 and the two railway cuttings, but from along the lane on the 400ft/122m contour, Rockshaw Road, can be seen the line of a hedge running diagonally and climbing slowly to the crest. The Greystone Lime Works afford another clue to the line of the road which is now lost.

From Merstham, the NDW follows the route of the PW to the A22 just E of Gravelly Hill. From the A23, then, turn E along Rockshaw Road, which begins just S of, and almost opposite, the church across the main road. Follow this road over the railway cuttings for ½ mile/800m and opposite a house called 'Noddyshall' on the right turn left along a grassy path, signposted 'Bridleway', beside two new bungalows, and follow this down the field to a gate leading to a subway under the M23 motorway. The massive M23/M25 intersection is just ½ mile/800m away.

Merstham to Westerham

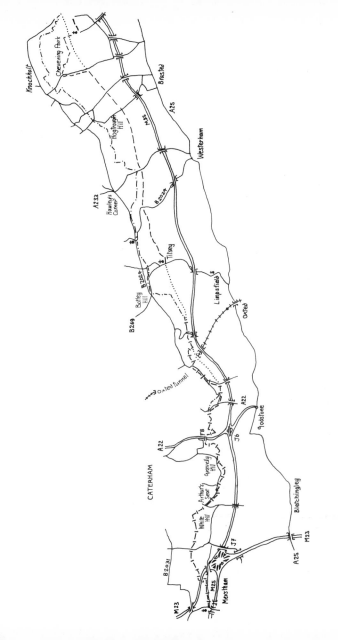

Follow the farm track, go through a gate and continue your direction diagonally across a sloping grass field on the bridleway, through a little wood to a large swing gate. If you look back from this point a continuous line of yews can be seen coming straight from Merstham church and right across the old lime pit. Ahead, the track continues to climb the face of the hill to an iron field-gate in the far corner at the top of the next field. Pass through the gate and turn right along a clear hedged track all the way past height 662ft/202m to the Chaldon-Bletchingly road.

One mile/1.6km down the road from this junction with Pilgrim Lane is the lovely church of Chaldon, which contains a unique thirteenth-century wall painting showing the tor-

Quality Street, Merstham

ment and punishment of the wicked and, on the upper section, the salvation of souls.

Cross the road into a lane opposite at Hilltop Farm, which after a while becomes a beautiful track (bridleway), passing the W.T. station on your left to Willey Park Farm. Keep the main farm building on your right, and after 20yds/18m or so, at a fork, take the bridleway bearing to the right to the summit of White Hill at the Stanstead Road junction. White Hill Tower, a four-storey flint-built folly erected by Jerimiah Long in 1862, stands just across the junction. Turn right along the road for a short distance, then straight ahead along War Coppice Road, passing to the N of Arthur's Seat, the spur on which stands a prehistoric camp. A most beautifully wooded road keeps along the high ridge bending and dipping for ½ mile/800m until the crossing of Weald Way and Hextalls Lane. The NDW turns off the road here, but the PW continues for one hundred yards/metres or so beyond the road junction and bears right along a broad path, a distinct terraceway on the spur of Gravelly Hill. Horses have cut up the surface of this chalky path rather badly, and it may be easier to use a parallel path a little lower down, to emerge in about ½ mile/800m on the grassy slopes of the famous Viewpoint.

The panorama from this ridge of Gravelly Hill stretches over the Weald from Tunbridge Wells in the E to Leith Hill in the W, 15 miles/24km away, with the South Downs forming the skyline, 25 miles/40km distant.

Gravelly Hill to Tandridge Hill 2 miles/3.2km

To the E of Gravelly Hill runs a long deep coombe, which may be called Caterham Coombe, up which runs one of the two Roman roads from the S and the modern London-Eastbourne road A22. On the steep western side of this coombe the old road is lost in the difficult undergrowth of Upwood Scrubs. It is probable that the old road went round the outer side of the hill 774ft/236m high rather than cross N of its summit, but all traces of evidence have been destroyed. The probable line can best be followed by taking the bridleway E of the Viewpoint, contouring round the spur of the hill, through the remnants of an old quarry occupied by a gypsy caravan site, to a road called Tupwood Lane. This is the route followed by the NDW.

Turn right in this road and reach the A22 Godstone Road, which runs in a deep cutting. The line of the old road cannot be easily found on the other side, so cross the new footbridge over the dual carriageway, and into the field ahead. Turn S on a grassy track, the old Roman road (a RUPP), then turn left on a track (footpath) doubling back past Quarry Farm to some industrial units sited in the disused Godstone Quarry.

Just S on A22, at the crossing of A25, lies the village of Godstone, with a large central green and a duck pond ringed by limes and chestnuts. The green was praised by Cobbett: the fine sixteenth-century timber-framed 'Clayton Arms' reflected in the pond was the 'White Hart' of Cobbett's *Rural Rides*. It was a famous coaching inn and (legend says) a stopping-place for the Tsar of Russia and his party in 1815 on his way to see a prize-fight at Blindley Heath. The name of the village is probably derived from the 'good' limestone that was once quarried here and used for the paving of Westminster Hall. Later, when the Wealden iron-smelting industry spread to Godstone, a gunpowder mill was founded in the village by Sir John Evelyn, half-brother to the father of John, the diarist, and the quarries declined. (His grandfather George Evelyn had introduced gunpowder into Britain towards the end of the sixteenth century. His vast fortune was divided among the 16 sons and 8 daughters he had by his two wives).

One mile/1.6 km N of the centre of Godstone we rejoin the old road at Godstone Quarry and turn right along a track (bridleway) skirting below Winders Hill. This lane is called Flower Lane and follows the 600ft/183m contour round the hill.

At the South Lodge of Marden Park (a Victorian Gothick mansion of 1879, now a Roman Catholic girls convent school), at a junction of tracks, the PW and the NDW part company. The PW track (bridleway) contours round, and within a few hundred yards/metres comes to a road above Flinthall Farm at the apex of a hairpin corner. The NDW crosses a stile and climbs up to and across the Downland, bearing right to descend to the road at a dangerous bend. The road between the apex of the hairpin and this bend is the line of the PW.

At this point on the road, at the bend on the 700ft/640m contour, the PW and the NDW continue ahead through the field along a bridleway below the plantation of Hanging Wood, coming soon to a bend in another road which leads up to Tandridge Hill. The M25 is just ¼ mile/400m to the S, running parallel to our path.

The Pilgrims' Way, east of Merstham

The Pilgrims' Way – Tandridge Hill to Oxted Road
1 mile/1.6km

From this point onwards for the next 3 miles/4.8km, the old road takes to rough ground, though its line cannot be followed by any definitive public footpath. The line can be traced along the 650ft/198m contour, passing below some old quarries, above the portals of the Oxted railway tunnel, and then alongside wire fences bounding fields, and the edge of a large quarry to reach a road coming up from under the motorway from Oxted station.

(The PW continues on page 154.)

The North Downs Way – Tandridge Hill to Oxted Road
1 mile/1.6km

At the road coming up from Tandridge the NDW takes a line generally higher than the PW, trying to reach and maintain the crest of the hills. A path runs parallel with the road, climbing transversely across the contours, until it emerges at a junction on Tandridge Hill, near an informal car park in the wood. Here you follow the road for 150yds/137m to where the NDW takes to the woods on the S side of the road, on a choice of paths, but keeping parallel to it, passing above some old quarries and through a small area of National Trust woodland at South Hawke. The storm damage of October 1987 to the beech woodland here is still very evident.

After having followed the cinder bridleway parallel to the road for ¼ mile/400m, to just below another informal car park at a bend in the road, the NDW goes down a long flight of 113 steps: here you are directly above the Oxted railway tunnel built in 1878. At the foot of the steps you follow the contour of the hill until your way ahead is barred by undergrowth on the edge of the Oxted chalk pits. Here you turn downhill, meeting the PW trackway.

Jeremiah Long's tower, White Hill

The North Downs Way – Oxted Road to Titsey
2 miles/3.2km

Across the road turn left and then right through a narrow gap in the hedge, across a field and then along the lower edge of Titsey Plantation. The PW trackway lies 100ft/30m lower down the hillside, running through the fields, and the M25 motorway runs a little further to the S but cannot be followed.

Across the private grounds of Titsey Park the track of the old road is clear, and passes just S of the site where the church of St James stood. The church was demolished by the Greshams in 1775 to make way for their country house, built in the same year, though the external appearance is stuccoed Gothic of 1832. The replacement church of St James was built in 1861 in harsh Victorian style with a shingled broad spire. It contains a monument to Sir John Gresham (d.1643) removed from the old church in the park. The new church stands in the small village of Titsey, little more than a few estate cottages on the edge of the park. In the grounds of the park was discovered and excavated in 1864 a Roman villa, dating from AD 166–80 and measuring 130ft × 55ft/40m × 17m.

When you reach the boundary of the Titsey Estate, just N of Limpsfield Lodge Farm, an attractive tile-hung building dating from 1700, you turn N on a track (RUPP) and climb up through the plantation gradually to the top of Bothey Hill at the junction of B269 and B2024. The B269, running E, gradually turns downhill to Titsey, and this will have to be used by those following the PW. The minor road coming in from the W is the one we left behind at Tandridge Hil: on maps it is marked as an ancient trackway, and it passes through Botley Hill along the B2024 as far as Hawley's Corner on the A233. It appears to have continuation further E to Knockholt Pound and to the 'Polhill Arms' on the A2028, heading for the Darent valley, to the S of Shoreham, but its line is fragmented and must be conjectural in parts. It bears no relationship to the PW which follows a lower line, but the NDW attempts to join

North Downs Way above Oxted railway tunnel

and follow this trackway above Otford and Kemsing.

(The NDW continues on page 161.)

The Pilgrims' Way – Titsey to Chevening 5 miles/8km

For the last 30 miles/48km the route we have been following has consisted mainly of rough tracks, bridleways, footpaths or no paths at all, and has sometimes been hard to find, yet E of Titsey the old road is well defined and often metalled for much of the way, making it easier to follow.

Half a mile/800m E of Titsey the Way passes Pilgrims' Farm, and after another mile/1.6km leaves Surrey and enters Kent at the crossing of the Westerham road B2024. At this crossroads the Kent County Council have erected a sign with which one is to become increasingly familiar along the next 50 miles/80km of the route – a plate bearing the lettering 'Pilgrims' Way' together with the symbol of the cockle or scallop shell of St James of Compostella in Spain. These signposts have been erected on the line of the route where it has been established beyond dispute, and sometimes also when it is in doubt. In many places they are falling into disrepair.

E of the county boundary the left-hand side of the road is lined with builders' allsorts and wirescape, and after ¾ mile/1200m of this we come to the crossing of the main road from London to Westerham, the A233.

E of the main road A233 the PW continues as a metalled road past a lane to Pilgrims' Farm and after another mile/1.6km comes to a crossroads below Hogtrough Hill, where the lane climbs the Downs from Brasted to Cudham. After another 1½ miles/2.4km we come to the fence of Chevening Park, where, by virtue of an Enclosure Act of 1785, the route has been barred to all traffic since 1792.

Westerham

A mile or so/2.3km to the S, on the edge of the greensand ridge, stands Westerham, a pleasant and unspoiled old market town and, as its name implies, the westernmost in Kent. Its well-kept green at the top of the hill is dominated by the statues of the town's two most famous men – General Wolfe, the victor of Quebec in 1759, and Sir Winston Churchill. Wolfe is seen leading his men to victory with drawn sword, while Churchill slumps back in a chair, his chin thrust aggressively forward.

Wolfe was born in 1727 at the Vicarage, but his mother lived at Quebec House, 1726–38, E of the town near the A25/B2026 junction. This is now National Trust property, is full of relics, and is open as a museum. Churchill lived at Chartwell, 2 miles/3.2km S of the town, in a house which he bought in 1922 and which was his home until his death in 1965. It too is National Trust property, full of memorabilia and also open as a museum.

Chevening

As the finely wooded grounds of Chevening Park are not open to the public, and as the route of the PW cannot be followed, the way on to Chevening church is as follows: Turn L up steep Sundridge Hill, past Sundridge Hill Farm and turn R on a bridleway into Park Wood, going SE. The bridleway ends but a public footpath continues, losing height, emerging from the wood then keeping alongside it, descending steadily SE. The path crosses the line of the PW directly in front of Chevening House but continues in the same line, reaching a long narrow belt of woodland, which is followed southwards to domestic outbuildings of the house and so into the church-yard at its NE corner.

The great mansion of Chevening has its main front facing N towards the heights of the Downs. The central block was built between 1616–1630 to a design by Inigo Jones for Richard Lennard, 13th Earl Dacre. After the death in 1715 of Lennard's grandson, 15th Baron Dacre, the estate was sold in 1717 for £28,000 (in 24 yearly instalments of £1,176) to James Stanhope, one of Marlborough's generals. Stanhope, George I's Foreign Secretary and Head of Government, was created the first Lord Stanhope in 1718, and he planned extensive additions to his new home. However, he died only three years later, leaving the vast alterations to be carried out by his widow. The original block, with its Palladian-type N front with Ionic pilasters, was extended to the E and W, and the great entrance forecourt was brought into being by flanking red-brick service blocks, with hipped roofs and bulls-eye dormer windows, joined to the central block by single-storey quadrants. The forecourt is enclosed by contemporary wrought-iron railings with splendid gates in three directions.

Had the great building so remained it would have ranked as one of the finest early Georgian mansions in England, but the 3rd Earl, 'Citizen' Charles Stanhope, the politician and inventor, changed its outward appearance drastically between 1786 and 1796 by refacing it in stone and cream-coloured fireproof mathematical tiles. He died in 1816 and lies buried beside the 1st Earl in the church.

In 1959 James Richard, 7th Earl Stanhope, gave his 3,500-acre/1,416ha estate to the nation, with an endowment of £250,000 for the upkeep of the mansion. It was his wish that it be used, following his death, by a Prime Minister of the day, or a Cabinet Minister, or a member of the Royal Family. The Earl died in 1967 and an Act enshrines his wish in law.

The original choice of occupant by Edward Heath, then Conservative Prime Minister, was Anthony Barber, then Chancellor of the Exchequer, and this nomination would have resulted in his joining the exclusive ranks of the Prime Minister and the Foreign Secretary in having his own official country home. However, when it was realised that the new occupant would have to pay tax in respect of residence there, Mr Barber had to decline the offer.

A special Act of Parliament was needed to overcome the tax problem, but then, as Mr Barber felt that it would be wrong for him to benefit from his own legislation, the House offered it to the Lord Chancellor, Lord Hailsham. He lived at Chevening for just six months, until the defeat of the Conservative government in February 1974.

Westerham to Wrotham

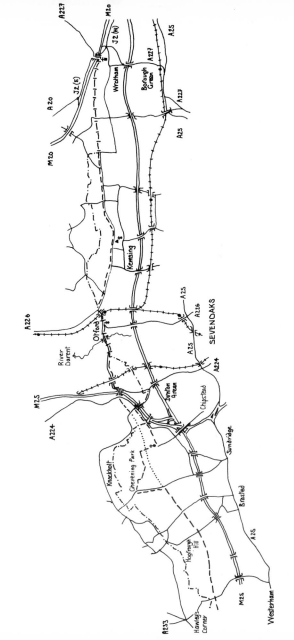

After Lord Hailsham's departure there was much speculation as to who would occupy the house. Lord Stanhope had not wished that the house be occupied 'by a succession of ministers' although it seemed that the likely choice would be a senior minister in Harold Wilson's Labour government. However, with such a slender majority in Parliament, the Prime Minister was obviously unwilling to commit someone to taking up a house which he might have to leave at short notice, and instead the house went to the Crown.

In May 1974 it was announced in Parliament that HRH The Prince of Wales, Prince Charles, had agreed to make Chevening his country house, thereby quashing rumours that he had declined an earlier offer because of his commitment to the Royal Navy. The Prince did indeed take up residence for a short while, but in 1980 he announced that he was to leave Chevening and make his new home instead at High Grove in Gloucestershire. The house remained empty for a long time but it is now used by the Foreign Secretary of the day.

The mansion has undergone extensive renovations since 1970, lasting four years and exhausting the endowment fund. The stone facings and cream-coloured tiles were removed, the brickwork restored, the fourth floor and flat roof removed and a new hipped roof, similar to the original, was built in its place. These extensive structural repairs won Chevening a place on a list of schemes of exceptional merit in a nationwide competition organized by the Civil Trust to coincide with European Architectural Heritage Year, 1975.

In the parish Church of St Botolph standing hard by the main gataes of the Park are a number of the tombs of the Stanhopes and the Leonards. If the church is locked, the key may be obtained from one of the red-brick estate cottages opposite the lych-gate.

The church had Norman beginnings, but has been greatly restored and altered. The long and narrow thirteenth-century nave has its arches on round piers, while the western,

Church of St Botolph, Chevening

battlemented and buttressed Perpendicular tower, in local ragstone, is a characteristic example of the fifteenth century. The altar frontal has the Tudor rose and crown of England in blue on a gold ground, having been made from a piece of the fabric which covered the stands in Westminster Abbey at the coronation of George VI. It will be noted that the S aisle is longer than the nave.

The church is rich in monuments and tombs. The Leonard monument is of John (d.1590), a high tomb-chest with four black obelisks topped by golden balls standing at the corners of a magnificent coffered canopy arch, topped by coats of arms. Reclining alabaster effigies of a knight in armour and his lady in a red robe lie above their eight kneeling children. The other, plainer, high tomb-chest with two reclining alabaster figures, is of Sampson Leonard (d.1615) erected by his wife, Lady Dacre in her own right.

Another tomb-chest is the white marble figure of Lady Frederica Louisa Stanhope, who died in childbirth in 1823, aged 23. She is on her couch asleep in a loose nightgown with her baby contentedly sleeping at her breast, a touching piece of wish-fulfilment. Above her, between the two chancel arches, hang the crested helmet, gauntlets, sword, stirrups and coronet of the 1st Earl Stanhope, captor of Barcelona, who died in 1721.

On the N wall of the sanctuary is the hanging monument of Ann Herrys (d.1613). This is a kneeling figure, in a ruff and farthingale, with two tiny children behind her and large angels on either side flamboyantly pulling back the curtains of a canopy. On the S wall is another hanging monument, this one of Robert Cranmer (d.1619) and his wife, kneeling together and flanked by black obelisks supporting a canopy carrying a coat of arms.

There is also a fine brass on the chancel floor: it is of Griffin Floyd, a former rector who died in 1596, and his wife and children – 7 boys (one is missing) and 2 girls.

It is held that St Botolph was a favourite dedication where travellers and pilgrims gathered. A St Botolph's church often stood at the gate of a city to welcome wayfarers, and it is said that there was once a St Botolph's at each gate of London. The one at Bishopsgate is a classic example of this association, and another stands at Aldgate. (The PW continues on page 163.)

The North Downs Way – Titsey to Chevening
7 miles/11.2km
Because the PW between Titsey and Chevening follows a public road, the NDW takes a route mostly on paths and

Church of St Botolph, Chevening

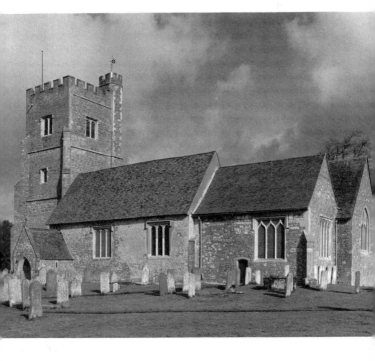

tracks, but it still cannot avoid following roads in parts.

From Botley Hill above Titsey Park you cross the B269 and follow a path which runs parallel with the road. When the road begins to bend S, turn left slightly uphill, go up some steps, over two stiles, and then right along the edge of woods to a lane. Cross this, and go through the woods and fields again to reach the B2024 at Clarks Lane Farm. Follow this road for 300yds/274m, then down steps and still parallel with the road, rejoining it at a fork, where a lane turns down to Tatsfield, past the church.

From the car park in the trees at the road junction, go on a road through the trees, and on reaching a T-junction, bear right to cross the Surrey/Kent border at Betson's Hill. This track continues gently downhill to the A233 at the bottom of

A Pilgrims' Way sign as found in Kent

Westerham Hill, at a point just above Betsonhill Farm where the PW crosses the main road.

Directly opposite the crossing of the A233, a stile gives access to a path which follows round the edges of fields below old quarries, before climbing the Downs to a junction of paths. Here turn right along the edges of a wood, reaching the boundary of Kent with Greater London. This boundary is followed for 3 miles/4.8km. Along this open stretch there are fine views over the Weald of Kent. The trackway goes past some houses, through a wood, and then on a path to the road coming up from over Hogtrough Hill. The path runs alongside the road as it climbs up to height 764ft/233m at a T-junction. Here you go straight across to Stoneings at another T-junction, and follow the road eastwards running towards Knockholt. When this road bends left after ¼ mile/400m, go straight ahead along a path, and follow field boundaries to near height 776ft/236m, to reach the road coming up from Sundridge at a point just S of Knockholt village.

At this point the NDW decides to keep to the top of the Downs, denying the walker the opportunity to use the path which runs down through Park Wood and past the front of Chevening House. Instead the path runs round the N sides of woods, and there is only one glimpse of the house through a break in the trees, known as 'The Keyhole'. On reaching a cross-track at the corner of the wood (where you could turn right and go directly down to Chevening church) the path continues ahead, contouring around the hillside above Minny Wood, and down across the PW to reach the B2211 between Turvin's Farm and Morants Court Farm, just E of Chevening.

(The NDW continues on page 165.)

The Pilgrims' Way – Chevening to Otford 3 miles/4.8km
The hamlet of Chevening stands just outside the Park and the road that leads up from Chipstead along the NE edge of the Park stops by the church. It was used extensively for the transportation of fish from the coast about Rye to the London market, but it fell into disuse when the Park was enclosed in 1785.

The carriageway drive leading N from the main entrance of Chevening House crossed the Pilgrims' Way about 300yds/ 274m N of the house by a brick bridge; although the bridge was demolished in 1841 that part of the Park is still called Bridge Lawn. The line of the PW passes along the northern boundary of a field to a small wood behind Turvins Farm and Morants Court Farm, crossing the NDW, then over what is now ploughed land along the line of a hawthorn hedge and barbed-wire fence until it strikes the byroad leading up to Knockholt Pound from Dunton Green. The PW cannot be followed until we reach this road. So from the church go E on a footpath to Turvins Farm and on the road past Morants Court Farm to the A224 roundabout. Here turn L on the minor road and take the track on the R.

Chevening House

Here the PW leads straight to the crossing of the River Darent down just such a spur as marked the crossing of the Mole. After a short while we pass by an old chalk pit, and the road is stopped off at the entrance to the business park. At some bollards a few yards/metres further on we reach the main highway from London to Sevenoaks, A224. The road lies below the level of the Way, so descend to the right to a gate, then go straight across to the continuation of the lane opposite. Go over the M25, turn L on Pilgrims Way West and follow it round. Pass under a railway arch, down the hill past some nondescript housing development to the valley and a bridge over the River Darent and into Otford.

(The PW continues on page 172.)

The NDW from Chevening, on the other hand, follows the

B221 past Morants Court Farm alongside the M25. At the roundabout of the A224 you turn R, cross the M25 and follow the road to Dunton Green. At the junction, where stands the 'Rose & Crown', turn N as far as the Donnington Manor Hotel. You leave the road by passing S of the hotel on a path which crosses fields N of Broughton House and across the railway line. Once across the railway you reach the outskirts of Otford, passing New Barns Farm to reach a housing estate road, and then to the main road, which is the PW, crossing the Darent and so into Otford.

(The NDW continues on page 175.)

The M25 from Godstone – the South London Orbital Motor-way – ends at Chevening (Junction 5) and continues as the M26 to Wrotham, there to join the M20 (Junction 3). The M26 was officially opened on 18 November 1980 by Mr Norman Fowler, the Minister of Transport. Motorists should note that there is no interchange between the M25/M26 with the A21 or A224 at Junction 5 – a decision which caused the Department of Transport to run into a storm of criticism – although an interchange is proposed between the M26 and the A225 near Otford. You either have to continue N on the M25 to Junction 4 at Knockholt (for Orpington or Sevenoaks) or E on the M26 to Junction 2A at Wrotham Heath.

Otford

From time immemorial the gap in the Downs through which the Darent flows N to join the Thames has formed a trunk artery of approach to the wide valley lands of the Weald beyond. Between the railway and the river lie the traditional sites of two great battles. In 774 Offa, King of Mercia, fought and conquered Aldric, King of Kent, and then in 1016 on a site $\frac{1}{2}$ mile/800m away Edmund Ironside had a great and successful struggle with Canute and his Danes, inflicting a crushing defeat upon them. Ironside followed his beaten foe as far as the Medway crossing at Alresford, when no doubt the Danish retreat was along the old road.

Trackways of prehistoric origin followed along each bank of

the Darent from that other great trunk route which became the Roman Watling Street to join the old road. Many travellers from London bound for East Kent chose to voyage down the Thames to Dartford or Greenwich and then follow the Darent to Otford in preference to riding along Watling Street, and then E along the old road. This was the choice of King Henry VIII on his way to France and the Field of the Cloth of Gold on 21 May 1520.

Today the Darent crossing at Otford is quite unspectacular. There is no attractive bridge and one is barely conscious of any river crossing at all. The road continues eastwards to the junction of the Sevenoaks road A225, which forms a roundabout around a most attractive and well-kept pond, fed with water from one of the many springs hereabouts. In the centre of the village is the Church of St Bartholomew and Archbishop Wareham's great Palace.

In 790 Offa gave land in the area to Christ Church, Canterbury, and soon after the Norman Conquest Lanfranc arranged that the property of Christ Church should be divided between the Monastery and the Archbishop. The manor of Otford fell to the latter and the power of the See of Canterbury and allegiance to the Archbishop became a strong influence.

The archbishops made Otford one of their places of residence – the medieval church could boast a chain of palaces from London to Canterbury, but they were more posting-houses than anything else. In the days when the roads were dangerous and insecure a small army of retainers, grooms and baggage porters would have to accompany the Archbishop, his messengers and guests from place to place on a journey to and fro between Canterbury and London. They demanded stabling, entertainment and food, and the so-called palaces were necessary to keep up the communications of the church life in those rough days. With the exception of Maidstone, all the palaces – Otford, Wrotham, Maidstone and Charing – stood directly upon the old road and are now in ruins. They were the chief centres of Kent S of the Downs, but they were destroyed by the new landlords of the Reformation and now lie forgotten.

Archbishop Wareham, prelate between 1503 and 1532, demolished the early manor house and at a present-day cost of £250,000 built the imposing palace, the fragmentary remains of which today bear witness to the ostentatious splendour customary among the late medieval church dignitaries.

The palace measured some 440ft × 220ft/134m × 67m and was two storeys high with tall towers at its corners, and some idea of its appearance may be gained from the existing ruin of the NW angle tower. The whole must have been a typical example of Tudor architecture; red-brick walls built in Old English Bond enlivened by a diamond pattern of purple headers, stone dressings to plinth, quoins and windows, tiled roofs and probably a forest of gracefully twisted chimneys rising from massive stacks.

Today in addition to the ruined tower, the only remains are the walls of the adjoining row of cottages fashioned from one of the original galleries.

The palace passed to Cranmer on Wareham's death and he was host to Henry VIII when he stayed here on his way to France with his retinue of 4,000, plus 1,000 attending his Queen Katherine. Whether his lavish entertainment here and the delights of Wrotham and Charing made Henry envious of the Archbishop's country palaces we do not know, but Cranmer handed them all over when Henry appointed himself Head of the Church of England.

Henry soon tired of the palace as he preferred Knowle and turned it into a residence for Princess Mary. Under Edward VI the lead was stripped from the roof and the house soon began to fall into decay. The palace and its domain remained with the Crown until the time of Elizabeth, but the queen sold it in 1601 to raise money to finance the Irish Expedition.

Today the tower has its roof open to the sky, with birds flying in at its windows and plants growing in its crannies, a poor neglected building and a pitiful sight.

Otford Palace

Just N of the old palace and facing the village green is the Church of St Bartholomew, with a timbered porch dating from 1637 leading into a squat, square, battlemented Norman tower, capped by a shingle spire. The new timbered porch leading into the nave was erected to mark the Silver Jubilee of George V in 1935, and bears an elegant little coat of arms. A fire in 1635 caused serious damage to the church, which was mainly repaired in brickwork, and it was later drastically 'restored' in 1863 by the Victorian ecclesiastical architect Street.

From the churchyard a path leads towards the railway station alongside a meadow, which contains behind some tall iron railings on the right-hand side Becket's Well.

The tradition concerning the origin of this spring is of considerable antiquity and Becket must have been familiar with the spot. The story is told that the Archbishop, in need of water close to the site of his building operations, and cursing the lack, struck the ground with his staff, whereupon water instantly flowed forth as it now does today. It has often been suggested, however, that the well was used in Roman times, and indeed, remains of a Roman villa have been found nearby.

There can be little doubt that this spring provided the only water supply at the time when the manor house was built. Excavations uncovered the massive stone lining of a great tank, measuring 36ft × 19ft/11m × 6m, and covered by a timber roof. The formidable iron railings which surround the site prevent the visitor from inspecting the well at close quarters.

Waymarking in Kent: The North Downs Way joins the Pilgrims' Way west of Wrotham

Part Four: River Darent to River Medway

8 Otford to the Medway 11 miles/17.6km

The Pilgrims' Way – Otford to Kemsing 2 miles/3.2km
From the centre of Otford the old road passes to the N of the
church in the form of the road A225, the main highway which
runs through the Darent valley connecting Dartford with
Sevenoaks. Beyond the railway station this main road bears
sharply left, and the PW continues ahead, bearing slightly
right, as a byroad passing beneath the shoulder of the Downs.

Within the next 6 miles/9.6km the old road exhibits nearly
all the points characteristic of its course, and these permit us
to deduce much that can be elsewhere applied to the less-
known sections of its course.

As throughout nearly the whole of its course between
Dorking and Chilham, the old road runs here upon the bare
hillside above the valley. The road appears to run at the same
level all along the hillside, but in reality it is rising as the floor
of the valley rises, in order to keep continually at the same
distance above it.

These 6 miles/9.6km may be divided into three nearly equal
parts to show the old road in each of its three historical
phases: first as the only artery of the countryside, then as a
way supplemented by a valley road, and finally as a decayed
and unused path whose value has been destroyed by the
alternative and more modern road below it.

The first stage of the route from Otford to Kemsing is of a
semi-urban character, where there must have been a considerable amount of ribbon development during the interwar years.
The road one follows is the only good road between these two
villages, but it lies above them both, and the Way can only be
reached from either by a short rising lane. If you desire to halt
you have to leave the old road and come down from it to the

village below, exactly as was done for centuries when the archbishops came up to London from Canterbury.

Kemsing

A visit to the charming village of Kemsing involves only a short descent, but is well worth the trouble. At the crossroads in the centre of the village is a simple war memorial cross standing above a spring, although its stone-ringed head is now covered in. This spring is St Edith's Well, which was named after the daughter of the Saxon King Edgar the Peaceful. She was born in Kemsing in 961 and died 24 years later, and the spring later gained local fame for the curing of sore eyes.

Further to the E and a little way N of the main village street is the snugly sheltered Church of St Mary the Virgin, of Norman origin but greatly restored and enlarged during the 1890s. The church has a shingled tower and turret and an interesting fourteenth-century porch, which leads us into a building full of the work of ancient craftsmen, rich, beautiful and colourful.

The lower part of the chancel screen was begun in the fourteenth century and the upper part, though restored in 1894, is rich with carving. The painted walls of the chancel are rich in colour and there is delicate carving everywhere. The silver chalice is exquisitely engraved by an Elizabethan craftsman, and within the altar rails on the sanctuary floor is perhaps the oldest priest brass in the country – a demi-effigy of the rector of Kemsing from 1341 to 1347. There is a brass to another vicar on the chancel floor.

The altar canopy is a magnificent sight, covered with 25 shields on which are painted the 30 pieces of silver, the crown of thorns, and all the other emblems of the Passion. On each side are niches in which are shown the Kings paying homage to the Child, and Our Lord transfigured in the clouds. The coats of arms decorating the chancel walls are of local families.

In the S wall is an Early English single lancet window dating from 1220 and containing perhaps the oldest glass in the country; a medallion of a Mother and Child. There are fragments of fifteenth-century glass in other windows, whilst that behind the altar shows Christ enthroned in majesty.

During the Middle Ages a shrine to St Edith stood to the S in the churchyard and was once a place of special devotion to the pilgrims and others who had been cured at her Well. It was destroyed during the Reformation.

A private drive leads up beside the churchyard to an imposing building which was once the vicarage. It is now a popular youth hostel, and the PW passes its gates.

Pilgrims' Way – Kemsing to Wrotham 3 miles/4.8km

Beyond Kemsing the Pilgrims' Way becomes a pleasant country lane lined by banks with hedges and trees. The 2 miles/3.2km to the grounds of St Clere show the second stage in the history of the road, for modern influences have provided an alternative. The Way runs along the hillside as a metalled lane, while below the old footpaths and cart-tracks have been united into a modern road, and a man going this way need not take to the old road above, but go straight along the lower level through Crowdleham and Heaverham.

The charming Stuart period mansion of St Clere was built during the reign of Charles I, in 1631 or 1632, for Sir John Sedley. It has finely proportioned elevations crowned by boldly massed chimney stacks above tiled roofs, and it can be seen from the roadside in its parkland setting.

Between St Clere and Wrotham is the section showing the final stage of the road, for here the more common condition of modern time asserts itself. The lower valley road now becomes the only important one, passing the Tudor house of Yaldham Manor; the old road dwindles first into a lane very little used and falling into decay, then as a path thick with brambles and almost impassable.

From St Clere the higher road is followed between hedges for ½ mile/800m to where it turns right. At this corner the NDW comes down from the Downs, and the two routes run together into Wrotham. The Way becomes a track once more (a BOAT), and we continue below the boldly rising escarpment of Wrotham Hill. Here a tall BBC mast with VHF transmitter erected on the crest comes into view, a prominent landmark, being typically characteristic of an age which decorates its landscape with gigantic electricity pylons and other similar monstrosities.

We follow this lovely track between the hedges and under great trees below the slope of the hill to a road coming up from Ightham. Cross this road and continue straight on again for another mile/1.6km along the beautifully hedged track between orchards, coming soon to a road at a corner. Continue ahead along this road to the crossing of the Old London Road. Go over this and along the Pilgrims' Way, passing playing-fields on your right-hand side. The road bends round, with a view of the church ahead, and enters Wrotham. If you continue ahead a new path goes up to the new A20 Wrotham Bypass.

(The PW continues on page 178.)

The North Downs Way – Otford to Wrotham 5 miles/8km
Beyond Otford railway station where the main road bears sharply left, bear right at the road junction and after a few yards/metres take a path which climbs up a spur of the Downs called Otford Mount. There is a good view back across the valley, and then the path enters the woods, passes a tumulus, and emerges at a road junction near height 669ft/204m. Go straight ahead along the road for 200yds/182m to find a path on the right, which you follow along the edge of the wood to reach a driveway S of Shorehill Farm.

When first designated the NDW had to follow a temporary route N of Hildenborough Hall (now called Otford Manor and used as a Christian conference centre) but it now goes S of it. The path turns R, SE, and descends the slope of Shore Hill then contours the hillside below the Manor, crossing a sunken path which comes up from Kemsing youth hostel, crosses a field, turns N and follows the N side of a wood to Cotmans Ash. Turn L at the road and at the corner of the road turn R.

From the farm a path runs along the edge of the wood, across two fields to enter Summeryards Wood and then along the ridge, again on the course of an old trackway, dropping down steeply across a road coming up diagonally from St Clere, and down to another road at a corner, joining the PW. The NDW follows the PW along the green lane (a BOAT) below the hills to Wrotham, for $1\frac{1}{2}$ miles/2.4km, passing some orchards on the way (see page 175).

(The NDW continues beyond Wrotham on page 186.)

Wrotham

Wrotham, pronounced 'Rootam', is an old village with russet roofs situated at the foot of the hill where ancient roads met. Mercifully it has been spared the rush and roar of the ceaseless motor traffic passing on the M20 motorway immediately to the N. The famous motor and motor-cycle track of Brands Hatch is not far away and on race weekends all roads in the area should be avoided. At these times home-bound motorists race along the narrow country lanes in souped-up family saloons, intent on emulating their idols on the track and avoiding the inevitable traffic jams.

The earlier Archbishops of Canterbury selected Wrotham for the site of one of their several palaces, which here provided a mid-way resting-place between Otford and Charing. The palace was demolished almost entirely by Archbishop Islip (1349–66) to provide material for his larger palace at Maidstone. Any remains which may be seen are now in the private gardens of a house behind the church.

The parish Church of St George in the centre of the village is of quite outstanding interest, and has one very peculiar and puzzling feature; an arch going through the base of the massive fifteenth-century western tower which rises hard against the highway. This vaulted passage, a rarity in England, was provided to enable the Sunday procession before High Mass in medieval times to circle the church without

Church of St George, Wrotham

leaving consecrated ground. This performance would other-wise have been impossible, but as the road was there before the church, why did the architect build right up to the road and then have to pierce his masonry to allow a passage round the building?

The bold S porch is a great two-storey affair with an angel in its vaulted roof and a bronze St George at the door. The upper chamber is reached by a curious stair-turret covered by a 'pepper-pot' roof. The earliest work in the church now remaining is the thirteenth-century nave arcading, but in the main Perpendicular period details prevail; the large fifteenth-century windows, for example, have replaced the older styles, and there are more modern ones showing the Shepherds and the Kings at Bethlehem.

A curious fifteenth-century newel staircase, approached from the E end of the S aisle, gave access to the rood-loft, long disappeared, and continued upwards to above the apex of the chancel arch into a nun's gallery in the N roof by a tiny passage. This passage is lit by three small windows or peep-holes, two looking into the nave and one into the chancel. The church is particularly rich in brasses, having a remarkable portrait gallery with about 50 figures of five families, and ranging in date from 1498 to 1615.

The Pilgrims' Way – Wrotham to Trottiscliffe
1½ miles/2.4km
Where the path meets the A20 turn L and go across the M20 to the roundabout of the A20 with the A227 Gravesend Road. Turn right here along the metalled road marked by the usual Kent County Council sign, and follow this narrow road for a little over a mile/1.6km along the 450ft/137m contour. All along this stretch are magnificent views over the wonderful valley spread out below. Across the Medway valley can be seen the distant heights of the Downs above Boxley and beyond to Charing Hill.

Wrotham to Kit's Coty

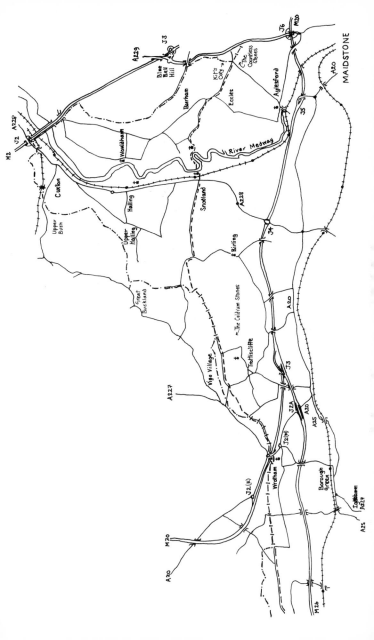

After Hognole Farm the metalled road bends sharply right to Wrotham Water, but you keep straight on along a clear track ahead. After 25yds/20m or so fork right on a hedgerow path, much overgrown, later widening into a grassy track, and follow this for ½ mile/800m or so until you reach a road coming up from Trottiscliffe to the Gravesend road A227 at the 'Vigo Inn'. In 1702 in an Anglo-Dutch battle against the Franco-Spanish, Admiral Rooke captured £1m worth of treasure and a veteran fighting with him spent his share of the booty buying this pub.

Turn right at this road and descend the hill slightly, passing on the left a charming old building called Pilgrim House, which was once an inn called the 'Kentish Drovers'.

(The PW continues on page 183.)

Trottiscliffe and the Coldrum Stones

Once more a village, lying in the shelter of the Downs but ½ mile/800m below the Way, tempts us to break our journey. Trottiscliffe, or 'Trosley' as it is known locally, is a quiet place of some charm grouped around the junction of several lanes. An attractive weatherboarded house near the centre of the village was the home of one of the greatest of our modern painters, Graham Sutherland. The village has an interesting church standing beside a large and handsome farmhouse which is the site of a palace once belonging to the bishops of Rochester. These two buildings lie beside the road about ½ mile/800m E of the 'centre' of the village.

The Church of St Peter and St Paul is small and unusual, a little museum containing many interesting features. The ground was given by Offa, King of Mercia, to the See of Rochester in AD 788. In 1100 Bishop Gundulf built the chancel in the Early Norman style upon Saxon foundations, and these walls and windows remain today as the best-preserved Norman walls in Kent. The nave was built about 1140 and the bold tower, serving also as a porch, was built in the four-teenth-century. The tower walls are 4ft/1.2m thick at the base, but taper as they rise in height. The buttresses were probably added in the early sixteenth century when other repairs were carried out.

The most beautiful possession of the church is the colossal pulpit brought from Westminster Abbey, elegant, delicately carved, with a beautiful canopy, and supported on a graceful branching pillar. The pulpit was designed in 1781 and removed from the Abbey in 1820 for the coronation of George IV. It was never re-erected, and probably without the knowledge of the Dean and Chapter it was given to Trottiscliffe church in 1824. About 100 years later a farthing dated 1799 and a scrap of paper dated 1803 were found between the joints of the finial crowning the pulpit canopy.

The attractive communion rail dates from 1700 and an unusual feature is the small alms box built into the rail to the left of the gate. In front of the altar rail lie a local landowner and his wife, their tombs marked by two brasses dated 1483. The church choir was accompanied by a violin, tambourine and clarinet before the days of the barrel organ. The barrel organ was replaced in 1937 and is now in Rochester Museum, while the musical instruments are preserved in cases in the N wall of the nave. Some prehistoric remains discovered during excavations of the Coldrum Stones in 1910 were placed in a case in the porch in 1932, but they are poorly displayed.

Immediately to the W of the church is the Manor House, an eighteenth-century building overwhelmed by vast new asbestos farm sheds. The house stands on the site of the palace built about 1187 in the time of Bishop Gilbert de Glanville (1185–1214). After the Reformation the bishops of Rochester ceased to reside there, and it was finally sold by them in 1867.

As we have already strayed this far from the Pilgrims' Way to visit the village and church, our next objective will naturally be the Coldrum Stones, which lie $\frac{1}{2}$ mile/800m to the E of the church. For 300yds/274m there is a good road which then turns sharply left and continues N past some 'Assorted Ideal Homes' up the slope of the Downs. At this right-angled bend a notice board indicates the direction in which the Stones may be found. A track, sometimes very muddy, leads for a full ¼ mile/400m to a car park, and the Stones lie less than 200yds/182m to the N beside the track.

The Coldrum Stones, or more properly the Coldrum Long Barrow, are the remains of a Neolithic burial chamber. They are today the property of the National Trust, given in 1926 as a memorial to the Kentish archaeologist and antiquary Benjamin Harrison (1837–1921), and a bronze plaque mounted on one of the stones near the path records this presentation.

Once the circle with the dolmen stood complete upon its raised knoll overlooking the Medway Gap – a circle of towering columns 160ft/48m in circumference. Now the eastern half of the knoll is gone, probably when chalk was being excavated or cut away when the road, now no more than a bridlepath, was made. Half the circle has fallen down as a result, but four

The Coldrum Stones, Trottiscliffe

massive sarsens about 12ft × 10ft/3.6m × 3m stand poised on the brink. The remainder of the circle lie prone in a more or less regular arrangement on top of the knoll – fallen giants of almost equal size strewn across the slope. Even now in its ruined state the monument is impressive and its site, facing the wide river valley, striking.

The remains of 22 Neolithic people, together with some bones of the ox, deer, rabbit, and fox ascribed to the period about 2000 BC were discovered here in 1910. Some bones are displayed in the British Museum.

The Coldrum Stones is a complex megalithic tomb and one of a remarkable group of dolmens found in this part of the Medway valley, between Wrotham and Boxley, described as the 'Kentish Stonehenge'. These structures were all of Neolithic origin and were, without exception, burial places. The great stones are all sarsens, and are comprised of sand hardened into masses by silica infiltration, the presence of iron often resulting in a yellow-brown staining. The stones are not of any composition quarried locally, and it is possible that they were strewn about during the ice age and collected together to be erected for this purpose.

The Pilgrims' Way – Trottiscliffe to Snodland
$4\frac{1}{2}$ miles/7.2km

We may return to the PW at Pilgrim House by retracing our steps through the village, or by turning N on the bridleway past the Coldrum Stones up to the Downs. Alternatively we may take the road northwards past a rash of architect-designed houses – complete with imitation sandstone and plastic gnomescape, and such imaginative and evocative names as Dawn, Stand-e-ze, Windrush, Hacienda, Bonavista, The Bungalow and Seven – to reach the Way below Great Wood.

Returning to the PW at Pilgrim House, we resume our journey eastwards along the upper of two tracks, a poor-surfaced road leading for nearly 1 mile/1.6km along the 400ft/122m contour past some isolated ribbon development. This stretch of the old road is in the nature of a terraceway, having been cut out of the hillside to form quite a considerable drop to the S. We soon come to a road junction a little way above a telephone kiosk, an unexpected but convenient amenity in this isolated spot, and from this point we may descend to visit Trottiscliffe church and the Coldrum Stones if we have not already done so. A little over ¼ mile/400m E of the telephone kiosk the hard road ends (turn right here down a bridleway to visit the Coldrum Stones) and the way once more becomes a terraced track between hedges.

This trackway is quite unspoilt, running green and straight for 2 miles/3.2km below Whitehorse Wood, and a delight to walk upon. It is enclosed for the most part by hedgerows and in places is overgrown, but one cannot fail to see a brick-built 'thing' on the left after 1 mile/1.6km or the gentle views on the right across the long narrow valley of Holmesdale.

When you reach the Birling-Vigo-Meopham road a track ahead is signposted 'Pilgrims' Way' but ignore this and turn right, passing an overgrown chalk pit on your left, and keep on down the road for about ¼ mile/400m and then turn left on the road through Paddlesworth to Snodland and the Medway.

From this point above Paddlesworth there is a wide prospect between two spurs of the Downs across the wide and tidal Medway. Much of the view is industrial, but distance here lends a peculiar enchantment to this unlovely scene. The new Medway bridge can sometimes be seen, a slim, mile-long thread built in 1963 to bypass the Medway Towns, with the silver towers of Grain Refinery catching the sun beyond. The gaunt cliffs of quarries at Halling and the long hangars of Rochester Airport on the opposing hill are often the limit of our view, as the smoke and dirt from paper mills and cement factories blot out the middle distance.

From a distance, Paddlesworth appears as a textbook example of a primitive community settlement, but the buildings lose much of their charm at close range, being dominated by electricity pylons and large asbestos sheds. There is a fine red-brick farmhouse and great timber barns on one side of the road and a small Norman church on the other. The tiny church of St Benedict is 45ft/13.7m long by 17ft/5m wide and of two-cell construction of chancel and nave, built of flint, rubble, brick, clunch and ragstone. It became deserted at the time of the Black Death and had been used as a barn for a long time, but it was saved and has been maintained since 1976 by the Redundant Churches Fund (as has the old parish church at Albury). (Open Saturdays and Sundays).

From Paddlesworth continue eastwards on the road down Constitution Hill to the main Rochester-Tonbridge road, A228, in the centre of Snodland, a depressing industrial village with cement works and paper mills. The less said about Snodland the better. It contains all the kinds of ugly housing produced in this country during the last 60 years, and even the Norman Church of All Saints contains little of interest.

Cross the main road and continue down High Street and over the railway by Snodland station, then by Mill Lane to the S of All Saints Church. The church has a fine tower, which has a priest's chamber with old oak seats in it and a fireplace. In the churchyard is a modern cross on the steps of the old market cross, and in the walls of the church are Roman tiles.

Outside the vestry door is the tomb of Lieutenant Waghorn; his portrait hangs in the National Portrait Gallery and his bronze statue stands outside Chatham station, for he was a famous man. This 'Marco Polo of the Medway' was born in Rochester in 1799. He entered the Navy as a boy of 12 at a time when it took ships three months to sail from London to India. Waghorn thought of halving the time by means of an overland route and the use of steam. Coal cost £30 a ton at Suez, but he convinced the Bombay Steam Company that the fuel could be carried across the desert and sold at £4 a ton. He did a journey from London to Bombay and back in three months, in 1845, to prove his point, and thereafter set himself to perfect his brave but hopeless scheme. He planned an Egyptian railway which did not materialize, so he went and lived with the Arabs and established fast caravan services from Cairo to Suez, with eight rest-houses on the way, and made travel as safe in Egypt as in England.

To the S of the church, a footpath leads to the bank of the River Medway. Medway mud is, almost without reservation, noxious; the flats revealed here when the river is low are evil smelling and repulsive, and one's enjoyment of the scene will depend on the state of the tide.

(The PW continues on page 203.)

The North Downs Way – Wrotham to the Medway
10 miles/16km

The NDW leaves Wrotham by the road which turns off the A227 immediately beyond the new motorway bridge and A20/A227 roundabout; this is the route of the PW. For the time being the NDW follows the metalled road until it bends sharply right to Wrotham Water: a new right of way has still not been negotiated to follow below the steeply wooded slopes from opposite Chaucers to beyond Hognore Farm.

From the hairpin corner between Hognore Farm and Wrotham Water, go ahead on a track, still the PW, and almost immediately branch off left to climb an attractive sunken track (BOAT) through Hognore Wood to emerge at a junction of roads with the A227 at the 'Vigo Inn'. Here turn right on the road to Trottiscliffe, turning off to the left just before the bridge over the road, to enter the Trosley Country Park. A long level track (footpath) along the 550ft/167m contour leads through Downs Wood and Great Wood below the new Vigo Village for 1 mile/1.6km, and when it reaches a junction with another track (BOAT) descend steeply to the PW directly above the Coldrum Stones (see page 000.) At this junction the Weald Way – an 80 mile/128km route from Gravesend to Eastbourne – follows the BOAT down to the Coldrum Stones. The route is waymarked with yellow arrows and the 'WW' logo. Here the route is also part of the London Countryway.

A delightful stretch of the PW is now followed (footpath) below Whitehorse Wood for a good 1 mile/1.6km, to a bridleway coming up diagonally from Park Farm. Follow the bridleway to the footpath coming up from Birling Place Farm. Here you leave the PW, to rejoin it at Hollingbourne beyond Maidstone. Turn uphill on the path and then right across a field, climbing quite steeply to reach the Birling-Vigo-Meopham road at the Holly Hill road junction. The road to Holly Hill, 643ft/196m, where there is an open space and a car park, is followed to just N of Holly Hill Farm, where the right fork is taken. The path (BOAT) to the left leads to Great Buckland village and the isolated Norman church of Dode. This tiny church is very similar to that of Paddlesworth (qv). The village of Dode 'disappeared' in the plague years of the Black Death.

The NDW then passes through a succession of woods and fields – on a BOAT through Greatpark Wood, then diagonally R across fields on a footpath under two rows of overhead cables into Ten Acre Wood, Horseholders Wood, Pastead Wood, Scrub Wood, Wingate Wood – passing above Upper Halling and its extensive chalk quarries. Beyond Wingate Wood, almost below an overhead electricity power line, at a junction of paths, the path turns NW across a valley, through North Wood on a ridge, and down to the hamlet of Upper Bush, where there is a well-restored Wealden house. A short distance down the lane, where it bends left to Lower Bush, the path goes off to the right to the road on the outskirts of Cuxton.

Almost as soon as it reaches the road at Cuxton the path climbs up behind the houses to cross the railway line and then it heads N across a valley, before veering E and NE. When it reaches a rough track serving Ranscombe Farm, the NDW turns SE alongside Merrals Shaw wood and down to the A228 Tonbridge-Rochester road, where it crosses the railway line. A path beside the main road takes you to the interchange of the A228 and M2, and another path takes you across the Medway Bridge.

The Medway Bridge carries the M2 motorway over the river to bypass the Medway Towns, and if you can ignore the noise and vibration from the traffic, and the wind which can funnel down between the hills on either side, the walk across can be quite enjoyable. The bridge is built of concrete, and carries the motorway over the marshy ground on close-set posts and lintels, but it leaps lightly across the river on a half, a whole, and a half elliptical arch, cantilevered from the slim pillars. The central span is as much as 500ft/152m.

There are interesting views downriver to Rochester castle and cathedral, and one may take time out to visit the town.

(The NDW continues on page 201.)

A Wealden House at Upper Bush

Rochester

Rochester has the advantage of compactness, forced on it by two reaches of the Medway which create a promontory on which the old town stands. As you approach Rochester from the W, across the river you are faced by the twin medieval grandeurs of castle and cathedral, standing side by side as reminders of secular and ecclesiastical power. The cathedral, low and stocky, is sheltered by the castle with its tall keep.

The Roman road Watling Street crossed the Medway here by a bridge, but not much of the town of Durobriuae survives. The hideous present bridge, built in iron in 1914, replaces a medieval bridge which crossed slightly upstream. A great stone bridge had been built in 1387, with eleven arches and a total length of 570ft/174m, vying with London Bridge, and at its end was built a Bridge Chapel, used by travellers for prayers of thanks for a safe arrival. This building was used by the Bridge Wardens who administered the bridge, and was restored in 1917. The Bridge Chapel next to the Bridge Chamber can be visited by request to the Rochester Bridge Trust, The Bridge Chamber, 5 Esplanade, Rochester. Displayed inside are plans and paintings of the bridge since Roman times. The old bridge was demolished in 1857 and replaced by Cubitt's bridge on the downstream side.

Christianity came to Rochester in 604, thus making it the second oldest see in England. St Augustine ordained Justus, one of the missionary monks who had sailed from Rome to settle with him in Canterbury, as the first Bishop of Rochester; King Ethelbert built him a small stone church, similar to those of St Pancras and St Mary in Canterbury.

During the Dark Ages Rochester was periodically attacked by the marauding Danes, and it was not until 1077 that the situation was taken in hand when Gundulf, a reforming bishop, was appointed by Lanfranc, Archbishop of Canterbury, to build a new church. Gundulf not only began building the present cathedral but also a monastery and the castle, and he later went on to build the White Tower in the Tower of London.

The Cathedral

Gundulf made a great reputation as a builder, but nothing much of his new cathedral church is left except the detached N tower and part of the crypt. Gundulf's tower stands between the N transept and the N choir aisle, strong and buttressed, like a fortress, in case anything went wrong with the Norman stronghold in this part of Kent. Nothing of Gundulf's church remains above ground, but part of his nave is incorporated into the S aisle wall of the nave. The nave is broad and low, not a distinguished piece of architecture, but nevertheless, the oldest one in England.

The W front is spectacular, one of the best Norman façades in the country, despite centuries of restoration. The nave and aisles have turrets at their outer angles – the N one square, the S one octagonal in the top two stages, with stairs inside them – and inner turrets slightly higher. The two inner and the two outer pinnacles did not reach their present state of satisfactory medieval symmetry until 1888–9, when they were restored by J. L. Pearson in accordance with the King's engraving of 1655. Most of the front is taken up with a great Perpendicular window, inserted in 1470.

The window dwarfs the richly-carved Norman doorway below it. The jamb-shafts, tympanum and five orders of radiating voussoirs of the central doorway are rich in sculpture – a tympanum of the seated Christ in Majesty, supported by angels, and flanked by the symbols of the evangelists, and the Twelve Apostles on the lintel. The voussoirs are carved into violently curving leaves and beasts viciously biting their tails or their backs. The jamb-shafts, five each side, are plain, with carved capitals and bosses, except that the second shaft on each side is carved into a statue – Solomon on the left and the Queen of Sheba on the right: although others have suggested King Henry I and Queen Matilda (Henry came through this door in 1130 when the cathedral was consecrated).

Early in the thirteenth century Rochester, like so many other cathedrals and abbeys, was reconstructed, and here the transepts were enlarged and a second pair of transepts built between the choir and presbytery. New building work started with the choir in 1227, and work was done in stages. It was financed by offerings made at the shrine of St William of Perth, a charitable Scottish baker who used to give every tenth loaf he baked to the poor. He was setting out in 1201 on a pilgrimage to the Holy Land, but was murdered in Rochester. The monks in Rochester eagerly seized on this possible rival to Canterbury's St Thomas: they buried him in style, set up a shrine to him, and conveniently miracles began to occur at his tomb. Rochester had a money-making martyr.

After the thirteenth century no additions were made to the cathedral, except for the Lady Chapel in the Late Perpendicular style in 1512–13, the occasional doorway here and there, a few larger windows, and the Perpendicular W window. Then came the drastic restorations in the nineteenth century. The central tower was rebuilt by Cottingham in 1825, followed by Sir G. G. Scott's new stonework and gables in 1870 and Pearson's W front in 1888. The central tower was again rebuilt in 1904–5 in the seventeenth-century style.

The total length of the cathedral is 305ft/93m, of the choir and presbytery 148ft/45m. The main transept is 120ft/36.5m across, the E transept 88ft/26.8m.

There is much to see inside the cathedral, but I shall only point out a few interesting things.

The nave is delightfully pure Norman, rising tier upon tier of arches to a magnificent oak roof supported by angels. The triforium has six double arches on each side, the tympanums packed with carving. Fragments of Gundulf's walls are exposed in the walls in the SE corner. The nave is 75ft/23m wide.

The stone choir screen was made by Sir G. G. Scott in 1876, but some of the choir stalls inside – those at the back – are the original choir fittings, c.1227, the earliest to survive in England. The other stalls by Scott are quite simple. The W end, and the N and S walls of the choir below first string-course, are completely painted, mostly in 1876, following traces of a medieval design – there are more than 100 alternating golden

lions and French fleur-de-lys on a red and blue background –
the arms adopted by Edward III in 1340.

Opposite the Bishops' Throne, on the NE pier, is a thirteenth-century painting of the Wheel of Fortune, or half of it,
a favourite medieval cautionary tale. It is very well preserved,
and of quite high quality. The Wheel is shown as a treadmill,
with the tall figure of Fortune standing inside the wheel; two
ambitious figures scramble upwards among the spokes, and a
king at the top looks anxiously down as he is about to be
toppled from his perch.

There are many tombs, but two are of particular interest. In
the NE transept is that of Bishop Walter de Merton (d.1277)
who is said to have been drowned in the Medway as a result
of his horse stumbling while fording the river. He was
Chancellor of England (1261–63) under Henry III, and Bishop
of Rochester (1274–77) under Edward I, and founder of
Merton College, Oxford. His tomb is a vaulted canopy on
clustered marble shafts, much restored. In front of it is a
carving of the purse he carried as Chancellor. His figure, in
Elizabethan robes, was made in 1598. In the presbytery is the
tomb of Bishop John de Northwoode of Sheppey, bishop from
1353–60 and also Lord Treasurer and Lord Chancellor in his
time. His effigy is richly painted in red and green: it was
discovered in the wall in 1825, which explains its good state
of preservation.

Bishop Sheppey's predecessor, Bishop Hamo de Hythe
(1319–52), built the Decorated door to the chapter house. It is
one of the finest examples of canopied doorways of its period,
the recesses filled with figures, and the moulding around
them entwined with elegant foliage and about 40 small faces.
Hythe lies under a canopy in the Pilgrims' Passage, the N
choir aisle where once stood the shrine of St William of Perth.

In the S transept there is a memorial tablet to Charles
Dickens, who lived nearby. Dickens made many references to
the city in his novels, calling it 'Dullborough' and 'Cloister-
ham'. The Bull Hotel was the setting for some of his scenes in
Pickwick Papers and *Great Expectations*. When he died in 1871 at

Higham, he wanted to be buried at Rochester, but he was in fact buried in Westminster Abbey.

The cathedral occupied the SW quarter of the Roman town, and the precincts were limited by the extent of the town walls. The precincts are entered from the High Street through the College Gate (called Jasper's Gate in Dickens' *Edwin Drood*), and on the left are a row of houses, with St Nicholas's church immediately N of the cathedral. On the S side of the cathedral – unusually adjoining the chancel rather than the nave – are the cloisters and the monastic buildings, entered from a gate on the S side or from the crypt. The remains of the monastic buildings on the E and S sides of the cloister are rather scanty, except that on the S side are the remains of the doorway and ruined walls of the refectory, over 124ft/38m long, up against the Roman wall. The refectory has the remains of the lavatorium at which the monks washed their hands as they went in to meals. On the E side the whole outer wall of the cloister walk remains. The chapter house had a passage which led from the dormitory above to the choir of the cathedral.

Beyond the cloister lawn is the castle ditch and outer wall, with the grey keep of the castle looming above it.

The Castle

Hours of Admission	Weekdays	Sundays
15 March–15 October	9.30–18.30	9.30–18.30
16 October–14 March	9.30–16.00	14.00–16.00

Closed 13.00–14.00 daily.

The Medway crossing was the most vulnerable part of Watling Street, and it needed to be protected by a strong castle. Small wonder, then, that the main road from London to Dover and the Continent was to be protected by one of the first Norman castles to be erected in Britain, and with one of the strongest keeps in the country: it is 70ft/21m square at the base with walls 12ft/3.6m thick, and is 125ft/38m high, making it the tallest keep in England. Gundulf's outer walls, built in 1087–9 enclose the outer bailey, roughly oval in shape, but the keep was built by William de Corbeuil, Archbishop of Canterbury, in 1127 following a grant by Henry I. A rectangular forebuilding reaches up two-thirds of the height of the N wall, and the keep is entered at the first floor. The hall occupies the third and fourth storeys. In 1215 the rebel barons held the castle for nearly two months against King John's seige weapons, despite the SE turret of the keep having been undermined, only surrendering upon near-starvation.

From the top of the keep there is a tremendous view in all directions, over the river, town and cathedral. Upstream you can see the M2 motorway bridge, and downriver the ships and mudflats of Chatham Reach.

Part Five: The Medway Crossing

The River Medway was the largest and most serious obstacle to pilgrims following the old road and it poses one of the biggest problems concerning the line of the Way.

At Wrotham the chalk cliffs turn away from their general line and reveal the wide Medway plain at your feet, but far off they continue their interminable line. Along those hills our way is clearly to be continued. Their trend is not due E, but they turn a little southerly, and the furthest visible height is not far distant from our goal.

On the far side of the valley the PW is recognized again, but in the interval between, across the broad flat valley, its passage has never been fixed. In so wide a gap as here made by the Medway a great difficulty arises, greater than any yet met. It is too easy to assume that the old road crosses in a straight line, and a longer search is necessary to find the true crossing-place of the river.

Far up the valley on each escarpment are the remnants of an ancient road, and as in the valleys of the Mole and Darent, difficulties increase because of other prehistoric tracks leading off northwards upon either side of the river.

The great main ridge of the chalk escarpment of the North Downs affords for 60 miles/96km a platform for the PW, but here at the Medway it is broken, for it turns N to form a 'funnel'. The interval between these hills, a distance of some 6 miles/9.6km, is the most considerable of any on our journey. Had there been no physical obstacles to intervene, the first travellers upon this track would have undoubtedly made a direct line from the projecting shoulder of Wrotham Hill to the somewhat less conspicuous turning-point of Blue-bell Hill. But serious obstacles do intervene: a broad river with a swift tidal current, flanked here and there by marshes, and a valley floor of clay, the crossing of which must prove far more lengthy and arduous than that of any hitherto encountered.

Oddly enough, the difficulty of rediscovering the original track by which the pilgrims crossed the Medway does not lie in the lack of evidence, but rather in the confusion arising from possible alternatives. In crossing such a major obstacle, and a tidal one at that, a very strong reason for one single track would be a valuable clue, for if one place of crossing had held a monopoly or even a pre-eminence, the evidence afforded by it would be of the utmost value; but an indication of this simplicity is completely lacking.

It is certain that the river has been crossed at four places, each of which may now lay a claim to be the original passage, and these places are Cuxton, Halling, Snodland and Aylesford. Furthermore, the two tracks of great antiquity on each side of the Medway are not only clearly defined but have each been given the traditional name of the Pilgrims' Way, and their presence adds a considerable embarrassment to the search for the original passage.

Let us now recall those certain features which we have discovered to be true of the road in the earlier part of its course where it had to cross a river, and certain other features which one may add and conjecture that the road would possess:

1 The road will attempt the shortest passage of the valley floor, the breadth being less of an obstacle than the damp soil.

2 The road will seek a ford.

3 Other things being equal, it will naturally cross a river as high upstream as possible, where the stream is likely to be less difficult to ford.

4 It will cross as close as possible to that height upon which survey could be made of the valley floor.

5 The nature of the river bed at the crossing will influence it greatly, whether the bottom be gravel, sand or mud.

6 A point of so much importance will probably be connected with religion, and almost always with some relic of habitation or defence.

7 It will often preserve in its place-name some record of the crossing.

8 It will choose a place where a spur on either side led down to the river.

To these eight points may be added for further consideration:

9 That whatever was the more usual crossing in early times affords something of a guide as to prehistoric habits.

10 Where a tidal river is concerned, the motives which were present for seeking a passage as far upstream as possible would be greatly strengthened, for the tide drowns a ford.

In the light of these principles, let us consider Belloc's view on the subject as to where a crossing is most likely to be found, and having discovered that, examine how far this is supported by other evidence. We know that the Medway has been crossed at four places since prehistoric times, and we shall study each of these in turn.

1 Cuxton

At this, the farthest point downstream, the river widens into a tidal estuary, though sheltered, with hills and firm ground leading right down to the river on either side. Ancient terraced trackways lead very near to the point of a possible crossing and indicate that traffic did go this far N, but they cannot be followed clearly. There is a constant tradition that the crossing of the river at this point by pilgrims was common, and this is the one favoured by Kent County Council. They have signposted the road passing through Upper Halling to its junction with the A228 at Cuxton as 'Pilgrims' Way', and the signposts next appear on the Rochester Road between Wouldham and Burham.

However, there is nothing like a ford at this place. The bottom is soft mud, the width of the river is very considerable, the tidal current strong, and of all the points at which the river might have been crossed, it is the most distant from the direct line; indeed, compared with the next point upstream,

Lower Halling, a traveller would add 5–6 miles/8–9km to his journey by crossing at this point.

2 Aylesford

This is the opposite extreme to Cuxton, being the highest point upstream, and it has several points in its favour. One of the strongest is that legend records a retreat of the Saxons from a defeat at Otford by Offa, King of Mercia, along some road to the Medway. Later the same thing happened when Ironside, after his great victory over the Danes at Otford in 1016, pursued them to Aylesford, where he was prevented from destroying them by their passage over the river. The Pilgrims' Way would have been a natural route along which the defeated armies could make their escape.

Aylesford also preserves the tradition of a ford in the last part of its name, though 'ford' in place-names by no means always signifies a ford, any more than 'bridge' signifies a bridge. In this case, however, we have historic knowledge that a ford existed, and, as is most frequently the case, the ford has been bridged, here by the finest medieval example remaining in SE England. When this bridge came into being it is reasonable to suppose that vehicular traffic would have found this more convenient to negotiate than a ford, and would have accepted the extra distance involved by diverging from the shortest line.

There are three strong arguments against these points, and one is that the valley is so wide (an immense tract of uncertain wooded land) as to give no view either of enemies or direction. Secondly, a belt of clay stretches all along the Downs just below the level of the chalk and here it is particularly wide. No straight line can be taken from Wrotham to the Aylesford gravels without crossing nearly 2 miles/3.2km of this wretched footing which, throughout its course, the road has most carefully avoided. Thirdly, a number of prehistoric remains lie to the N of such a crossing, and in order to reach Boxley, a site undoubtedly dependent upon the prehistoric road, one would have had to turn back upon the original and generally eastern direction.

If Cuxton and Aylesford are to be discounted as being too far off the general line (as Belloc thinks they certainly must be), there remain only Halling and Snodland.

3 Halling

One might conclude that this was the original crossing of the Medway, for there was a good surface from the track on the hills above right down to the river bank at this point. No clay intervenes between the chalk and the gravel and one would have had fairly dry land underfoot all the way down to the river. Even beyond the river, the belt of alluvial soil is less broad than it is at Snodland, and if the geological argument alone were to be considered, the decision would undoubtedly be given to this place.

4 Snodland

Claims are asserted for this crossing by a number of points, individually slight but convincing on the whole, and these must be examined in more detail:

1 The spur which leaves the main ridge of the hills for the river (as at Shalford and Dorking, attracting the Pilgrims' Way to it) touches both Snodland and Halling on either side, but Snodland is on the S and Halling on the N of the slight ridge. The southern side would dry quicker in winter, and in a dry summer it mattered little whether the slope was partly of clay (as is the descent to Snodland) or of chalk (as is that to Halling). During more than half a year, therefore, the descent to Snodland was preferable, and during the other half indifferent.

2 Antiquities are numerous in the locality of Snodland. An ancient chapel marks the descent from the hills at Paddlesworth, while beyond the river a Roman villa was unearthed in 1896 precisely upon the road that would lead from such a crossing of the Medway to the track upon the hill at Burham.

3 The crossing at Snodland is shallower than that at Halling, and at this point is a natural outcrop of greensand which

has defied all dredging operations in the past. A ferry no doubt adequately provided for the needs of foot travellers in the Middle Ages, as in fact it continued to do until quite recently, while those on horseback would have had no difficulty in crossing here by the ford at low tide.

4 There stands at Snodland a church, past the southern porch of which goes a road, and when the river is crossed and the same alignment followed along the bank upon the further side for a little way, the track again passes by a church, and again by its southern porch.

5 The 'Horseshoe Reach' of the Medway has always marked the limit between Rochester's jurisdiction over the lower, and Maidstone's over the upper reaches of the river. This fact is of great importance. All our tidal rivers have a sea-town and a land-town; the limits up to which the seaport has control is nearly always the traditional crossing-place of the river – London and the Thames has the best example of all in Staines.

6 The megalithic monument of the Coldrum Stones corresponds to that of Kit's Coty House on the opposite shoulder beyond the valley. Both monuments are within sight of the old road, and this relative position may have something to do with the alignment of the route through Snodland. There is a tradition that an avenue of stones stretched from one monument to the other and thus marked out a crossing from one line of hills to the other in a zone where the hillside is no longer a guide to the position of the road. The river crossing at Snodland would be a natural route between the two. The stones are now gone, if ever they existed.

These converging lines of proof, or suggestion, would seem to settle the discussion in the favour of Snodland, but in all probability these different crossings were used from time to time as conditions of the river bed and tidal water varied. It would be misleading to point to any one spot as 'the' crossing.

Part Six: River Medway to River Stour

9 The Medway to Charing 16 miles/25km

The North Downs Way – Medway to Kit's Coty 5 miles/8km
At the E end of the Medway Bridge there are two roads which
follow the valley below the Downs, one passing through
Wouldham, and both passing through Burham to reach Kit's
Coty. The NDW decides to follow neither and climbs the
Downs, to find a level of nearly 600ft/183m before dropping
down from Bluebell Hill to Kit's Coty.

The village of Wouldham lies on a bend in the Medway, its
church right on the bank of the river. A ferry once crossed
from Halling, and we have seen that this might have been a
crossing-point of the PW. The village has little to offer, apart
from All Saints Church.

The church has a battlemented fifteenth-century tower with
outsize turret, abutting the church on the N side. There was a
Saxon church on the site, and there are Saxon windows in the
S wall, and twelfth-century chalk pillars inside. The whole
place has a rough-hewn effect, with the chancel walls leaning
alarmingly outwards. In the chancel is an unusual brass of
1602, with inscriptions in four languages, to a brother and a
sister: Morley Manox 'a youth of excellent hopes', aged 23,
and his sister Margaret, who died at the age of 5 in 1579. Let
into the wall of the chancel arch is the dainty sculpture of two
kneeling figures – William Bewley and his wife, dating from
1613.

Below the W window of the S aisle are two cannon-balls
said to be from the *Victory*, and just outside the church, beside
the path leading to its door, is the grave of Walter Burke, the
purser on the *Victory*, who stayed with Nelson after he was
mortally wounded, and held him in his arms as he died.
Burke himself died 10 years later, on 12 September 1815, aged

70; which means that he must have been 60 at the time of Trafalgar, well past the normal age of active service. A special service is held in the church each Trafalgar Day. Burke lived in a lovely Tudor cottage next to the church, which has been removed and taken to Sussex.

From the Medway Bridge, then, the NDW crosses the Chatham-Wouldham road and takes the lane from Borstal Court Farm beside the motorway as far as Nashenden Farm, where you turn away from the motorway, pass between the cottages, and go up the hillside. On the L is the village of Borstal, now part of Rochester, and its Fort Borstal, built as a defence against a possible invasion by Napoleon. It became a detention centre for young people and gave its name to this type of institution nationwide. The path goes up a spur of the hill and alongside a copse, where there is a tumulus, then climbs steadily over Wouldham Common. To the SW the Downs drop steeply in a series of wooded coombes, and there are views of the upper Medway valley, while to the NE the slopes are more gradual.

The route becomes Hill Road (a BOAT) passing Burham Hill Farm, becomes a metalled road as it passes the isolated Robin Hood Inn, then runs over Burham Common towards Bluebell Hill. When some houses appear on the left, and just before some 30 m.p.h. signs, leave the road on the right by a stile and walk parallel with it through the Bluebell Hill picnic area (parking and toilets), returning to the road at its junction with the A229, just ½ mile/800m S of its interchange with the M2, at the 'Upper Bell' public house.

At this point the NDW takes a turn for the worse – not only does it drop down from 597ft/182m to 192ft/58m in ¾ mile/ 1200m, only to climb up again to 625ft/190m after another mile/1.6m, but it also follows the busy A229 for part of the way between the two intersections with the M2 and M20 motorways. The sole reason for making this turn must be to visit Kit's Coty, and to give some opportunity for visiting the nearby Countless Stones. However, a far better alternative is to cross over the A229 on the minor road Mill Lane behind the

'Upper Bell', and where this bends S – Warren Road, the old Roman road going down to Maidstone – go through fields alongside the crematorium, through Frith Wood above the M2, past the radio station to Crossington Fields Farm, then S across Lower Warren Road (BOAT) to Westfield Wood, joining the official NDW again. This alternative saves ½ mile/800m, is virtually on the level, and avoids 405ft/124m descent and 433ft/132m ascent.

From Bluebell Hill the official NDW goes downhill on the old A229, now a metalled bridleway, after a footbridge, becoming Old Chatham Road after ½ mile/800m. Go down some steps to follow a path past Kit's Coty and down to meet the PW at a junction of roads. (Kit's Coty – see page 208.)

(The NDW continues on page 218.)

The Pilgrims' Way – Snodland to Burham 1½ miles/2.4km

It is unfortunate that the one-time ferry at Snodland no longer operates. In the absence of any means of crossing the Medway at this point, the modern traveller is faced with a long detour before he can resume his journey from the E bank. The nearest bridge crossings are either by footpath beside the M2 Motorway near Rochester downstream or Aylesford upstream, and as Snodland lies midway between these two points there is no difference in the choice of either bridge.

The more interesting of the two possibilities is the Aylesford crossing. From Snodland follow the footpath parallel to the railway line southwards, past the Blue Circle Lakes and into Aylesford, crossing the railway at New Hythe station, then alongside the massive Reeds Paper mill. Follow the river bank. Aylesford Priory is on the opposite bank, a Carmelite Priory (open to guests and visitors all the year round) founded here in 1242. The priory was dispossessed at the dissolution of the monasteries by Henry VIII but re-established in 1949. (Free admission to showroom and tea room, 1000–1645 daily).

If one chooses the Aylesford crossing, there is the temptation to cut out that section of the Way between the river bank opposite Snodland and Bluebell Hill, but in doing so one would miss a fine section of the old road and a magnificent retrospective view of the Medway as the gradual climb is made towards the Downs.

It is, of course, possible, in fact probable, that the river has during the centuries altered its course to some extent and the great bend of the 'Horseshoe Reach' – where the meander of the Medway doubles back to within 100yds/91m of itself – may be very different from what it was in medieval or prehistoric times. Nevertheless, the site of the ferry (which plies no more) represented a traditional crossing-place at Snodland, the point where the old road strikes the river bank having passed immediately south of the church. On the eastern shore an embankment runs round the bend until it reaches a spot close to Burham Court.

Scattered throughout the Burham marshland are the grim

The River Medway at Snodland

Burham Churches   Bluebell Hill

remains of disused lime kilns and cement-works. Although many factories are in view, they are safely out of reach and the riverside is peaceful. The only sounds nearby are the rustle of the tall waving reeds screening the margins of the river and the 'kraak' of a tall grey heron disturbed from one of the numerous pools left by former industrial workings.

At Burham Court Farm the river embankment runs into a made road which almost certainly must be part of the old road, and here the ancient parish Church of St Mary's stands hard against the farm buildings. This Norman edifice with a fifteenth-century Perpendicular western tower is now empty and deserted for today a modern church serves the village 1 mile/1.6km away. The church stands on ground just above the flood level of the river close to the crossing, a lone sentinel here in the marshes. The church was rescued from dereliction in 1956.

Beyond the churchyard the road begins the ascent gradually towards the foot of the downland scarp. It has all the characteristics of an early trackway, such as we can recognize in many places on this journey to Canterbury; the track or path raised above the fields on the S or right-hand side, and a steep bank on the left, the terrace thus formed having been cut or worn out from the sloping ground.

After a while we pass near to Burham village and there are magnificent views across the Medway, particularly towards Snodland and the great chalk scar of Holborough Knob showing brilliantly white against the green background of the Downs which extend as a skyline to Wrotham in the far distance. A graveyard of factories down on the marshes, evidence of the cement industry of the last century, is backed by the paper mills at New Hythe and Snodland beyond the fantastic contortions of the river. In the evening sunlight, with the dusty smoke of the active cement works drifting across the river, these shattered ruins have an air of unreality.

The Pilgrims' Way – Burham to Boxley 3 miles/4.8km

Burham is an ugly village, beautifully set under the Downs. St Mary's, the impressive but not very attractive Gothic revival church, was built in 1881 to replace the one down by the river. Close to the roadside S of the village near Petts Farm, a Roman building was discovered during 1896.

Beyond the junction to Eccles the road becomes a dual carriageway and rises gently towards Bluebell Hill to reach the Aylesford road at a corner. At this point the NDW comes down from the N, having passed Kit's Coty. No part of Kent is so rich in prehistoric remains as the district we are now approaching. There is the Coffin Stone at Tottington and 500yds/450m to the E are the Countless Stones, Fallen Stones or Lower Kit's Coty House, as they have variously been called. This latter group is now preserved as an ancient

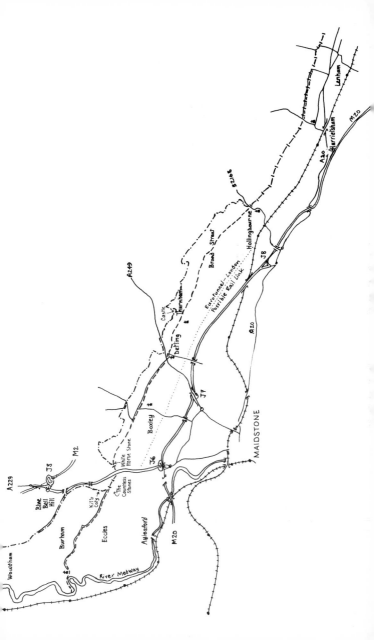

monument in common with the more imposing Upper Kit's Coty House.

A few hundred yards/metres down the Aylesford road on the left-hand side, just beyond the pylons, will be seen the group of fallen megaliths known as the Countless Stones (signposted Little Kit's Coty), the ruined burial chamber of a prehistoric long barrow. It is so called because it is said that no one has been able to number them correctly, or no two people arrive at the same answer when they try. There are not many of them and they are all in a heap, and it is difficult to know if two stones counted are really opposite ends of the same stone sticking out of the ground.

A little further to the S still, a track on the right-hand side of the Aylesford road leads between a hop field and an orchard to the Pilgrims' Spring, the Coffin Stone at Tottington Stone Circle.

Back at the Aylesford road and the junction of the dual carriageway to Burham, a signposted path leads up between high hedgerows to Kit's Coty House, the remains of which will be found in a field on the left. These Neolithic remains consist of three upright stones, 7–8ft/2.2m high, surmounted by a capstone nearly 13ft/4m long. They formed the central compartment of the burial chamber and were once enclosed by an earthen mound covering 180ft/55m long but this has been completely eroded away. The Ministry in whose care the monument now rests has, with quite remarkable insensitivity, thought fit to 'protect' it with a hideous iron cage.

It is significant to note that both groups of monuments – Kit's Coty House and the Coldrum Stones – are on prominent sites, although well below the downland escarpment, with magnificent views down upon the river and the whole extent of the Medway Gap; approximately on the same level on the sides of the valley; each visible from the other; and both having another stone circle a short distance to the S – here are the Countless Stones and on the other side are the Addington Stones.

Both monuments are dolmens – i.e. two massive upright

Church of St Mary, Burham

stones raised to support a horizontal table-stone. At Coldrum the table-stone has fallen, but at Kit's Coty House the arrangement is complete. It is the generally accepted opinion that these structures, after internments had taken place beneath them, were covered with mounds of earth, and around them was placed a circle of standing or recumbent stones, such a circle being termed a 'cromlech'.

For the traveller who is unable to recognize the affinity between the monuments of Coldrum and Kit's Coty House and, those of the Rhineland and the Low Countries, and their dissimilarity to those of Wiltshire, their principal appeal will lie in the vast scale and the splendour of their settings.

After Kit's Coty House return to the PW and take the hedged and signposted track (BOAT – although it's too narrow for vehicles, and a fence at the far end bars exit) for ½ mile/

Kit's Coty

800m to emerge at the old Rochester-Maidstone road. Turn L, then R through the underpass below the A229, then turn R up to a petrol filling station with a well-stocked shop and toilets.

From the crossing of the A229 the old road presents little for comment, save that over the next 15 miles/24km it is more direct, more conspicuously marked and better preserved than in any other similar stretch of its whole course. Nothing of its ancient character has been lost: it is not a permanent road as is the section between Alton and Farnham, but on the other hand it is not – except in two very short places – interfered with by cultivation or private enclosure. This stretch of road is a model to scale, preserved from modern changes and even from decay, but exhibiting those examples of disuse which are characteristic of its history.

The road goes parallel to and above the line where the sharp spring of the hills leaves the valley floor; it commands a sufficient view of what lies ahead; it is well on the chalk, just too high to interfere with cultivation (or at least with the cultivation of those lower levels to which the Middle Ages confined themselves); it is well dried and drained by the south slope and the porous soil; it is uninterrupted by coombes or any jutting promontories, for the range of the hills here is exactly even. In short, it here possesses every character which may be regarded as normal to the original trail from the west of England to the Straits of Dover.

The villages which lie immediately below the Way are all at much the same distance, and all but one lies just to the S. These villages – Boxley, Detling, Hollingbourne, Harriestham, Lenham and Charing – are now connected by the modern highway A20 which joins up the valley settlements which were once, it may be presumed, isolated from each other by the common fields of each village. They may have depended for their intercommunication upon the old road for many centuries, for each of them possesses a definitely marked line of approach to it; the old road remains the typical main artery, which passes near, but not through, the places it serves.

The crossing of the Rochester-Maidstone highway A229 occurs some 600yds/548m below the 'Lower Bell' Inn, by an underpass. Keep the petrol filling station on your R and keep to the track, a BOAT as far as Boxley. Where the tarmacadam ends, past a house, the old PW comes in from the R.

After some 250yds/228m the Way enters the fringe of the large Westfield Wood, which covers all the downland to the N. Just beyond this point, where four steps lead off L, will be found another megalith, the White Horse Stone.

Like the coincidence of the Coldrum Stones and Kit's Coty House, the coincidence of the name White Horse Stone here and White Horse Wood above the Coldrum Stones is significant.

(The NDW continues on page 218.)

The White Horse Stone

For a while the Way passes through the fringes of the wood past an area of open hillside, a spot beloved by motorcycle trial-riders. Here the Downs rise for 600ft/182m or more, a level maintained as far as Charing and beyond. Further on the woodland again drops close to the Way at Boarley Scrubs and we reach the road coming up from Sandling and Boxley Abbey. At this point we must once more break our journey, as so many other travellers must have done, to visit the scanty remains of the once-prosperous Boxley Abbey and the village of Boxley itself.

Boxley

A vast throng of devout and superstitious pilgrims would have been drawn to Boxley Abbey to gaze upon the supposedly miraculous Rood of Grace and the figure of St Rumbold. This Cistercian Abbey was founded by William de Ypres in 1146 – one of the earliest of the Order to be found in England, the only one in Kent and second only in importance to Waverley Abbey near Farnham – and was destined to grow in importance and the wealth of its possessions until it was unrivalled among the other great monastic settlements of Kent. It was the Abbot of Boxley who conducted the service over Becket when they laid him in the crypt at Canterbury.

An enormous stone-built tithe barn, 186ft/56m long, built about 1280, and stone walls which enclose 17 acres/6.8ha of land, are now all that is left of the abbey, which stood 1 mile/1.6km S of the Way near the village of Sandling.

The story of the Rood of Grace has often been told; how the monks acquired a figure of Christ fixed to the cross from a craftsman, with an ingenious mechanical device which enabled the figure to roll his eyes and bow his head by means of a complex system of concealed wires, and how for so long they imposed on the ignorant its 'supernatural' properties, and how it was eventually seized in 1539 by the King's Commissioners and ignominiously burned before a London crowd in St Paul's Churchyard.

The abbey was ruthlessly destroyed by Henry VIII at the

Dissolution. The abbey had been in his bad books for some time, for it was here that the court sat by order of the Pope under the presidency of Cardinal Campeggio. The adjudicators were against Henry's 'divorce' from Katherine; the King must have decided to have revenge some day, and his charge was that the monastery had been wasting its revenue by planting 'gilly flowers and roses' in the rich soil of its grounds! The abbey met the same fate as all the other monastic houses of the country, passing to the Crown and subsequently by the King's grant into private hands.

Boxley village and its church lie about 1 mile/1.6km to the E of the abbey and much nearer the Way. A footpath runs from the Abbey to Boxley, emerging from behind the 'King's Arms', opposite the church. We must return to the point above Boarley farmhouse and resume out eastward journey. For the next 500yds/457m the old road is part of the road from Sandling to Bredhurst, and 500yds/457m further E at a signpost we drop down again to Boxley village.

Boxley Abbey   *Church of St Mary and All Saints, Boxley*

Boxley is a small and quiet place beautifully situated near the foot of the steeply wooded Downs, from which issue several springs to feed a modest tributary of the Medway. The village has so far resisted development and takes its name, like Box Hill in Surrey, from the box trees that flourish on the Downs.

In 1840 Alfred Tennyson the poet came to live at Park House and the fair countryside is featured in many of his poems – *Prologue to the Princes*, *In Memoriam* – and many believe that one of the local streams inspired him to write *The Brook*, in 1855:

> I steal by lawns and grassy plots,
> I slide by hazel covers;
> I move the sweet forget-me-nots
> That grow for happy lovers.

As so often in Kent, it is as the focal point of a delightful scene, rather than as a distinguished building in itself, that Boxley church is so valuable. There is a charming village green and a pond, and by a group of stately elms and an old yew stands the church of St Mary the Virgin and All Saints. It exhibits work of all periods, but its most striking feature is the unusual narthex or chapel attached to the bold, Perpendicular period W tower. Apparently this may once have had a gallery from which sermons were preached or relics shown to pilgrims. This is supposed to be the nave of the original Norman church which became too small so the 'new' church was built behind it in the thirteenth century. There are some fine decorated windows, particularly the one at the W end of the N aisle, and there are two interesting brasses. In the chancel is a monument with the family tree of Sir Francis Wiat (1575–1644), Governor of Virginia from 1621, who is buried in the church. Tennyson's sister Cecilia married Edmund Lushington and is buried alongside other members of the Lushington family in the Lady Chapel.

The Pilgrims' Way – Boxley to Detling 1½ miles/2.4km
The wooded hills above Boxley make a most beautiful skyline
and there are little green rides from time to time through the
densely wooded slopes ascending to the crown of the ridge.
The chalk here is rich in wild flowers, including some rare
orchids. The woods are largely of beech mixed with box,
producing most spectacular contrasts in colour at many seasons, especially in autumn.

The Way becomes a tunnel of foliage below Boxley Warren
and at the junction of Harpole Lane the width increases and
we come out at the foot of Detling Hill where the main
Maidstone-Sittingbourne highway, A249, rises steeply to
bypass Detling.

Cross the dual carriageway – there is the largest ever
Pilgrims' Way sign here! – and after 50yds/45m or so, round a
slight bend, we see the jumbled roofs of the 'Cock Horse' inn.
A 'cock horse' was a specially-bred powerful horse used in
coaching days to lead a team of horses up steep hills – one
was needed at Detling to pull coaches up the Sittingbourne
turnpike. We now enter the village of Detling, where immediately there are two features of interest. One is the charming
timbered house which stands immediately to the S of the Way
and the other is a very attractive old red-brick Tudor gateway
that gives access to the grounds of East Court, a mansion
which was demolished about 150 years ago.

Detling is a quiet hamlet grouped round the Norman church
of St Martin of Tours. The church is not a big one and
architecturally is of no particular interest, except that the flint
tower is capped by a helmet-like broach spire which is of
unusual pattern for Kent. Let into the wall of the N aisle is a
remarkable piece of stone, a 600-year old carving of the face
of a man, with his hands clasped in prayer, but the most
striking possession is perhaps the oak lectern, a remarkable
work, carved about 1340, which probably came from Boxley
Abbey. It has a beautifully carved pedestal with four book-
rests, the sloping sides of which are enriched with period
tracery of varied pattern – an intricate design made up of

abstract patterning, flowers, grotesque faces among foliage, and animals, including an elephant with a howdah on its back.

(The PW continues on page 219.)

The North Downs Way – Kit's Coty to Detling

4½ miles/7.2km

Just below Kit's Coty the NDW joins the PW at a road junction – one road (the PW) coming in from the right from Burham, and the other coming up from Aylesford. The NDW and PW run together on a hedged track (a BOAT) to the A229 Rochester-Maidstone road, pass under it by a subway, and continue together until just after the White Horse Stone. The PW continues ahead on the track, but the NDW branches off,

The Cock Horse Inn, Detling

climbing steeply up through the woods, on a spur of the Downs. At the highest point, on the 625ft/190m contour, you join the path coming in from Cossington Fields, my suggested alternative route.

Maps show an ancient trackway along the top of the Downs leading SE towards Detling, but the NDW chooses not to follow this at first; it goes round field edges and through woods above Boarley Scrubs, only to join it before it passes through Harp Farm to a road. Why keep to the shade of the wood, unless it is for shelter from wind, rain or sun? The NDW follows the road for a short way to a T-junction with another road, then goes straight ahead on a muddy track (bridleway) through the woods above Boxley. After 1½ miles/ 2.4km this track makes a T-junction with a lane – Hermitage Lane – and this is followed S for a few yards/metres to where it bends back into the woods. Here you climb a stile, cross a field, descending steeply through a wood on a footpath to reach the A249. Oddly, you do not cross this road to the top of the Detling's main street, but go up the main road towards Sittingbourne village. (The NDW continues on page 221.)

The Pilgrims' Way – Detling to Hollingbourne
4 miles/6.4km
From Detling the PW continues as a typical byroad, very little frequented, such as we have often encountered previously. To the N, as always, are the rising heights of the Downs, while to the S lie orchards and open arable fields, in summer golden with ripening corn.

After about 1 mile/1.6km from Detling we come to a crossroads and the centre of the small village of Thurnham, where stands Friars Place, a lovely half-timbered and herring-bone-brick house, built early this century in the Tudor style re-using old timber and bricks. The church of St Mary the Virgin stands a few hundred yards/metres S of the 'Black Horse' down the hill, but it possesses few features of particular architectural interest to merit a special visit. Of interest to cricketers, however, is the grave of Alfred Mynn, one of the fathers of Kent cricket, who died in 1861. The inscription on his tombstone says, with typical Victorian thoroughness, that '400 persons have united to erect this tombstone, and to found in honour of a name so celebrated the Mynn Memorial Benevolent Institute of Kentish Cricketers'. Even the sum raised is specified – £121 10s invested in India 5% stock!

We rejoin the PW below the castle in Thurnham and follow the road for a further 3 miles/4.8km between hedges and open banks with the fields falling away gently to the S. We pass through the tiny hamlet of Broad Street, an attractive hamlet with some good buildings, including a fine black and white Tudor farmhouse. In a little over 1 mile/1.6km we reach the Hollingbourne-Sittingbourne road, B2163, at the foot of the steep Hollingbourne Hill at the 'Pilgrims' Rest' pub. If we turn right here into the centre of the village we will pass on our right Hollingbourne Manor. Only part of the great house, built by the Culpeppers in 1560, remains, but even so that which survives is a fine period building. It is said to be haunted by the ghost of Catherine Howard, whose mother was a Culpepper.

Hollingbourne is a small village nestling under the Downs. The green-tree'd hills provide the backcloth to red roofs, mellow brick and black-and-white timber-framed buildings which add much to the character and charm of the street architecture. The Perpendicular period Church of All Saints stands at the upper end of the straggling village in an attractive setting, and has several interesting features. There are three stained-glass windows in the S wall with pictures of Bible scenes and national saints: one with St George in gold, St Patrick in red and St Andrew in green; another with the Madonna, St Catherine and St Margaret; and another in the chancel with the Feast of Canaan and a scene of Abraham burying his wife.

The chapel is raised to the level of the altar and has 124 shields around its walls, but only two of them are decorated with coats of arms. There are many family memorials to the

Culpeppers, who once lived at the Manor and once at Green-way Court, and the most notable tomb is that of Lady Elizabeth, who died in 1638. She lies, a life-size figure chiselled in white marble, with her head on a pillow and her feet resting on a most peculiar heraldic beast, vaguely dog-like but with large spots and cloven hooves. Lady Elizabeth's four daughters made the altar cloths for which Hollingbourne is famous, but they are exhibited only during the principal festivals of the church. These two magnificent pieces – hangings for the altar table and pulpit – are the most treasured possessions of the church, and represent thousands of hours of needlework stitched by the young ladies over a period of 12 years, during the Commonwealth. The altar cloth has a border with the 12 fruits of the Tree of Life (Revelations 22:2). There are oak leaves and acorns, apples and cherries, quinces and pomegranates, all bordered round with winged cherubs.

(The PW continues on page 223, with the NDW.)

The North Downs Way – Detling to Hollingbourne
4 miles/6.4km

Since its conception the NDW was intended to run along the crest of the hills but for more than 20 years it followed a 'temporary' route between Detling and Broad Street, not along the PW – because here it is a minor highway – but on a line parallel to and just S of it.

However, the NDW now follows its intended line, rights of way having been negotiated, contouring round the coombes to Thurnham Castle, then to climb higher and wind in and out of the woods on the slopes, for 2 miles/3.2km to Broad Street.

Cross the A249 above Detling – where it is intended to provide a footbridge – and go down some concrete steps, through some scrub woodland and into an open field with a view over the Weald. The path comes to a road which descends to Thurnham. The road descends steeply to a hairpin bend, defining on the left the edge of Thurnham Castle's earthworks, a castle once built and occupied by one

Robert de Thurnham in the reign of Henry II.

The castle is a Norman defensive work of typical motte-and-bailey type. The only fragments of masonry left are flint walls, some 3ft/1m thick, and these are so hidden that it is difficult to find them among the trees. The castle was built up and fashioned out of a natural spur of the Downs. To the S and E the position was defended naturally by the steep fall of the hillside, but its appearance has been much altered by chalk quarrying and by the deeply cut road on the W side. The entrenchments consist of a mound, more or less natural. To the N and W was a fosse, which with the passage of time has been nearly filled up, while a rampart was provided at the summit around the weaker sides. To the W of the mount a bailey or court was protected by a massive stone wall which may have been continued up the hillside to join one encircling the top.

It is probable that this castle was built upon the foundations of earlier structures to guard an ancient trackway over the ridge from Maidstone to the coast near Sittingbourne, a track used for the transport of salt. No doubt this castle, or fort, or watch-tower guarded the crossing of the two roads, and at a place that, on account of its position, was a good look-out station. From the castle summit the view over the Weald is magnificent.

The NDW turns up into a coombe on the E side of Thurnham Castle then turns E through Civiley Wood, crosses a minor road, and passes through more scrub and woodland to reach a road coming up from Broad Street. A stile takes the path through scrub and wood to a sunken trackway, often muddy, which brings a bridlepath up from Allington Farm. Here you turn left and, after about 100yds/91m, turn right through a gate marked 'Private' to follow a clear path leading out on to the open downland above Hollingbourne, giving superb views over the Weald. The path contours above a deep coombe, and then descends steeply to the crossroads in Hollingbourne village.

Hollingbourne to Lenham 3 miles/4.8km

Beyond Hollingbourne there is a long section of trackway, mostly still leafy paths between fields, running for 12 miles/ 19.2km past Charing to Boughton Lees. This track, in places a metalled road and elsewhere a BOAT, is the PW, and both routes run together for this distance. Although the route runs parallel and close to the busy A20 and M20, it is generally remarkably quiet and peaceful.

E of Hollingbourne the 'No Through Road' degenerates into a rough track, although lawfully it is a BOAT. For the first few hundred yards/metres this is surfaced, and from the spot where this surfacing ends there is a fine prospect to the W of Hollingbourne church and manor with distant downland hills, blue in the distance where lies the Medway Gap. The next 2 miles/3.2km or so is one of the finest stretches of a grassy hedged track, a bridlepath sometimes skirting open meadows and arable land to the S, at others passing below the tangled branches of trees and hedgerows.

The old road between Hollingbourne and Harrietsham was duplicated to the S by another and possibly equally ancient track. Greenway Court stands on its line at the end of the road 1 mile/1.6km E of Hollingbourne, and beyond it continues as a grass path to Harrietsham church, becoming a road again and forming the modern highway A20 to Charing. This grass way was more generally called 'The Greenway' – hence Greenway Court – but in earlier times it was known as the 'Welcumeweye'.

We come soon to a crossing road which descends steeply towards Harrietsham, a village consisting of two hamlets bisected by the A20 running between Maidstone and Canterbury. East Street is the more attractive of the two parts of the village, possessing a number of charming seventeenth-century cottages, now mainly dressed up in Georgian frills, and a group of twelve almshouses built in 1642 by Mark Quested for the Worshipful Company of Fishmongers of London. They were rebuilt in 1770. Old Bell Farm opposite the Quested Almshouses is an unusually well-preserved eighteenth-cen-

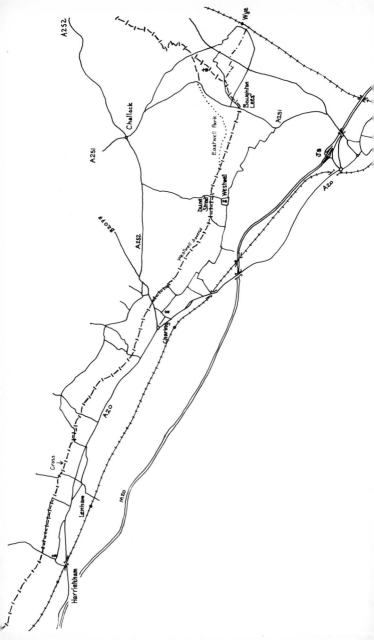

tury Wealden house (i.e. not restored), probably the most complete one left in Kent.

The parish Church of St John the Baptist stands upon the line of 'The Greenway', away from the old village but not yet submerged by the new. It is perhaps one of the most interesting and attractive along this section of the route as it has, or had, two towers. The original Norman church lay on the N side of the present chancel, and the remains of its W tower now form a chamber above the vestry at the E end of the N aisle of the present nave, which was built in 1360.

The tall, Perpendicular W tower of the present church was built about 1480, and is an impressive and beautiful example of its period. On the S side of the Early English chancel is a chapel of 1320 which contains a number of memorials to the Stede family, who lived at Stede Hill on the crest above the village. The oldest and best of the several tombs is that of Sir William Stede, who died in 1574. The unusual Norman font is one of the finest in Kent. The sundial above the porch, put up in 1853, is said to be accurate to within five minutes.

Immediately beyond the crossing of the steep ascent from Harrietsham the PW passes S of the private grounds of the one-time home of the Stede family, whose tombs we saw in the church below. At the eastern boundary of Stede Hill Park the Way resumes its normal character of a narrow byroad. Even as late as 1810 it was recorded by the then owner of Stede Hill that a 'Sheer Way' or 'Shire Way', now called the Pilgrims' Way, was the only through road from Hollingbourne to Charing.

In half a mile/800m we come to Marley Court, a farmhouse with buildings of eighteenth-century character, though perhaps now best distinguished by the odour arising from the many poultry houses around it. Opposite the farm, between the PW and the main road, spread the extensive buildings of a factory manufacturing concrete roofing tiles. The shortage of clay for roof tiles during the First World War led to the

Harrietsham to Boughton Lees

introduction of the concrete variety, and the Marley Tile Company is now world famous, turning out a wide range of products.

Half a mile/800m beyond Marley Court, the Way once more becomes a track (BOAT) when the road makes a right-angled bend to the right, and we continue ahead for a few hundred yards/metres to join another road at a corner on Lenham Hill. Follow this road for a few yards/metres and where it turns right we may follow it downhill to the village of Lenham.

Lenham

Lenham was once a flourishing market town on the old coach road, but it is now only a village bypassed by the main Maidstone-Folkestone highway A20. Henry III granted a market by charter and the spacious market square indicates the importance of the place when it was the agricultural centre for all the surrounding countryside. On the N side, screened by a row of lime trees, is a charming row of old houses, some now converted into shops. In one corner is the Saxon Pharmacy, named after a Saxon grave discovered outside in the course of restoration work. The Pharmacy is part of a typical Wealden timber-framed house, with a tall medieval window, and a kingpost roof rising above the glowing glass bottles and blue drug-jars of an old-style chemist's shop. It was restored from dereliction in the 1940s by Robert H. Goodsall, the local historian, who had previously bought and restored Stede Hill, above Harrietsham.

Occupying the W side of the square is the long, low, white 'Dog & Bear', with a brilliant royal arms over the door, commemorating Queen Anne's stay there. There are several remarkable fifteenth- and sixteenth-century timber-framed buildings in the village and some of these have Georgian or Early Victorian shopfronts.

The original church of St Mary's was maliciously burnt down in 1297, and though the arsonists were excommunicated by the Archbishop, they were never discovered. The present building consists of a nave and N aisle, with a good Perpendicular W tower. It still has its medieval stone altar-slab, which was let into the floor, and thus survived the destruction of the Reformation. N of the altar is the tombstone to the prolific Mary Honywood, who died in 1620 aged 92, leaving behind her a village-sized population of 367 descendants – 16 children, 114 grandchildren, 228 great-grandchildren and 9 great-great-grandchildren. The ornately carved Elizabethan oak pulpit probably dates from 1622. Two comical figures bear up the book rests, and two others hold the canopy,while all around are 26 smaller figures among foliage and little birds. There are few finer pulpits in Kent. The medieval lectern may once have been a 'singing desk' or music stand for the choristers. On the S wall of the nave is a faded medieval mural showing St Michael weighing souls.

Lenham is on a watershed which causes streams to drain W to the Medway and E to the Stour, but the ridge is hardly discernible from the old road. The watersheds of south-eastern England are low; the bold ranges of the Downs do not divide the river-basins because the water system is geologically older than the chalk hills.

Lenham to Charing 3 miles/4.8km

The Way leaves Lenham Hill as a tarmacked lane leading past a big disused chalk pit and a few houses, then a field gate gives access to a fine stretch of downland turf, in which is cut the great Lenham Cross. This well-known landmark was established immediately after the First World War and can be seen from considerable distances to the S. An iron railing at its foot once enclosed a granite block recording the names of those who fell in the two World Wars. The granite block was removed to Lenham churchyard in 1960 and as the railings no longer serve their purpose they ought to be removed.

Beyond the Cross we come to another field gate, and the Way now passes along a length of waste bordered on either side by bushes and small trees. You emerge at the Lenham-Warren Street road, which we follow for the next ¼ mile/400m until it sweeps round some extensive chalk workings (now

filled in), then it continues as a track bordered by hedges for
⅓ mile/480m to the next crossing road. At the end of this short
section are several houses built for staff of the Lenham
Sanatorium. The former Lenham Chest Hospital is now empty
and becoming derelict, forming a prominent landmark on the
crest above, from which can be seen a magnificent panorama
over the Weald to the distant Channel horizon.

For 100yds/91m E of the road junction the Way is a rough
track (BOAT), then for the next 300yds/274m or so it becomes
a pleasant pathway alongside a field. Beyond, it is in the form
of a terraceway raised 8 or 9ft/2m above the ground to the S.
The path passes a row of tall pine trees then runs across open
ground to Cobham Farm.

Pass through a corner of the farmyard and take up the
distinct line of the old road again passing between fields and
through wicket gates to a concrete road at Hart Hill, ¾ mile/
1200m further on. Beyond the first field the Way is tree-lined,
similar to the other stretches we have found, then for the last
400yds/121m it crosses open pasture and arable land as a
terraceway without hedges.

When the Way emerges on to Hart Hill it proceeds down
the hill for a short distance, not directly across or up as has
been its custom. Then, immediately below a house, it passes
along the top of a deep dell much overgrown by trees. This
may have been an ancient chalk working, but all signs have
been covered in by soil washed down the hillside. Just above
the Way at this point is a prominent chalk pit, but it is no
longer worked.

The spinney of trees on your right thins out and then the
church tower and russet roofs of Charing village appear. We
follow the tree-lined path for just over 1 mile/1.6km towards
Charing Hill, and soon the path leads us into a track passing
a waterworks building and a few houses, to reach the Canterbury road A252 by a tile-hung cottage. The PW continues on
the other side of the main road, but here let us turn right
down A252, then left along B2077 into the centre of Charing
village.

Charing is an attractive village which has long enjoyed the advantage of a bypass. It is situated at the fork of two main roads to the coast and the main village street is thus preserved from the worst of the horrors of through traffic. There are some good houses of unpretentious brick or black-and-white timbering in the High Street, broken here and there by the grander places like the gabled Peirce House set back a little from the road, or the fine Georgian Wakeley and Ludwell Houses. Hidden behind their façade is an estate of hideous concrete-panel utility houses, fortunately not noticed by the traveller on the PW, but a regrettable foreground to the village when approaching by main road from the W.

Gatehouse and Porter's Lodge, Charing Palace

Charing

Charing was a place of some importance, for it possessed the greatest of those archiepiscopal palaces, the string of which we came on first at Otford, and it was also the last convenient halting-place for those pilgrims on the journey to Canterbury.

The archbishop's palace was built by Archbishop John Stratford (1333–48), although little of the once considerable establishment now remains standing. Beside the approach road to the church from the village street are the ivy-covered remains of the fourteenth-century gatehouse and porter's lodge, and a range of domestic buildings now converted into cottages in one block. Behind this range was an irregular courtyard, now the farmyard, which contained on the N side the residential portion of the palace, now represented by the Tudor brick farmhouse of 1586. The once imposing fourteenth-century Great Hall to the E has become a barn. On the N side of the main block was the chapel, some traces of the undercroft remain, whilst elsewhere round the perimeter of the grounds are traces of the original boundary walling.

The Great Hall must have been the scene of lavish hospitality in its day. It is known that Henry VII was entertained here by Archbishop Wareham on 24 March 1507, and Wareham was also host to Henry VIII, who rested here one night when on his way to the Field of the Cloth of Gold in 1520. The palace remained in possession of the See of Canterbury until Cranmer resigned and handed it over to Henry VIII. The palace stayed in the hands of the Crown until the reign of Charles I, who sold it into private hands in 1692.

The Church of St Peter and St Paul dates from the middle-thirteenth century, though there may have been an earlier church on this site. The fine fifteenth-century tower is built in the characteristic Kent Perpendicular style; square, with angle

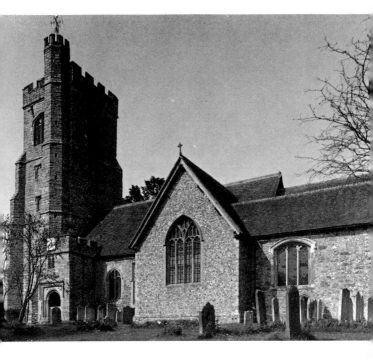

Church of St Peter and Paul, Charing

buttresses and beacon turret. There is an embattled porch
with a vaulted roof dating from the same period. The church
has no aisles but consists of a nave and transepts, with
windows ranging from Early English lancets to the latest of
square Perpendicular shapes. The arch from the tower to the
nave is enormously high and graceful. The nave and other
parts of the fabric were seriously damaged by a fire in 1590,
and the present nave roof, a magnificent and lofty span, with
painted oak beams on fine carved brackets, dates from 1592.

The ornamental roof in the chancel was built in 1620.

The church once possessed the block upon which St John the Baptist lost his head. This much-revered relic was brought back by Richard Coeur de Lion and presented to the archbishops of Canterbury, but it was removed by the Dissolution and has never been seen since. In the vestry is preserved a rare musical instrument, the long trumpet or vamping horn, through which a loud humming noise was made to accompany the orchestras of the seventeenth and eighteenth centuries. Only six are now in existence – five in England and one in Germany.

Charing to Eastwell 4 miles/6.6km
At Charing the great chalk hills turn a corner, where the River Great Stour passes through a wide gap on its way to Canterbury. The Downs continue their general line above Wye to the Channel Coast at Folkestone and this is the line followed by the main route of the NDW, but here the PW has reached the end of that long, clean-cut ridge which we have followed all the way from Farnham.

Beyond the crossing of A252 on Charing Hill the Way is clearly marked by one of the Kent County Council signs, and once more we are on a clearly marked country lane with banks on either side. The road continues for a full mile/1.6km as far as Burnthouse Farm, so named perhaps from its association with the adjacent limeworks.

Immediately beyond the farmhouse the track bends sharply to the left and then to the right, and we come quite suddenly upon the lime-works hidden at the edge of the wood. At the eastern end of the large chalk pit, after 150yds/137m or so, the Way divides into a fork. There is no Kent County Council sign at this spot and it is easy to take the wrong path. The right-hand one is the one to follow, a rough track (BOAT) continuing at much the same height as before, a terraceway bordered by trees and bushes.

This is one of the most attractive spots along the old road we have encountered since leaving the wooded slopes above

Boxley. The path runs through a great beech wood, then we
unexpectedly come upon an ancient chalk working which is
completely overgrown and forms a deep coombe on the right.
A little way beyond, near height 426ft/130m, a road comes up
from the S and once more we are on a metalled highway
which continues as far as Dunn Street, where it runs into the
road from Westwell to Challock.

Westwell is a pretty little village, with St Mary's Church
whose unpromising exterior of flint, cement render and brick
buttresses hides a beautiful, spacious interior. A broach spire
is awkwardly perched on a modest, narrow and unbuttressed
W tower. Inside there is a wonderful forest of columns,
alternating round and octagonal in the arcades, leading to a
rare stone-vaulted Early English chancel, with an additional
pair of columns in the chancel arch to take the weight of the
vaulting. There is a rare stone chancel screen, and in the
chancel are fine triple sedilia. The Rev Richard Harris Barham
(1788–1845), the author of the *Ingoldsby Legends* (1840–47) was
curate here from 1814–17.

From Dunn Street the old road enters Eastwell Park and
turns a gradual corner, following the course of the Stour
Valley. The modern road from Charing, the A252, cuts off this
corner and saves a good 2 or 3 miles/4km to Chilham, but the
reasons which caused men to take the longer course are not
easily overlooked:

1 The universal motive, the dryness of the road, which
could only be maintained upon the southern side of the hills.

2 The slopes down to the Stour were open when the plateau
above was dense forest, and this in turn would mean a group
of villages, which are absent from the line of the main road.

3 The water supply of the plateau was stagnant and bad;
that of the valley was a good running stream.

From Dunn Street the line of the Way is difficult to negotiate, for it passes through a long wood and is obstructed by
many trees and much tangled undergrowth. Fortunately a
well-established farm road runs parallel with it along the N
edge of the wood. Leave the road, therefore, and curve left,

then right, on a track past a large asbestos barn, then along the N edge of the wood to a railway level-crossing-type gate.

Ordnance Survey maps for this stretch east of Dunn Street don't help either. The 1/50,000 Landranger shows the old trackway to be the right of way (footpath) while the 1/25,000 Pathfinder shows the farm road to be the right of way. Both maps are correct where the path turns right at the next gate through the wood, then left to the end of the wood. The line of the old road travels across three fields marked by tubular steel field gates, to reach the track to Walnut Tree Farm just N of Eastwell Church.

Eastwell Park

Eastwell

The fifteenth century St Mary's Church now stands in ruins beside the edge of the lake. The roof of the church collapsed through neglect and war damage, and pushed over the walls, leaving only the Perpendicular tower with angle buttresses, and some of the W wall, standing.

The most imposing feature of the church was a great tomb with fine recumbent marble effigies, but these were removed in 1968 to the Victoria & Albert Museum. One of these would be the tomb of Sir Walter Moyle (died 1480), Earl of Winchelsea, and his wife, who lived at Eastwell House, while another

is of Sir Thomas Moyle, speaker of the House of Commons, who rebuilt Eastwell House. Another tomb is reputed to be that of Richard Plantagenet, son of Richard III, who died in 1550. When the Plantagenets lost the day to the Tudors at the Battle of Bosworth Field and Richard III was killed, Richard, then aged 16, escaped and made his way into Kent in disguise. He worked as a mason and bricklayer on the Eastwell estate and when he died a record of his passing was made in the parish register and his body laid in the church. In his memory the well near Boughton Lees was later renamed Plantagenet's Well.

Eastwell Lake was formed in the park as part of the landscape improvements of the eighteenth century and covers some 40 acres/16ha. The whole of the park was under requisition by the army during the war and on the great lake Bailey bridges were tried out and troops trained in their use. After the war, during cleaning-up operations, a number of bicycles were fished out of the lake and the previously unexplained fate of the many bicycles reported missing after dark from the streets of Ashford was made abundantly clear!

The grounds of Eastwell were enclosed in the reign of Elizabeth I, and it may well have been this act which caused the old road to fall into disuse and so accounted for the present doubt as to its original line. It is worth noting that no part of the old road is enclosed for so great a length as that which passes through Eastwell Park, where nearly 2 miles/3.2km lie within the fence of a private owner.

The first house was built in Eastwell Park in the middle of the sixteenth-century, but on several occasions the mansion has been altered or rebuilt. The ninth Earl of Winchelsea demolished and rebuilt between 1793 and 1799 and again rebuilt in 1825. The property remained in the hands of the Earls of Winchelsea until 1900 and on the change of ownership the mansion was once more demolished and rebuilt, as we

Church of St Mary, Eastwell

see it today, in imitation of the Tudor style. It is now a luxury hotel.

The line of the PW is lost after Eastwell church, but after a distance of about 2 miles/3.2km the line is recovered, above the valley of the Stour on Soakham Downs. There are two possible routes between these points and they will be examined in Part Eight: The Canterbury Loop. It is sufficient to say here that the route favoured by the Kent County Council, as far as the A251 at Boughton Lees, is also the route of the NDW: follow the road lined with poplar trees past the church to a junction, then continue straight ahead by a fence, following FP 213, veering left at a solitary tree to cross the driveway coming in from the Park Lodge, to cross diagonally opposite, emerging on the A251 at Boughton Lees, beside a whitewashed brick chapel.

Eastwell Park Lodge is a monstrous flint and stone neo-Jacobean gatehouse, built in 1843 – an unforgettable sight as you leave Ashford on the A251. It has big rampant lions on a huge coat of arms over the arch, and four octagonal towers.

It is at Boughton Lees that the PW and the NDW part company; the PW going on to Canterbury, and the NDW continuing the south-easterly course along the Downs to Folkestone and Dover. The Canterbury Loop is a device engineered by the Countryside Commission to take the NDW on an alternative route to Dover via Canterbury, enabling it to follow the PW as far as the outskirts of the cathedral city for the early part of its course.

Those who want to follow the NDW via Folkestone to Dover should continue with Part Seven, while those who want to follow the PW to Canterbury, or the NDW via Canterbury to Dover, should continue with Part Eight.

Boughton Lees to Etchinghill

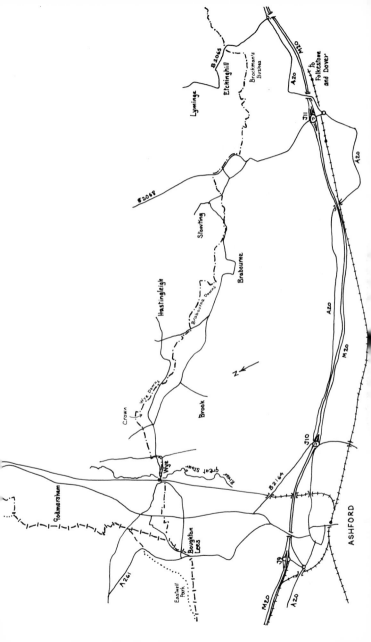

Part Seven: River Stour to the coast 22 miles/35km

11 River Stour to Folkestone 17 miles/27km

Eastwell to Wye 2½ miles/4km

The NDW emerges from Eastwell Park on the A251 in Boughton Lees at a corner of its broad, triangular green. Cross the main road and follow the road along the E side of the green towards Boughton Aulph, alongside orchards. Just past the entrance to Brewhouse Farm, the Canterbury Loop Path strikes off NE, but for Wye and Folkestone we continue along the road for 100 yards/metres or so to the next bend, where a stile gives access to a path around two sides of an orchard, first SE and then N. At a gateway, turn right on a footpath beside another field to a stile on the A28 Ashford-Canterbury road, opposite Perry Court Farm, just ½ mile/800m N of Kempe's Corner. Just N of the farm you follow paths through the orchards in a reasonably straight line, and go across fields to join a road near Wye railway station.

Wye

'Wye', wrote Leland, 'is a pratie market townlet', and so it is today, delightfully compact and small in scale, lying between the placid waters of the Great Stour and the steep scarp of the Downs. It is now chiefly known as the home of one of the country's main agricultural colleges, and its most prominent landmark is a large crown carved in the chalk up on the hillside behind. Our route takes us through the centre of this smart little Georgian country town before climbing the Downs above.

   The Stour is crossed by a five-arched stone bridge, built in 1638 and repaired in 1684, with the names of the six men who repaired it. Beside the bridge is a charming mill and a mid-Georgian mill-house in red brick and white boarding, with an

Ionic doorcase with an enriched frieze. Bridge Street runs up into the town past several pleasing cottages. Notice on the right Nos. 134–40, originally one tall timber-framed building, on which the seventeenth-century brackets to the overhang of No. 134, and the hood of the doorway to No. 138, are carved into grotesque crouching human figures and gryphons respectively.

You turn left into Church Street, the main street of the town, starting as a funnel and widening out as it approaches the church. In the narrow part Georgian cottages crowd close up to the pavement: on the right side is the wide, flat, red-brick front of Little Lords, and on the left the three-storey, black-and-white painted Swan House, with an Ionic doorcase. As the street widens out there is, on the left, the 'King's

Church Street, Wye

Head', rebuilt after a fire c.1870, the only jarring building in the town.

At the mouth of the funnel is the churchyard and church of St Gregory & St Martin, a building reflecting the disasters of its history. It was originally a large cruciform building of about 1300: four bays of the nave and part of a fifth, together with their aisles, survive from this period. In 1572 the steeple was struck by lightning and set on fire, and in 1686 the central tower collapsed, bringing down the transepts and the chancel. This was never rebuilt. It was probably Kempe (of whom more below) who remodelled the nave in the mid-fifteenth century to give it more light; and then between 1701–6 the demolished E end was replaced. The present little apsidal chancel was built where the old tower once stood, and the massively buttressed and pinnacled tower was built over the site of the original transept arch.

There are hardly any monuments, but there is a good set of funeral hatchments below the big clerestory windows. There is a splendid brass with 14 figures on it: Alice Palmer with her two husbands and a charming group of their 11 children.

Wye claims to be the birthplace, in 1640, of Mrs Aphra Behn, the Mata Hari of Restoration England, who spied for Charles II in Antwerp. She was the first Englishwoman to become a professional writer, and she is buried in Westminster Abbey.

Our path takes us from the main gate diagonally through the churchyard behind the college buildings to the northern side of the town on Olantigh Road.

Wye College – the College of St Gregory & St Martin – has now expanded far beyond its medieval beginnings at the corner of the churchyard. It was founded by Cardinal John Kempe, friend of Henry V, and who was in his time Lord Chancellor to Henry VI, Bishop of Rochester, Chichester and London, and Archbishop of York and Canterbury, who had been born in Wye. In 1432 Kempe obtained a licence to found a college, which he did in 1447. By 1448 the staff were appointed – a master, a master of grammar, six clerks and two choristers.

Kempe's college is immediately E of the churchyard, from which it is entered. It lies round three sides of a small quadrangle, with the hall on the fourth side, furthest from the church, on the road-side. The oblong, one-storeyed, building was no doubt intended from the start as the schoolroom. The upper storeys of the other three sides of the quadrangle, originally half-timbered, were rebuilt in 1739 in red brick, the brickwork even at this late date still bonded in the English fashion.

At the Reformation the college for secular priests was disbanded, but the college survived because the buildings were granted to Katherine Parr's secretary, on condition that he maintained the grammar school. The grammar school survived until 1893, when the buildings were turned into an agricultural college for the SE, and later into the agricultural college of London University, including a 720-acre/290ha farm. Four more college quadrangles have since sprung up – building taking place in 1901, 1903–6, and 1912–4. Students come here from forty countries worldwide to study or to undertake research on agriculture and land use management.

Withersdane Hall, ½ mile/800m SE of the town, is a hostel for the agricultural college, built c.1950; and the college also has a museum. This is in the village of Brook, 2 miles/3.2km to the SE, and is open on Wednesday afternoons between June and September, and additionally on Saturdays in August. A vast medieval barn houses a collection of every sort of farming bygone, from carts to ploughs; and an oasthouse at the back has smaller exhibits such as sickles and bird scares.

Wye to Stowting 7 miles/11.2km

From the crossing of the Olantigh Road on the N side of the town, the path goes E on a straight track (RUPP) through the college farm, heading for the Downs. Cross another road and climb more steeply up through the Juniper Wood, and on a spur of the Downs pointing NW. You then meet a road leading to Down Farm and Pett Street, but you keep the edge of the wood on your right, up on to Wye Downs above the memorial crown. This large crown was carved in the chalk by students of the college to commemorate Edward VII's coronation in 1902, and is a landmark for traffic on the Ashford road.

Beyond the crown you continue in a south-easterly direction on the crest of the Downs, where there are superb views, even the first view of the sea, passing above the tumulus called the Giant's Grave; and after about ½ mile/800m you come to a road junction. Cross the road here and climb a stile to enter the Wye & Crundale Downs National Nature Reserve. This was established in two stages – in 1961 and 1967 – 'to maintain a good example of chalk downland and woodland and its characteristic flora and fauna'. The Reserve covers 250 acres/100ha. The chalk turf is rich in wild flowers, grasses and herbs – 17 species of orchids occur in the Reserve – and the flora supports many species of moth, butterfly, beetle and bug. Forty per cent of the Reserve is woodland, predominantly ash, with hazel coppice and occasional whitebeam, yew, and beech. In the scrub of hawthorn, blackthorn, and dogwood breed whitethroat, blackcap, and willow warbler.

It is sad to reflect that nowhere else on our walk along the North Downs have we encountered any 'natural' downland: almost everywhere it has been cultivated or planted, and this short stretch has been preserved from agricultural improvement.

You head in a southerly direction, passing a round barrow 35ft/10.6m in diameter and 4ft/1.2m high. Excavation revealed a pit containing fragmentary human remains, but no grave goods.

Keep to the edge of the ridge, which falls away spectacularly at one point, and you soon reach open downland on Broad Downs. Here the Nature Conservancy Council has established a small information centre which is open during most summer months. During this time a self-guiding nature trail is open, and descriptive leaflets are available. Access to the Reserve is limited to public footpaths – including the NDW – otherwise by permit.

The Devil's Kneading Trough, Broad Downs, Wye

These Downs have steep coombes on their SW flanks, and you contour round the head of the Devil's Kneading Trough, a popular picnic spot, accessed from a busy car park, with a restaurant nearby. You leave the crest of the Downs, past Cold Blow Farm, and beside a field edge to a road. Follow this road S for ¼ mile/400m to a T-junction near New Barn Farm. You turn left at this junction, and follow this road E, to South Hill Farm, and, when it turns N to Hastingleigh, you continue ahead on a trackway above Brabourne Downs.

The trackway is marked on Ordnance Survey maps in 'olde Englishe' lettering, to indicate its antiquity, and it follows the crest of the Downs parallel to the road which hugs its base some 150ft/45m below. The road is marked 'Pilgrims' Way' but there is doubt about its historical authenticity. At the end of the track, at a road, turn S, cresting the highest point of the Downs hereabouts at 597ft/182m, to reach an OS triangulation pillar at 584ft/178m, directly above Brabourne.

Brabourne is a compact little village, with St Mary's Church unexpectedly awe-inspiring, its enormously wide massively buttressed low tower making it look almost square. The Norman chancel arch has intricately carved capitals, and the whole N wall of the chancel is Norman work. The E window on the N side of the chancel still has its original twelfth-century stained glass – a simple piece of pattern-making, believed to be the oldest complete Norman window anywhere in England: deeply splayed, small and narrow, glowing with red, green and gold.

Eighteen generations of the famous Scott family, descended from Baliol, are buried in this church. By the door opening into the S chapel is a small throne-like altar, with a recess at the back for a heart encased in silver or ivory – almost certainly the 'heart-shrine' of John de Baliol, founder of Balliol College, Oxford, who died in 1269. Baliol's son, John Baliol de Scott, King of Scotland, may well have brought the heart with him after his defeat by Edward I, and entrusted it to his brother, Alexander Baliol, who lived at Chilham.

In the N wall of the chancel is a fine Perpendicular tomb of the 'Easter Sepulchre' type to Sir John Scott (d. 17 October 1485), a Lord Warden of the Cinque Ports, who was also Comptroller of the Household to Edward IV: the helmet above the tomb was probably that of Sir Edward Thomas Scott, commander of the forces in Kent in Elizabethan times. He was so powerful in Kent that he raised 4,000 men in 24 hours when the Spanish Armada came. The helmet on the S wall of the chancel is that of Sir William Scott who was with Henry VIII in the Field of the Cloth of Gold in 1520. He built the Scott chapel on the S side of the church, and died in 1524. The arms of the Scotts from 1290 are displayed on the altar, with text from Tyndale's Bible.

From the trig-point on Brabourne Downs you follow the road to a bend halfway down the steep hill, and then you turn left along a farm track (RUPP) rising to the crest of the Downs. After ¾ mile/1200m you cross the Brabourne-Stowting Common road, and, going straight across, go down the hill to another road, to Stowting Court and the 'Anchor Inn'. The village of Stowting lies a little to the N, ringed on three sides by the Downs. The church of St Mary's has been restored so many times – 1843–4, 1876 and 1890 – that there is nothing of interest left in it.

Stowting to Folkestone 9 miles/14.5km
It becomes increasingly difficult for the NDW to find a route along public footpaths as it approaches the coast, and of the next 9 miles/14.5km to the A260 outside Folkestone, no less than 3.5 miles/5.6km are on the highway. There is then another good mile/1.6km of road before you reach Dover.

From Stowting Court and the 'Anchor Inn' you follow the road for ¼ mile/400m to approach a Y-junction, but just before this is reached, a sunken path goes off left across another road and climbs up Cobb's Hill, out of the bowl in the Downs in which Stowting is situated. The path goes up the spur of the hill, from the top of which there are very good views, and then it reaches the B2068 Lympne-Canterbury road, the Roman road Stane Street. This road ran from the Roman fort of Lemanis near Lympne direct to Canterbury, and apart from a kink in it at Newingreen, and a bend near Farthing Common – where it climbs up the Downs – it is as straight as an arrow for 11 miles/17.6km.

The Way turns S and runs parallel to the road, rather than along it, for ½ mile/800m past the Farthing Common, Monks Horton picnic area at a road junction, then round a long bend. The Way crosses the road across the headland of the Downs, and the sea properly comes into view, with the buildings of Dungeness nuclear power station on the horizon. The Way drops down about 180ft/55m into a dry valley, and then climbs up, to contour round two prominent hills in front, just above Postling, where there are good views over the village and Romney Marsh beyond. You may descend to Postling from here, or double back along the road from Staple Farm, to where the Way drops down to a junction on the B2065 road.

Postling is a beautiful hamlet, with black-and-white cottages nestling in the apple orchards. Postling Court is a charming Tudor house, one of the most attractive timbered farmsteads S of Canterbury, its courtyard now tastefully developed. The Norman church with shingle spire is unusually dedicated, to St Mary & St Radegund: at one time it belonged to St Radegund's Abbey, 2–3 miles/4km W of Dover. (St Radegund was a German princess, born about AD 520, who founded an abbey at Poitiers.) The church's dedication stone, a rare survival, is on the N wall of the chancel. Small, square, and perfectly preserved in Caen stone, it is inscribed with the date of its dedication – 19 days before the Kalends of September (i.e., 14 August, the day of St Eusebius the Confessor) – but not, intriguingly, the year. It is twelfth century. There are traces of medieval twelfth-century painting in the SW nave, and on either side of the chancel are the sawn-off ends of the rood beams, still painted.

Joseph Conrad chose the seclusion of Postling to write some of his greatest novels: between 1898 and 1907 he rented Pent Farm, outside the village at the junction with the B2068, and wrote *Lord Jim, Typhoon, Nostromo*, and *Mirror of the Sea* while living there. He moved to Bishopsbourne (qv) in 1920.

To the N of Postling is Lyminge (pronounced 'Limmindge'), a large and dour village, but one of the early shrines of Christianity in Kent. In 633 Ethelburga – daughter of King Ethelbert, the founder of Canterbury, the wife of the founder of York – and Bishop Paulinus founded an abbey here for men and women. Its last known charter was granted in 964 – part of the original abbey church can be traced, from its apsidal E end beside the S porch of the present church, to its excavated E end SW of the tower. The first church was destroyed by the Danes about 840 and the present church of St Mary & St Ethelburga was built c.965 by Dunstan, Archbishop of Canterbury, who rebuilt the ruined earlier church. It has a good deal of later Saxon work in the nave and chancel, and was added to by Lanfranc when he removed the remains of Ethelburga to Canterbury, c.1180. The flying buttress at the E end was added in the late fifteenth-century, and the low sturdy tower was built between 1508 and 1527. A plaque on the S wall of the church marks the original burial place of Queen Ethelburga.

E of Postling a large spur juts out, just before the Downs finally reach the sea. The unusually named Brockman's Bushes is the highest point on these hills, but nowhere on this stretch of the Downs from Wye do we climb higher than 600ft/182m.

From Staple Farm, at the Sandling/Postling/Lyminge road junction, a path climbs these hills to a Post Office tele-communications station, with its impressive array of dished receiving aerials on a concrete pylon, standing just N of the highest point of 595ft/181m. Adjoining it is a joint Ministry of Defence/Civil Aviation Authority air-traffic radio station (Swingfield or Tolsford Radio Station). The NDW is joined here by the Saxon Shore Way, which follows our route all the way to Dover.

The North Downs above Postling

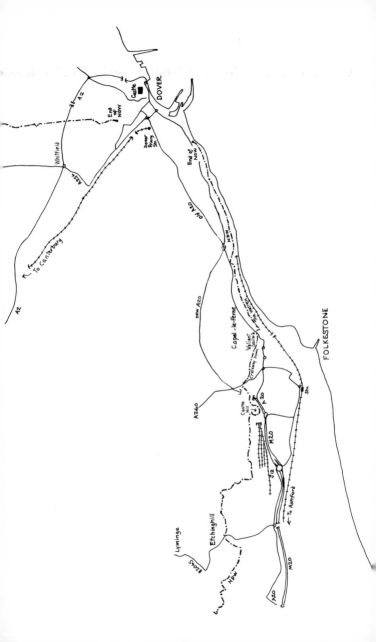

Beyond the wireless station on Brockman's Bushes the Way passes along the edge of a MOD training area (keep the fences to your right), and the path is very muddy through the scrub until you meet a wood. It improves as you go through the edge of the wood above the park of Beachborough, and it then runs down to the B2065 Newington-Lyminge road just outside Edginghill, an unprepossessing village dominated by a large hospital. You cross the road and go down a track towards Coombe Farm, but just before you reach the farm you take a path diversion around its N side, and pass under the disused Folkestone-Canterbury railway.

Beyond here the Way makes its last climb up the Downs, going steeply up a dry valley from 300ft/91m to 581ft/177m, crossing fields at the top to reach a bridleway at a bend in the road to Paddlesworth. This bridleway leads SE to another road on Hungar Down. Follow the road S for a short way then continue on a track to Pean Quarry. Here turn E, generally on the 500ft/152m contour, along the edge of fields to join the road to Cheriton Hill.

At Cheriton Hill the road makes a T-junction with another coming in from the N, but just before this junction the path leaves the road, running parallel to it on the top of the Downs to another road junction, a Y-fork, above the deep coombe between Cherry Garden Hill and Castle Hill. All along this section there are good views down into Folkestone.

Here you can look down onto the M20 and the Folkestone terminal of the Channel Tunnel.

Construction work on the project began in 1987 and is due to be completed in the summer of 1993 when the Single European Market comes into effect. As a result of one of the biggest engineering works this century The Tunnel will provide the first-ever fixed link between Great Britain and the Continent, connecting the road and rail networks of Europe. In twin tunnels trains will operate on a shuttle system transferring all kinds of road vehicles from this terminal to

Etchinghill to Dover

Coquelles in France, and the vast marshalling yards and transfer decks are needed to cater for all the expected traffic.

High-speed through-passenger trains are intended to run between London and Paris or Brussels but the new or improved rail links between the Folkestone Terminal and London have not yet been built. There has been a lengthy dispute between the government and prospective contenders as to which route the rail link should take but no decision has yet been made. However, there seems to be general agreement that the link should follow the present line as far as Ashford then run alongside the M20 up to Detling, the portal for the tunnel section under the North Downs. From here the government's preferred route is to cross the Medway between the M2 bridge and Halling, while British Rail's preferred route crosses between Halling and Snodland. The former would approach London from the east through Stratford whilst the latter would make a southerly approach to Kings Cross and Waterloo from Deptford.

Given that the speed of the shuttle determines the Tunnel's throughput, it is estimated that the line will be able to handle 140 trains each way each day. These trains would carry an estimated (most pessimistic forecast) 13.4 million international passengers and 6.1 million tonnes of freight during the opening year, rising to an estimated (most optimistic forecast) 31.9 million passengers and 16 million tonnes within 30 years. The new lines would be equipped with overhead lines supplying power and trains would travel at speeds up to 140 mph. Whichever route is chosen there is no doubt that it will have a considerable impact on the Kent countryside.

At Cheriton, on the outskirts of Folkestone overlooking the Folkestone Terminal, is the Eurotunnel Exhibition Centre, showing how the tunnel was built and how it will be used. It has a full-size mock-up of a section of the shuttle trains, displays and models of construction work and a 32m-long model (one of the biggest N-gauge model railway layouts in the country) of the terminals and tunnels in action. (Open Tuesdays to Sundays throughout the year. Closed on Mondays except Bank Holidays. 1000–1800 in summer, 1000–1700 in winter).

Castle Hill is also called Caesar's Camp, the name given locally to the early fortifications on the top of the chalk hill. The ditches round the top may be Iron Age or medieval; they are certainly not Roman. The Way goes round the S side of Castle Hill and Round Hill, where considerable disruption is caused by the construction of the new A20 from Dover, which drops down to join the M20 below Castle Hill. Go on to the A260 N of Sugarloaf Hill. This smooth conical hill is supposed to be man-made, but no one knows why, or when.

One can drop down into Folkestone from the A260 Canterbury Road but we shall do so shortly. Go up the road a short way, then over a fence on the R to follow a path through the gorse bushes parallel to the road along the crest of the Cretway Downs for another good 1 mile/2km to reach the A20 Dover Road at the 'Valiant Sailor' public house. Accommodation on the outskirts of Folkestone is scarce, and a descent into the town centre means a long climb up the following day.

12 Folkestone to Dover 5 miles/8km

Folkestone

In the Middle Ages Folkestone was important enough to be made a 'limb' of the Cinque Port of Dover, but after that, until the nineteenth century, it was hardly more than a few rows of fishermen's cottages down by the harbour, and a scatter of houses up the hill between the harbour and the church. Defoe called it 'a miserable town', and apparently it remained so until the railway was opened in 1843 and it was turned into a fashionable seaside resort.

From our vantage-point high up on the crest of the Downs we can see, in the centre of the town, William Cubitt's superb railway viaduct of 1843 which spans the valley around which the town is centred. It has 19 slender brick arches, nearly 100ft/30m high in the centre. Its litheness comes from the fact that the piers taper from front to back as well as at the sides. Newman, in *The Buildings of England*, calls it 'the most exciting piece of architecture in the town'.

Guarding the town are four Martello Towers, two below Dover Hill on Copt Point and two at Sandgate, and they too can be seen from the NDW. The round, three-storeyed towers were built in 1806 as gun-posts against a possible Napoleonic invasion. Twenty-five towers were built along the coast between Folkestone and Lillestone. The name is taken from the Torre della Mortella in Corsica, which had resisted an English attack in 1794. In the 1820s they were used to accommodate the Coast Blockade, a naval force set up to combat smuggling, which became the forerunner of the present Coast Guard.

As a fishing port, Folkestone can claim more than respectable antiquity, but the harbour, designed by Telford in 1807, is well-nigh useless because of the eastward drift of shingle which still causes so much anxiety to all towns along this SE coast. It was the railway which made Folkestone what it is today. The old harbour was bought in 1842 by the South Eastern Railway Company, whose directors were quick to see the advantage of an alternative through-route to the Continent. They cleared away the silted-up harbour, erected landing-stages, and soon established a ferry service: the first steamer sailed from Folkestone to Boulogne on 28 June 1843, taking 4 hours, and a regular service was inaugurated on 1 August. In less than 20 years the population of the town doubled; the town became a fashionable, if staid, seaside resort, and has remained so ever since. Further development followed, so that today Folkestone holds a high position in cross-Channel traffic: the journey now takes $1\frac{1}{2}$ hours and the Folkestone-Boulogne route from London to Paris is shorter by 28 miles/45km than that via Dover-Calais.

Folkestone is a good place to stay for the last leg of the journey, if you can bear that long descent into the town and the necessary climb up the following day! Although it is only about 5 miles/8km to Dover, we have come 16 miles/25km from Wye, and it will be pleasant to spend the last day on the coast exploring these two towns. To rejoin the Way where we left it, you go straight up the Dover Road from the old town.

Folkestone to Dover 5 miles/8km

From the 'Valiant Sailor' on the A20 Dover Road, on the outskirts of Folkestone, the NDW lies along the cliff top to the western outskirts of Dover. There are good views of France on a clear day, and of the never-ceasing stream of vessels, compelled by the narrowness of the Channel to pass close to land.

The Way begins this final section by following a path to the cliff edge above The Warren, the greatest classic landslip in the country. The gault clay, which underlies the chalk, is impervious to the water which percolates through the chalk, and this has caused the cliffs to slip into the sea. The fallen debris in this vast area is covered with trees and scrub growth, and is a favourite area for lovers of wild flowers. There is access to it from Folkestone, and from a path which descends the steep cliff from a point near Capel-le-Ferne village.

The cliff-top path runs parallel to a minor road on the edge of Capel-le-Ferne village for 1½ miles/2.4km, passing bungalows and cafés, a country club, then through a caravan park to the prominent Abbotscliffe House, close to the A20 at a point 3 miles/4.8km out of Folkestone, 3½ miles/5.6km from Dover. Here you pass on the inland side of the house, to the main road.

The Lydden Spout rifle range is no more, but it has been replaced by another intrusive user of land, the new A20, which services the Channel Tunnel at Shakespeare Cliff.

The coast is then followed, above Abbot's Cliff and past Lydden Spout, and overlooking the coastal railway line where it emerges from its tunnels. At the foot of the cliffs, as you approach Dover, the construction site for the Channel Tunnel can be seen. There are earlier borings made as long ago as

Shakespeare Cliff, Dover

1880, which extended for over 1 mile/2km towards France. The spoil from the present project, used as a vast construction site for six years up to 1993, will be landscaped and used for public recreation when the project is completed.

The NDW descends Shakespeare Cliff past allotments and ends at the Old Folkestone Road. Shakespeare Cliff is where the blind Earl of Gloucester in Shakespeare's *King Lear* tried to jump. This sharply-pointed peak is one of the first objects a Channel voyager looks for, when approaching Dover.

Although the path ends on the outskirts of Dover – on the Old Folkestone Road – we cannot stop here. We must get down into the town in order to find transport to get us home, and, while waiting for that bus or train, we must go and look at the castle.

Dover

Dover is every traveller's goal: its White Cliffs gladdened the heart of every loyal Englishman returning from across the sea, for this is, after all, the traditional first sight of England. As the gateway to England for over 2,000 years, Dover has been the place of passage for kings, armies, pilgrims, but because the town is not a particularly attractive place to visit for its own sake today's ever-increasing tide of international holiday-makers, and those who merely pass through it, will probably fail to appreciate the part it has played in our island's history, which is a pity.

Unfortunately, the walker cannot approach Dover by the right and proper way – the sea – but he can appreciate best its splendid situation between two great chalk headlands. On one side is the white precipice of Shakespeare Cliff and the green brow of the Western Heights, and on the other the heights of East Cliff and the mass of the enormously powerful castle. Between is the River Dour, with the mass of the town spilling inland up the valley. At one time the sea flowed for some distance up this valley and formed a secluded haven – a vast Roman timber jetty near Phoenix Street and a wharf of about the second or third centuries in Stembrook Street have been discovered – but it began to silt up in Norman times as a result of the formation of a shingle bar across the mouth. For a few hundred years an entrance was kept open, but a landslip in the fifteenth-century effectively stopped up the mouth of the old harbour, which was then replaced by a system of docks.

Dover's history is based on the constantly evolving harbour, and the fortifications which were built to defend it. Not much of the town remains that is worth seeing: the heavy wartime shelling and piece-meal rebuilding has seen to that.

As we descend from Shakespeare Cliff we get a good view of the Western Heights and the huge harbour, and we shall make a brief tour of the town, including the promenade, before climbing up Castle Hill to visit the magnificent fortress of Dover Castle.

Cross the new A20 and go up South Military Road opposite up to the Western Heights which provide a magnificent view over the town and harbour. At the top of the road on the left, just after a viewpoint car park, are the remains of the Knights Templar Church which were uncovered in 1806. It was established c.1128: not only was it one of the smallest in the country, 32ft/9.75m long, but it was one of the very few round churches built in England. The foundations, repaired in 1913, show the characteristic circular nave modelled on the plan of the Church of the Holy Sepulchre at Jerusalem. To the W of the Knights Templar church is some drab housing occupied by staff serving the HM Young Offenders Institution (formerly called Borstal) housed in The Citadel, the major fortress of the Western Heights. It can only be visited by those having a legitimate purpose – i.e., visiting inmates.

The Western Heights

The Western Heights are topped by the Napoleonic War fortifications (now commonly called the Western Heights) which complement the magnificent Norman castle on the other side of the valley. Although the fortifications of the Western Heights are much larger than the Norman castle they are hidden from casual view behind walls, vast brick-lined ditches and grassy embankments, and they turned the hill into a single, huge fortress complex.

In 1793 the new Republic of France, with the brilliant young Napoleon at the head of her forces, seemed to threaten the safety of all Europe. It was assumed that, should an invasion ever be mounted against England, the French troops would land on the marshes between Hythe and Rye. In due course the Royal Military Canal and a string of Martello Towers were constructed to make such a landing hazardous for the enemy. It was concluded that Dover must be the last stronghold of the British Army, and a base from which an enemy advancing on London could be cut off from the sea, but Cobbett argued that its purpose would be useless, as the enemy had many suitable landing-places to choose from.

The medieval castle on the east side of the town was modified to make it a vast mount for guns and the Western Heights were hollowed out to accommodate a sizeable part of the British Army within them, and to provide the Army with a second vantage point from which to cover the town and the valley running down into it.

The plan was for a major defence complex consisting of two independent forts, or redoubts – The Citadel to the west and the Drop Redoubt to the east – linked by a deep moat with a smaller fort, or bastion, halfway between the two. Work began in 1804, with the Drop Redoubt being completed in 1808 and The Citadel in 1815.

Initially the only access into the impregnable fortress was by two long, steeply winding roads – the South and the North Military Roads – and the troops in the barracks were unfortunately a long way from the harbour, where an attack would be expected. So the third element of the scheme was the construction of the Grand Shaft as the most direct link between the fortifications and the town and harbour. The military wanted to have a quick response to any attack on the harbour as well as allow a fast retreat to the safety of the Heights if necessary. Sir Thomas Hyde Page had the unique notion to design a triple spiral staircase, which was built between 1806–9. The Grand Shaft is 140ft/42.6m deep and 26ft/8m in diameter. It consists of two brick cylinders, one inside the other, with the interlocking stairs between them, its core open to the sky as a lightwell. The tunnel at the bottom led out into Snargate Street, opposite the entrance to the present Hoverport.

Upon the signing of the Treaty of Paris on 30 May 1814 it became clear that the Dover defences would not be needed. By that time, as Cobbett characteristically estimated, the quantity of brick buried in the hill would have built a cottage for every farm labourer in Sussex and Kent. 'Either madness most humiliating or profligacy the most scandalous must have been at work here for years', he fumed.

After the war ended in 1815 the fortifications were left to decay, except for the retention of the barracks, but in 1850, during the unrest in Europe, it was decided to renovate and complete the fortifications. The Citadel was made the nucleus of the scheme (completed between 1853–5) and The Drop Redoubt was modernised according to the principles of Vauban, the seventeenth-century French military engineer. At the Drop Redoubt a series of cavernous underground chambers were constructed, linked to form roughly a five-pointed star with fortlets or carponiers at four of the projecting corners. Myriads of 30ft/9m deep brick-faced ditches or 'lines' for gunfire were dug, making a crazy web over the hillside. Every inch of the ditches was covered by gunfire from the carponiers so that any attacker, once enticed into the ditches, would be gunned down. The Western Heights became an impregnable vantage-point controlling the whole town: the maniacal scale and thoroughness of it are still oppressively apparent.

Between 1860–74 a further fort was built on the northern side of the hill to defend the area between The Citadel and Grand Redoubt from any attack on the landward side, but by 1920 the fortifications had fallen into disuse. During the Second World War the Redoubt, the batteries and the barracks

were put to use again. The barracks were demolished in 1965
but many pill-boxes and gun emplacements of that period, as
well as the two main forts, the bastions and most of the
batteries and ditches are still in excellent condition.

The District Council have provided a self-guided Western
Heights Trail that explains the development of the fortifications. Use of the Trail and access to the Western Heights is
free and can be enjoyed all year round at any time (except HM
Borstal). The Grand Shaft is open by the museum service for
a small charge (Open May to September, Wednesdays to
Sundays, 1400–1700, and also Bank Holiday Mondays
1000–1700).

Tour of the Town

From the Western Heights descend North Military Road and
Durham Hill to reach the dual-carriageway York Street just
south of the roundabout of the A20 Folkestone Road. From
the roundabout continue in the same direction as before, now
with the flow of one-way traffic into Priory Road. On the right
hand side is St Edmund's Chapel, consecrated in 1253 and
considered to be the smallest church in England still in regular
use. It measures only 26ft/8m by 14ft/4m and in the nineteenth
century was converted into a house. Only when scheduled
for demolition in the 1960s was it rediscovered: it was saved
and restored and reconsecrated in 1968.

Priory Road runs into High Street and at its junction with
Ladywell is the incongruous Victorian town hall. The town
hall incorporates part of the Maison Dieu, built in 1203 as a
hospice for travellers and pilgrims, but closed at the Dissolution. In part of the town hall, with access off Biggin Street, is
the Old Town Gaol: here you can experience the horror of
Victorian prison life by walking through Dover's reconstructed
prison cells, brought vividly to life by the latest animation and
audio-visual techniques. You can even be locked up in a 6 ×
4 cell! (Open throughout the year).

Turn S down Biggin Street, here pedestrianised. On the L
next to the town hall is Maison Dieu House, a fine house built

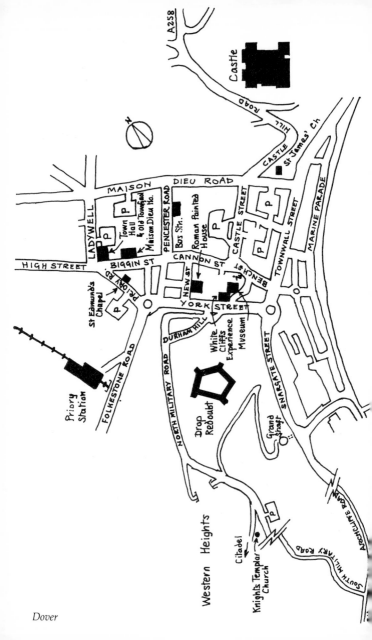

Dover

in 1665 in the Dutch gabled style as the residence of the Agent Victualler for the English Fleet. It now houses the town's public library.

Cross Penchester Road and continue S down pedestrianised Cannon Street. To the R, in New Street, is the Roman Painted House, sometimes referred to as 'Britain's Buried Pompeii.' In 1970 archaeologists made a remarkable discovery when a multi-storey car park was being planned. They came across three rooms of a great mansion, or hotel built for official travellers, built by the Romans about AD 200 just outside their naval fort of Dubris. The house was lavishly decorated with plaster walls but it was demolished c. AD 270 when the Romans enlarged their fort. The unique wall paintings are the most extensive surviving anywhere north of the Alps. (Open daily except Mondays, April to October, 1000–1700).

Return to Cannon Street and continue southwards to the Market Square, where a Victorian facade provides the entrance to a complex of new buildings containing the TIC, the Dover Museum and the White Cliffs Experience.

The TIC occupies part of the ground floor of the museum, containing three floors of Dover's history. (Open throughout the year). Behind the museum, through a connecting coffee shop and bistro is an historium containing the White Cliffs Experience. This 'Visitor Attraction of the Year' (no year stated) is built over the remains of the Roman fleet head-quarters Classis Britannica. Operated by the same company that manages Canterbury Tales in Canterbury this centre tells Dover's history with stage effects in an entertaining way. (Open 24 February–28 March daily 1000–1500; 29 March–8 November daily 1000–1700; 11 November–24 February Wednesdays to Saturdays, 1000–1700).

From the Market Square continue seawards down Bench Street and across Townwall Street to the seafront promenade. To the R are the Western Docks and Hoverport and to the L are the Eastern Docks, and the Promenade provides a pleasant walk from one side of the harbour to the other.

The prosperous Port of Dover has grown from the little

haven at the mouth of the Dour to one of the largest artificial harbours in Europe. The docks, harbours and piers are full of every type of craft. Each year millions of passengers are carried on hovercraft, jet-foil and modern super-ferries: modern vessels to anticipate the challenge of the Eurotunnel.

Standing in front of the toilets on Marine Parade, a bronze statue of the Hon. Charles Stuart Rolls looks out to France: he is wearing the flying helmet and gaiters of those early days of aviation. On 2 June 1910 he crossed the Channel and returned in a single flight, capping Bleriot's flight of the year before. (M. Louis Bleriot's monoplane landed at Dover after his historic flight across the Channel on Sunday morning, 25 July 1909. The spot in the turf where he landed is marked by granite slabs, and is immediately below the castle on the northern side, where Northfall Meadow extends to the cliff: access from the A258 Deal Road.)

A few hundred yards/metres to the E of Rolls's statue, the mustachioed bust of Captain Matthew Webb eyes the swimmers in the harbour. On 24–25 August 1875, using the breast-stroke and without wearing goggles, Webb made the first cross-Channel swim, spending nearly 22 hours in the water. It is said that he kept out the cold 'by doses of cod-liver oil, beef tea, brandy, coffee, and strong old ale'. Though he won his share of fame and fortune, Webb was a spendthrift. In a desperate attempt to restore his finances, he went to Canada in 1883 to attempt the impossible – swimming the rapids at the foot of the Niagara Falls. His strength failed him when he reached the central whirlpool, and he was sucked down and drowned.

From the Rolls statue on Marine Parade, go into Townwall Street via Dour Place to the Sports Centre and swimming-pool. Behind its car parks are the ruins of St James's Church, which was bombed during the 1939–45 War. This and St Mary's in the town are the only two remaining of the four original churches of the town. Enough is preserved to show that it was a sizeable early Norman church with central tower between chancel and nave, but with no transepts. All that now remains is the W front in Caen stone, with a pair of windows above a shafted doorway, and parts of the N and E walls.

Behind St James's a pathway rises up to join Castle Hill, and the stone bulk of the castle, its towers and ramparts, rise up in front of you through the trees as you climb the hill. You may continue up Castle Hill to the main entrance of Dover Castle, but it is more convenient for us to take the signposted path and flight of steps up to Canon's Gate Road, and enter the castle by Canon's Gate.

Dover Castle

Admission. The castle is open daily throughout the year. Charges are made for entry to the keep and underground works.

Keep & Underground Passages	*Weekdays*	*Sundays*
1 April–30 September	1000–1800	1000–1600
1 October–31 March	1000–1600	1000–1600

Historical Outline

The Channel at Dover is little more than 22 miles/35km wide, and the coast of France is visible, as often as not. As the front door of England, Dover has had to be prepared to receive any who tried to enter the harbour, and by the Iron Age an extensive area on top of the cliffs here was already enclosed by massive earth ramparts. The Romans built a lighthouse, or Pharos, within it towards the latter end of the first century, and another on Western Heights, to guide cross-Channel shipping. The Saxons had a burgh or fortified township, for which a church was built *in castro* – i.e., within the old Roman walls – in the latter part of the tenth century. The church was not monastic in foundation, but must have been built to serve the garrison of the castle and not the inhabitants of the harbour town below.

The main castle dates from the period following the Norman invasion, or perhaps just before it, since some areas were under strong Norman influence even during the reign of

Edward the Confessor. In 1064 King Harold promised to hand over the castle to William the Conqueror, who had professed to derive his 'right' to England, and expressly stipulated that he build up, on the Confessor's death, a 'Castell of Dover, with a well of water in it'.

After his victory at Senlac, the Conqueror landed at Hastings: he left the battlefield and marched directly on Dover and spent 8 days strengthening the fortification of it. All traces of the first Norman castle have gone: it was probably built of timber pallisades.

The present castle dates from the reign of Henry II (1154–89) with most of the work dating from 1168–88; and it was continued during the reign of Richard I. Henry built a new inner bailey at the NW end of the old inner ward, with a barbican in front of each of its N and S gateways, and raised the great rectangular keep c.1181–2, in the centre of the courtyard. By 1185 the keep was garrisoned, and by 1190 the

The Castle, Town and Docks from the Western Heights, Dover

total cost of the works was just under £7,000, an enormous sum of money in the twelfth century. (The estimated annual income of the Crown at that time was less than £10,000.) Maurice the Engineer was paid 8d a day, later raised to 1s, and built a splendidly broad and sturdy tower keep, a complete curtain wall with towers incorporated within it, defining the edge of the artificial earthwork, and two gates; the N King's Gate, and the S Palace Gate. Both gates had barbicans, but only the northern one survives. Maurice also began a second curtain wall to the NE, following the line of the Iron Age earthworks, blocking the entrance to the Iron Age fortress.

Henry II's castle – a keep within a curtain wall – was something novel in Europe in the 1180s. The combination of keep with concentric walls is very rare. A keep needs no defensive walls, but evidently Henry thought otherwise. The Crusaders in the Holy Land had been repulsed and impressed by the castles of the Infidel, which consisted of enclosing walls punctuated by square defensible towers in the standard pattern of a Roman *castrum*, and, most memorably, by the pattern of the walls of Constantinople of c.400. It was at Dover that the system was first revived in the W, and perhaps naturally Henry was not prepared to put all his eggs in this new basket the very first time.

The circuit of the outer defensive curtain, with its towers and gateways, was continued during John's reign, c.1204, extending southwards on either side to the edge of the cliff. No wall was built to the S.

The castle's strength was put to the test in 1216, when Prince Louis, Dauphin of France, and his troops in support of the insurgent barons, besieged it; Hubert de Burgh only just managed to hold them off. Louis used exceptionally powerful *petravia* and other siege engines to make a violent and incessant attack on the walls, and he mined the northern gate. Hubert replied with such devastating effect that the French, feeling their loss, moved both their engines and their camp further back. Meanwhile King John died, and Louis and his allied barons, thinking that England was now in their power, called upon Hubert to surrender, offering him great honours and high position. But the Constable refused to give up the castle, and Louis had to call off his troops and leave Hubert in full possession.

After the fighting was over Hubert made determined efforts to repair and strengthen the northern area. During the 1216 siege Hubert constructed some underground earthworks, and afterwards built up an outwork in front of the N gate, which was blocked up. Further towers were erected to complete a most formidable defence. Henry III had the curtain wall extended, and by 1256 it reached the cliff edge on both ends; although that on the E has largely gone, that on the W is still in good repair. No wall was built to the S: St Mary's Church and the Pharos were protected only by a steep earth bank. The castle was then essentially the same size as that seen today.

In the fifteenth century, further work was carried out, and in Tudor times the defences were kept in good repair and strengthened for fear of a French or Spanish invasion. During the English civil wars the townspeople took over the castle in the name of the Parliament, and consequently it was not slighted after the war. For a century the castle was left in peace, but in 1745 it was brought up to date, and some quite savage 'modernisation' was undertaken. The entire southern barbican was removed, together with associated towers; the keep was strengthened to withstand heavy artillery; the eastern curtain wall was demolished; and most of the surviving towers were reduced in height.

The castle grounds occupy about 35 acres/14ha, and entrance can be gained either by the Canon's Gate or the massive Constable's Tower, immediately beneath the keep.

Tour of the Castle

We shall begin our tour of the castle at the Canon's Gate and then make our way N along the wall to the Constable's Tower, continuing around the outer curtain wall. We shall then visit the underground defences, and, returning to the surface, enter the inner bailey by the North Barbican and Kings Gate. After having visited the keep we shall leave by the Palace Gate, and make our way to the Church of St Mary in Castro and the Roman Pharos.

Just inside Canon's Gate, on a platform, stands the famous Queen Elizabeth's Pocket Pistol, its muzzle pointing seaward. Cast in Utrecht in 1544, it was presented to Elizabeth by the State of Holland in gratitude for the help she had given them against the Spanish. It is a magnificent gun, with a wealth of Renaissance ornament in relief: it is 24ft/7.3m long, and is said to be capable of firing a 12lb/5.4kg ball for 7 miles/11.2km.

From the cliff edge and Canon's Gate the walls and towers are greatly reduced in height as far as Peverell's Tower, which incorporates an arched gateway, and once had a drawbridge. It marks the spot where the outer curtain was returned to join the S Barbican of the inner curtain. The outer curtain between Peverell's Tower and the next, Queen Mary's Tower, is eighteenth-century brickwork.

Next comes the Constable's Tower, the principal entrance into the outer bailey and one of the most impressive gate-houses in the country. After the keep, it is the most imposing thing in the whole castle, and in some ways is even more spectacular than the keep.

It was let into the wall by Henry III between 1221–27 and rises sheer from the moat, exceedingly strong, with five towers all united to form a hall and guard-chambers. Having been in continuous use as a residence from the time of its construction to the present day, it has been subjected to much alteration and addition, but its original parts can still be identified. If you can ignore the sash windows and eighteenth-century brick galleries, you can see the gate-tower and residence as an exceptionally complex piece of thirteenth-century fortification.

This gate is of most unusual design: the core of it is one of King John's wall-towers. In front of this was placed a flat-faced tower, to form a porch at right-angles to the axis of the gateway. It was rounded at the ends, so that the arrow slits in it cover long stretches of the wall to both sides. In turn, this is flanked by wings on either side, with rounded turrets, rising via chamfers from square bases, that on the N being given a subsidiary turret as it is much wider. The original height was two storeys: in modern times, probably in the eighteenth-century, the earlier central tower was raised, and on the inner side was built a whole range of rooms to link the porch to the lateral towers.

Rising from the wide and deep ditch, the gatehouse is a formidable affair. It was approached from a long barbican of later date now in ruins, and the moat was crossed by a drawbridge. The first part of the gateway passage is a long and narrow porch, set cross-wise with the gateway; the porch is still covered by its roughly ribbed vault. The entrance doorway to the porch has been altered and its defences obscured. The gateway passage was defended by a portcullis and a two-leaved door; beyond the door it widens out from 9ft/2.7m to 15ft/4.5m, seats for the guard being provided in long recesses on either side. The floor rises 6ft/2m from the outer to the inner ends of the passage.

The Constable's residence consisted of a large and lofty hall over the gateway, an entrance room on the S, a vaulted chamber on the N, and a guard-room over the porch. The entrance was from the wall-walk on the curtain between the Constable's quarters and the flanking tower on the N; the present passage between was driven through the wall at a later period. The N Tower, with its latrine turret, was distinctly for the accommodation of the troops guarding this point. Further, there was no direct connection between the upper and lower rooms of the tower itself. The lower guard-room of the N tower was entered from the courtyard, and from it a spiral stairway rises to the battlements of the tower without any intervening doorway to the first floor. The first floor itself was entered from the wall-walk on the curtain running northward. There was no access from this room to the battlements above. Therefore all three doorways of the N tower, which is sufficiently spacious to accommodate a large body of men, were under the direct surveillance of the guard on the battlements of the residence. The Constable, from his post, could not only direct operations against a common enemy, but could also defend himself against the possible treachery of his own troops.

Continuing along the outer curtain N of the Constable's Tower, we come to the polygonal Treasurer's Tower, rebuilt by Edward IV. Next is the rectangular Godsfoe's Tower, followed by Crevecoeur Tower, the best of the early thirteenth-century towers for studying the internal arrangements for the defenders. The outer curtain between the Constable's Tower and Fitzwilliam Gate was essentially created by Hubert de Burgh, Constable of Dover, under King John, between 1204–15, and strengthened at three crucial points – the Constable's Tower, Norfolk Towers, and Fitzwilliam Gate, after Prince Louis of France had in 1216 all but forced an entrance into the castle from the N. The characteristic difference between the twelfth- and thirteenth-century designs is in the shape of the mural towers; the rectangular plan gives way to D-shape, which had the advantage that it was without corners vulnerable to undermining. The tops of the towers were cut off, c.1800, to make mounts for guns. Godsfoe's Tower and Crevecoeur Tower may have been affected by the domestic requirements for the hall built for King John. A garderobe and a well, as well as other domestic buildings, were attached to the wall at this point, in the thirteenth-century.

Next come the Norfolk Towers where King John made his gateway into the castle. This was imprudent, for here alone can an attacker command the castle from higher ground. Louis's force in 1216 had succeeded in demolishing one of the gate-towers; so when it came to repairing the damage, the main gateway was shifted to the W (the present Constable's Tower), where the land falls steeply, naturally, down into the town. The old N gateway was blocked and turned into the kernel of a massive system of fortification, designed to deprive an enemy of the high ground to the N. A monumental beaked projection plugged the gateway between the twin towers, and two more D-shaped turrets were thrown out to the E. The outer ditch was greatly deepened, and in the bottom of it the circular St John's Tower reinforced the battery further; beyond that a vast earthern spur was thrown up. The result is intimidating enough when seen from the N, but the full ingenuity and interlocking functions of all the parts can only be appreciated underground. We shall return to this point for a tour of the underground defences shortly.

The remainder of the outer curtain, from Fitzwilliam Gate SE to the Avranches Tower, was the only stretch which Henry II managed to build. The Fitzwilliam Gate has a pair of rounded towers, a postern gate inserted in the 1220s. Under it runs a covered passage, now partly exposed, by means of which defenders might sally forth to attack the enemy from the rear, a subordinate assistant to the main outflanking system to the N. The Avranches Tower is polygonal, and covers the entrance to the Iron Age earthworks. On the stretch of wall between these two towers, the arrow-slits are in groups of three, and pierce the walls as well as the towers.

From the Outer Bailey you can get the best view of the walls of the Middle Bailey. The battlements, as on all the walls, were shaved off during the nineteenth century adaptations, but one can see that these walls are contemporary with the keep. The intermediate towers are all rectangular, with arrow slits in pairs low down, both facing outwards and for infilading the walls.

Returning to the Norfolk Towers, we can break off and make a tour of the underground outworks. At present they are approached by a modern entrance near the barbican; originally they were controlled from the Norfolk Towers. In the 1790s they were considerable extended, with many new devices for eliminating an intruder – grenade shafts for blowing trapped troops to pieces, for example – and the spur and underground passages were cased in brick. The thirteenth-century passages were cut clean through the chalk, the first leading straight down to St John's Tower. (This has a basement with doorways into the ditch and three upper storeys, no longer with original floors. Double doors protected it within, a portcullis and a *meurtrière* from the outside). The continuation of the passage northwards is all Napoleonic, pierced by slits alternately for guns and muskets. The thirteenth-century passage ends in a chamber, or assembly point, originally vaulted, from which passages branching three ways led to points of exit to the spur, whence sallies could be made in the enemy's rear. The finale of the Napoleonic modifications is the booby-trap at the end of the L passage, closed by three doors operated by remote control from the guard-room nearby, for taking prisoners without danger.

Back on the surface, we can now visit the keep, by climbing the stairs and taking the ramp to the barbican protecting the King's Gate on the N side of the Middle Bailey: it remains almost intact.

The massive keep is a classic of castle building, combining immense strength with magnificent living accommodation. Built by Henry II, c.1180–86, at the then colossal cost of £3,000, it is one of the best preserved in the country.

The keep is of three storeys and rises, with two offsets, to a height of 83ft/25m: square angle-turrets at the corners rise 12ft/3.5m higher. In plan it is almost square, 98 × 96ft/29 × 28 m, and the walls are immensely thick, between 17ft/5m and 21ft/6.4m. In the middle of each wall are turret-like buttresses, the N one accommodating all the garderobes in the keep.

On the E face, and continuing partly round the corner to the S face, is an extremely strong and elaborate forebuilding protecting the entrance on the ground floor. It gives room for a straight flight of steps up to the entrance, and two chapels – one above the other – a more complex version of what was built at Newcastle-upon-Tyne, but nowhere else. The turrets here commanded the stairs, which were originally open to the sky. At the foot of the stairs is the entrance to the basement, in a particularly vulnerable position: hence the triple door to it – see the drawbar sockets. The first floor of the keep was also originally entered from the forebuilding, but not now.

The present ticket office, placed where the doorway once was, makes the lower chapel, as a result, seem more isolated than it really was.

The lowest flight of stairs is on the S side and rises to the Lower Chapel, richly decorated with clustered pillars and chevron-moulded arches – fine Norman ornamentation of the 1180s. On the other side of the chapel vestibule, to the SW, is a miniscule tunnel-vaulted chamber, assumed to be the porter's lodge. A doorway in the corner of the vestibule opens to the second flight which has, midway in its height, a postern leading out from the second storey of the keep. At the head of the second flight there was a drawbridge and a doorway, and at the top of the third flight a guard-room and the entrance to the keep at third-storey level. The guard-room looks directly down on, and commands, the flight of steps of approach.

You enter the second floor apartments, and in a chamber left of the entrance passage is the Well, called Harold's Well, sinking deep down into the chalk cliff. It is about 350ft/106m deep, and is lined with stone to a depth of 172ft/52m. In the recess to the left are the mouths of two lead pipes, part of an elaborate system for conveying water to other parts of the keep – another of Dover's sophisticated pieces of engineering.

The main hall contains the armoury – a formidable collection of armour, pikes, maces and muskets. The hall is divided into two by a wall, and alterations by Edward IV provided the rooms with fireplaces. The rooms was built two-storeyed, and had a gallery running round them, but the brick vaults, inserted c.1800 to support guns on the roof, drastically reduce the height and all but obscure the wall-galleries. Edward also provided fireplaces in the mural chambers.

A narrow and tortuous passage leads from one of the spacious chambers within the depths of the walls to the Upper Chapel, directly above the Lower Chapel, and also finely decorated. Within the keep, access from floor to floor is by the two spiral staircases in the SW and NE turrets. On the first floor the double-hall and mural-chamber layout is repeated, to make a second complete suite of living rooms. The chief attraction at this level is a scale model of the Battle of Waterloo, made in the 1830s. The staircases go down to basement level. During Marlborough's wars against France at the beginning of the eighteenth century, the basement was used for prisoners-of-war, and the walls are covered with the names of Frenchmen incarcerated here. Spiral stairs leading up from the second floor to the roof were alterations made by Edward IV.

The keep at Dover was one of the largest and most elaborate of these great structures, and it was one of the last to be built.

Our exit from the Middle Bailey is by the Palace Gate in the SW corner, which is no longer masked by its two-storeyed barbican. As we turn S across the car park, we see ahead of us Colton's Gate, the now isolated gate-tower which stood in the thirteenth-century wall which enclosed the Church of St Mary-in-Castro and the Pharos.

The Church of St Mary-in-Castro is surrounded by a high bank from which there is a tremendous view across the harbour. Named to distinguish it from the St Mary's in the town, Castro is *the* outstanding late Saxon building in the country, dating from about 1000. (In the nineteenth century it was believed to be Roman, as it uses Roman tiles, but it is now thought to incorporate re-used portions of the Roman fort.) It is cruciform in plan, with nave, chancel, transepts, and a low central tower. The tower does not spring from the crossing, but stands on the ground. The nave is as wide as the tower, and the nave and chancel arches are broad and tall, but the arches to the transepts were modified c.1190 – they are pointed, whereas the original Saxon ones were low and rounded. The details – dogtooth on the ribs, trefoil leaves on the shaft capitals – suggest work by the same mason who worked on the chapels in the castle keep.

The church was semi-derelict in the seventeenth century, and in 1860–62 it was 'restored' in a singularly hideous way by Sir George Gilbert Scott – he smothered the interior with weird mosaics (by Butterfield, 1888) in chancel and nave, quite exceptionally unsympathetic.

Adjoining the church at its western end is the stump of a tower, the remains of the Roman Pharos, or lighthouse, one of the most remarkable buildings of Roman Britain. In its patched-up state, it stands to a height of 62ft/18.8m, but the top 19ft/5.8m is medieval. The lower Roman work is magnificently preserved: it consists of a hollow tower 14ft/4.2m square internally but octagonal externally, originally diminishing in width in a series of steps. The walls are built in the typical Roman manner, with coursed rubble faced with greensand and tufa ashlar, set in hard pink mortar, with bonding courses of tiles at regular intervals. It probably stood to a height of 80ft/24m in its original form.

Built soon after the Roman conquest in AD 43, it blazed on the hilltop as a beacon for the galleys coming over from Gaul. Presumably, with the similar lighthouse on the Western Heights, and the Tour d'Ordre at Boulogne, this lighthouse served to guide ships across the Channel between the two ports.

The Roman Pharos is witness to all those men who have come and gone from this shore, men who have laid the foundations of civilization in these islands. It has seen the Romans go, and the Saxons and the Normans come; it saw Henry V arrive from Agincourt, Edward III embarking from France, and Henry VIII sailing for the Field of the Cloth of Gold. It has seen the landing of Charles II, and it has towered over a million men returning from the greatest war ever fought. It has seen many travellers come and go, and as we turn back upon it, we have completed our journey.

Part Eight: The Canterbury Loop

13 River Stour to Canterbury 11 miles/17.6m

Eastwell Park to Soakham Downs 2 miles/3.2km
The line of the Pilgrims' Way is lost after Eastwell church, but after a distance of about 2 miles/3.2km the line is recovered above the valley of the Stour on Soakham Downs. There are two possible routes between these points and these must be examined before we can proceed.

1 Through Boughton Lees and Boughton Aluph to Soakham Farm
This is the route favoured by the Kent County Council and is the official route of the NDW Canterbury Loop. The supposed line of the PW runs from Eastwell church along a road lined with poplar trees to emerge at a lodge beside the main road A251 in Boughton Lees. Here it turns a right-angle, squarely to the left, along the road on the E side of the village green to a crossroads. Take the road straight ahead leading to Boughton Aluph, KCC signpost, and after nearly ½ mile/800m a sign points along a footpath beween some orchard trees to just S of Boughton Aluph church. This path then continues across fields to White Hill at a road leading to Wye. Here, just S of a quarry, is another KCC sign at the entrance of the track to Soakham Farm.

2 Through Eastwell Park, above Boughton Aluph to Soakham Farm
From Eastwell church the old road may have taken a slightly higher line diagonally across the field to the left of the road to pass in front of the mansion, then along an avenue of beech trees where there is an existing 'surfaced' park road to join the A251 Ashford-Faversham highway at a sharp bend in the

road. There is a rough byway leading almost due E from a house beside the A251, and if this line is continued across the re-entrant coombe below Warren Farm it will strike the Wye road below the quarry at White Hill.

In some respects this latter is the more convincing alignment for Boughton Aluph church, like many others we have found, is passed to the N rather than to the S as the former line would make it do.

Warren Farm and Soakham Farm lie in deep coombes, while the lane from Wye to Challock and the main road A251 run up projecting spurs. We have found that when the old road came to obstacles of this kind it made for the neck of the promontory and cut off the detour by passing just N of the crest, but at Soakham Farm the track turns straight up the hill, as a diagonal approach is not possible.

Just beyond Soakham Farm curve with the track along the edge of a field to an old sign beside a sheep dip. A yew tree marks the ascent up a steep and deeply cut gully lined with beech trees, and this curves up the hillside to the edge of a wood, which it enters. The footpath, however, keeps to the edge of the field then enters the wood to join the old road leading up to the crest of the Downs. The route of the NDW from the highway at Soakham Farm to the outskirts of Chilham is a BOAT.

Perhaps the real explanation for these two routes is to be found in the crossing of the River Stour by ford, prior to the building of a bridge at Wye. Wye lay on an ancient and busy route along the Downs to the Channel ports, continuing the south-easterly course we have been following from the Medway and Stour crossings through Wye, Brabourne and Monks Horton to reach the coast near Folkestone and Dover. Obviously travellers on this important trackway from the W to the coast would have sought the crossing of the Stour via Boughton Lees and Kempe's Corner; those who were bound for Canterbury would have kept more to the N above Boughton Aluph to Soakham Downs.

But why should there be alternative routes on this Canterbury division? Perhaps strangers from the W might have found a road junction at Eastwell, but, lacking guidance, followed a more prominent southern course intended for those making for Wye. On having reached Boughton Lees and the lower level they would have discovered their mistake and so be forced to take the obvious line back to the downland crest – through Boughton Aluph.

It must not be forgotten that the traffic was not all from W to E. One making the journey from Canterbury with the object of crossing the Stour at Wye for some destination to the SW would have followed the old road down to Soakham Farm and then turned off for the ford. Those continuing west towards Charing would keep on the higher level above Boughton Aluph.

All evidence points therefore to the choice of the higher-level route; it is more direct, avoids any sharp bends, avoids unnecessary descent and ascent and passes N of the church.

Soakham Downs to Chilham 3 miles/4.8km

As we have seen before, the road does not take to the crest of a hill without good reason, but once there it often remains, especially if there is a spur upon which it can fall gently down to the lower levels, in this case straight to Chilham.

At the top of the wood above Soakham Farm the Way keeps just on the edge of a big meadow on Soakham Downs and turns E to a gate. Here we enter a very considerable area of forest, some 5,000 acres/2,023ha, formerly known as King's Wood and now renamed the 'State Forest of Challock'. One hundred yards/metres after the fire warning sign at the gate, fork left at a KCC sign and then, a little further on at the crossing of a broad forestry road coming in from the left, carry straight ahead, slightly downhill. After 100yds/91m, by a fire warning sign at a fork, bear up the left-hand path, soon gaining the ridge where there are views down over Godmersham Park.

The view across Godmersham Park is one of great beauty,

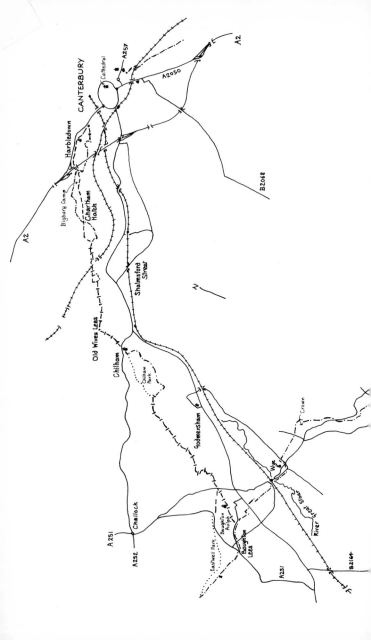

with the Georgian Palladian mansion embowered in the trees below the great sweep of the Downs. The house was built in 1732 in a refined and consciously designed landscape by one Thomas Brodnax, who had changed his name first to May to inherit a fortune and then to Knight. His son, being childless, adopted a distant cousin, Edward Austen, as heir. Edward changed his name to Knight to ensure his inheritance and when his wife died his sister sometimes came to stay and keep house for him during the years 1794–1813. Her name was Jane Austen, whom we have already met, and the society she discovered here fascinated her and provided raw material for her novels.

The flint church of St Lawrence, Godmersham, stands in trees near the bridge over the Stour beside the main valley road A28. On the S wall of the choir is a remarkable twelfth-century bas-relief of St Thomas Becket vested as archbishop with mitre and crook, seated below his cathedral. This is the earliest known sculpture of the martyr and the only image known to have survived the efficient destruction of the Reformation.

The Way leads through the woods for almost 2 miles/3.2km along the heights above Godmersham Park. After the first mile/1.6km the ground becomes open and cleared on the right and you may get occasional glimpses of Canterbury Cathedral through the trees. Just on the right over the old wooden fence can be seen traces of the old road. After a further ½ mile/800m a forestry road comes up from the left, and on the right is a faded painted Pilgrims' Way sign. After another ½ mile/800m the track bears right down to Hurst Farm and leaves the forest by a fire-warning sign.

Continue ahead on a footpath and after a few hundred yards/metres reach another footpath which crosses the hillside from Dane Street on the N to the ford across the Stour S of Hurst Farm. This crossing is marked by a stile in a fence spread around a thin plantation on the site of an Iron Age

Godmersham to Barham

settlement. From this point there is very little trace of the further course of the Way, but the woodland ride ahead is an easily recognizable landmark. If you were to continue ahead through the plantation you would reach a wide grassy ride which runs down the spur of the hill all the way to Chilham, but this is private ground.

At the T-junction of paths from Dane Street to Godmersham turn R and continue down the woodland track towards Hurst Farm, then turn along the road to Mountain Street and so into Chilham.

Chilham

From whichever side you enter the village you will climb up past old doorways and gables with projecting windows to emerge into a diminutive square. On the two long sides are more of these old houses and shops of contrasting styles and periods forming a continuous façade. They are built in half-timber and plaster, brick and stone, and have tiled roofs; most are without front gardens, but some have unfenced flower strips. All the views out of the village square are closed, but note the surprising axial arrangement of the castle and the church, both seen among trees through gaps at the end of the square. The blending and composition of materials, styles and proportions makes Chilham a masterpiece of unconscious planning.

Chilham claims to be the prettiest village in Kent and the full horror of this claim may be realized when the village square is seen choked with traffic and the clicking of camera shutters is deafening. The houses are mainly tearooms, and antique shops, and those residents who derive no commercial benefit from this invasion must curse those who have popularized this lovely village among the hop fields and orchards of Kent.

The fifteenth-century Perpendicular-style Church of St Mary's stands at the E end of the square, with its low embattled flint and stone chequered tower reaching through the trees. There is a porch with a parvis, or upper chamber, and up near the roof of the nave are some excellent carvings.

The church is notable for its monuments, all of interest and some of quality. One is to Sir Francis Chantrey (1781–1841) who left his fortune to found the art collection which formed the basis of the Tate Gallery in London. Most of the rest are to the Digges family, formerly residents of the castle. That of Margaret, Lady Palmer (Sir Dudley's sister, d.1619, N aisle) is typical of its period. The polished Bethersden marble has been cut away in an intricate arabesque and diaper pattern to give a luxuriously inlaid effect. Lady Margaret was, according to the inscription 'fayrer than most women and wiser than most men'. The monument in the S chapel to Lady Mary Digges (d.1631) is a tall black marble Ionic column, 11ft/3.3m high with an urn on top. Lady Mary is likened to Rachel, upon whose grave her husband Jacob set up a pillar (Genesis 35:16–20). Round the column are four tall pedestals, with the

The Square, Chilham

alabaster figures of the cardinal virtues – Justice, Prudence, Temperance and Fortitude. In the N Chapel is a sentimental memorial to the Hardy boys, sons of the owner of the castle, who died in 1858. Victorian pathos shows the children nestling affectionately against one another, reading *The Babes in the Wood* while their battledore and shuttlecock lie on the ground beside them. The fifteenth-century sarcophagus of Purbeck marble here was long thought to contain the remains of St Augustine, whose shrine was brought to the church after the dissolution of St Augustine's Abbey at Canterbury, but when it was opened in 1948 it was found to contain only records of previous openings – in 1914, 1904 and 1883!

At the W end of the square are the gates to Chilham Castle, home of the Viscount Massereene and Ferrard, DL. The 300-acre/121ha park is private property, but when the castle and gardens are open to the public – gardens open daily, castle open Tuesdays, Wednesdays and Thursdays from 1 June to 31 August – we may walk through the mile-long park to search for the line of the old road.

Chilham Park is heavily timbered and proper identification of the old road in this section is most misleading. It is fairly likely, however, that the old road ran straight down the centre of the ridge in a direct line towards the castle. For the last few hundred yards/metres the centre of the saddleback is all open ground. Beyond rise the grey walls of the ancient castle among the trees, while close by the mellow brickwork of the stately mansion shows richly colourful above the green lawn and the terraced and topiary gardens which were designed by 'Capability' Brown. Here were planted the first mulberry and wisteria in Britain, while in the park is a mile-long avenue of Spanish chestnuts and the oldest and largest heronry in England.

That the Romans established a station at Chilham and an important trackway passed immediately through, or near the site, seems to suggest that its choice as a defensive position must date far back into history. Commanding as it does the eastern end of the great Wye Gap, the break in the Downs through which the Stour finds outlet to the sea, such a choice was an obvious one. It is reasonably safe to assume therefore that the late Bronze Age people had a hill fort here on the site of which the Romans established a station, later converted by the Saxons for their own use.

The massive octagonal keep which survives today dates from the middle twelfth century. This is enclosed by a fourteenth-century curtain wall to form a more or less rectangular bailey, but raised upon twelfth-century foundations. On the NE side of the keep is an annexe, which when excavated in 1926 was discovered to be the remains of an eleventh-century dungeon, containing fifteen skeletons.

The owners of Chilham had varying misfortunes. John, Earl of Athol, was unfortunate enough to be rashly involved in the Scottish wars against Edward I and as a result paid the penalty with his life. His successor, Bartholomew of Badlesmere, for refusing Queen Isobel, consort of Edward II, entry to his castle of Leeds (near Maidstone), met a similar fate. Then Thomas, Lord Roos, having backed the House of Lancaster in the Wars of the Roses, had his property seized by the Crown. Later Henry VIII granted the estate to Sir Thomas Cheney, who proceeded to demolish as much of the castle as he could to rebuild his new mansion on the Isle of Sheppey. The remains were purchased by Sir Thomas Kempe and in due course his estates passed through inheritance to one of his daughters, who was wife of Sir Dudley Digges.

Sir Dudley Digges was a highly successful diplomat and lawyer, and he commissioned Inigo Jones to rebuild the mansion, a brick Jacobean house, which was completed in 1616. In 1618 Sir Dudley went on a deputation to Moscow for James I, and he later held the office of the Master of the Rolls. He died in 1639.

Like so many of its time, the building tries to reconcile the English Gothic tradition with Renaissance ideas of classical design, with pleasingly homely results. The design is on a revolutionary plan illustrating the mathematical fancies of the age – a regular hexagon with one side omitted. Above the door is the inscription 'Dudley Digges AD 1616 Mary Kempe', together with the pious phrase 'The Lord is my house of defence and my castle'. In this house was born Edward Digges, who became the Governor of Virginia in 1655–8.

It is now impossible to determine exactly how the line of the old road continued after passing the keep, for the building of the house and the creation of the terraced gardens has obliterated all the evidence. Probably it passed to the N of the house to the present village square, for here travellers, arriving too late in the day to complete the journey to Canterbury, would have found welcome rest and refreshment.

Chilham to Canterbury 6 miles/9.6km
Much uncertainty exists as to how the Way continued from Chilham to Bigbury, and for the first 2 miles/3.2km, until the crossing of the London-Canterbury-Dover railway line, the line is almost lost.

There is a tradition that the pilgrims of the later Middle Ages passed down Church Hill – the lane leading out of Chilham square on the NW side of the churchyard – crossed the Maidstone-Canterbury road A252 in the valley below and ascended the opposite hillside by a lane to the hamlet of Old Wives Lees. This is the diversion favoured by the Kent County Council, and is the route of the 'official' Canterbury Loop, for the road is signposted at the A252 junction in Chilham, in Old Wives Lees, and again on the A28 near Shalmsford Street. However, the NDW from Chilham goes up the road to Old Wives Lees, then E along the road for ½ mile/800m to where it turns down to Shalmsford Street. A path then runs through orchards and hop fields to cross the railway line just W of the archway leading to Nickle Farm.

The pilgrims may have made the detour for the purpose of visiting some special shrine or for some other reason (as they did at Compton), but the route turns a sharp corner to cross the damp and northern side of a loamy hill in so doing. The known path before Chilham goes S of the castle mound and this would lead through the square and S of the church, down

the lane to the 'Woolpack' and so over the southern shoulder
of the hill towards Shalmsford Street. The inn would seem to
bear a significant name, although when it was first so called is
doubtful; traditionally it is said to have been the home of the
master-builder employed by Sir Dudley Digges on his
mansion.

Cultivation and extensive road widening of the present
highway has swept away all traces of the old road where it
continues round the steep bank on the curve to Whitehill.
Bygone travellers, taking the line of least resistance, would
have kept below this high bank rather than attempt to climb
its steep side. At this point there is a group of old cottages,
and a back lane running in the direction of Shalmsford Street
continues the line. One old name for this was 'Pikey Lane'
(piker = a tramp), suggesting that local tradition associated it
with travellers, and it is now known as 'Pilgrims' Lane'. An
obvious depression in the lawn of a house garden situated
immediately opposite the commencement of Pilgrims' Lane is
on the same alignment, and a series of tests have proved that
below the surface of the depression, which is about 10ft/3m
wide, lay the surface of a forgotten road. At the far end of
Pilgrims' Lane we join the road leading down from Old Wives
Lees and then there are a few fields before Shalmsford Manor
is reached; but immediately beyond the manor-house garden
where the ground rises there are unmistakable signs of an old
cart track again.

This spot, close to the river, must have been one of
considerable importance, for hard against the bridge is the
ford which provides the place-name in 'Shalmsford Street'. It
is reasonable to assume that the ford was used a great deal in
medieval times by travellers bound towards the Channel
coast, and possibly as an alternative route towards Canterbury
through Chartham. In 1908 a find made near some cottages in
Shalmsford Street would seem to indicate some pilgrim traffic
S of the Great Stour, for the object discovered has been
identified at the Canterbury Museum as a brass matrix of the
seal of the Prior of the Order of Hermit Friars of St Augustine's

Winchester, dated about 1480.

At Shalmsford Street the present highway A28 coincides with the old road for 600yds/546m or so beyond the manor house to where the road makes a neat right-angled bend within a few yards/metres of the river. On the left-hand side is a tall and very steep bank along the base of which the Great Stour must have once flowed. Any margin of level ground at this point would have been marshy or liable to flooding, a most unlikely place for a track to have been established, particularly when a dry and easy path could have been found on the higher ground above.

In actual fact, beyond the strip of orchard land which runs in a north-easterly direction from a house garden a short distance back, there seems to be an obvious terraceway immediately below a grass-covered bank some 100ft/30m above the level of the river. This crosses the face of the hillside in the direction of Nickle Farm, where a rounded spur of the hill drops into a shallow orchard-clad valley before the high railway embankment and the farm is reached. If the Way crossed this land all traces of it have been obliterated by cultivation, and the construction of the railway embankment adds to the difficulty of identifying any sort of continuous line. However, the lane leading from the main highway to Nickle Farm passes through a brick archway in the railway embankment and this was almost certainly built to preserve the ancient approach. It seems significant that the short length of road beyond the railway arch lies in the same line as Shalmsford Manor; the railway arch must stand over the route of the old road. Just beyond the arch the lane comes to the junction with several farm tracks. The NDW comes in from the W. The track going E climbs the hillside to the edge of Fright Wood. It is deeply sunken and has every appearance of great antiquity. It is signposted at the start 'Pilgrims' Way'. This is now followed by the NDW.

At the top of the climb a concrete road is reached and 100yds/91m or so beyond are two old, lone dwellings called 'Puddledock Cottages', now modernized and picturesque in their quiet seclusion among the apple trees. The significance of their name becomes understandable when we approach the spot and find some springs which rise here below the wood. Immediately to the E the track forks and we continue the natural line along the northern reach to Hatch House and a gate, and when it emerges on the highway we find the KCC nameplate. (The official NDW however forks right along the concrete road to Hatch Farm, and then follows New Town Street opposite, passes the 'Chapter Arms' and enters the centre of Chartham Hatch.)

From Chartham Hatch the NDW takes a metalled path on the corner with Nightingale Close, and then goes by the recreation ground before entering the woods. After an orchard, the path branches N to continue through mainly coppiced woodland to the northern side of the earthworks of Bigbury Camp, then reaches a road. (The earthworks of Bigbury Camp can be seen in an area of cleared woodland on the R). The PW, on the other hand, takes Bigberry Road (note the incorrect spelling) from the village, past an assortment of builder's allsorts ribboning out along the straight and level road, to the eastern edge of the ridge where the road cuts right through the earthwork of Bigbury Camp, the last and the greatest of the prehistoric remains upon the line of the old road.

Bigbury Camp

The remains at Bigbury are a typical example of an early Iron Age hill fort, most likely thrown up against the attacks of the Belgae, invaders from northern France who managed to settle in Kent in the first-century. The lines of the camp are not easy to trace on the ground, being so much obscured by woodland undergrowth, old gravel workings and houses.

The camp occupies the eastern extremity of a gravel-capped spur some 250ft/76m high. It is almost 25 acres/10ha in extent, of irregular polygon shape with entrances at both E and W ends. The Way passes through the western one, but appears to have left the camp at a point somewhere S of the E gate.

The road to Harbledown uses the E gate, and where there is a very sharp 'S' bend and a steep drop the defences, consisting of two deep ditches, can be seen quite clearly. The two high eastern banks separated by a deep ditch which formed the defensive ring can be traced nearly all round the perimeter of the camp, but cultivation has severely cut into them on the southern side. The banks were probably faced with a timber stockade, for no trace of stone walls has been found.

Bigbury was the scene of Caesar's victory over the native forces which opposed his second landing in Kent in 54 BC. Caesar landed on the Channel coast somewhere between Thanet and Walmer. Following a night march inland of about 12 miles/18km, the Roman troops came upon the chariots and cavalry of the defenders advancing to meet them from some high land across the river, the Great Stour, perhaps near Tonford.

The numerous relics belonging to the pre-Roman people who occupied this important stronghold were mainly found in the gravel workings between 1861 and 1895. These include pottery objects and a few weapons, but principally they were iron agricultural tools; sickles, plough-shares, a plough coulter, and hammers and chisels. There was also a good deal of horse and chariot gear, equipment used for cooking, such as pot-hooks and tripods, and slave collars and chains. Many of these finds are now in the Canterbury and Maidstone Museums.

Bigbury to Canterbury 2 miles/3.2km
The Pilgrims' Way took the left hand fork past Bigbury Camp in the direction of Harbledown, but at the Z-bend turn R, signposted Tonford Lane and 'No Through Road'. Where this road bends sharp R, at Pilgrims Cottage, the PW is on your L, where there is a KCC sign again.

This path is a 'modern' route, running parallel to and on the northern side of the original Way. This has come into being because the old road, here part terraceway and part sunken, is completely overgrown and it is impossible to walk the original line. There is an orchard behind a tall wire fence on the L and a belt of trees on the R, but the A2 Harbledown Bypass intervenes and the footpath has been stopped off. Unless you are prepared to find your own way across this busy road to the path continuation opposite, you have to double back at Pilgrims Cottage on a path through the orchard to the road over the bypass. (Therefore, to save unnecessary walking, at the Z-bend continue with the road to its crossing over the A2).

Go over the bypass bridge and immediately turn R to follow the NDW alongside the A2 in its cutting. At the end of the cutting bear L along the original line of the PW across open country to a fertile valley on a green lane heading for Golden Hill opposite.

We have been descending the ridge from Bigbury Camp to the valley in which the small Cranbourne stream meanders on its course to the Great Stour. The old road once crossed this brook by a ford, but today a footbridge has been provided for the modern traveller. I have been reluctant to advocate too many detours from the Way itself, but at this point it is obviously convenient to break the journey in order to visit the village of Harbledown.

It is possible that some pilgrims after leaving Bigbury Camp took the northern fork to join Watling Street near Harbledown, and then turned E with the main throng from Chatham. The Watling Street on its way eastwards crosses a series of ridges, and the village of Harbledown was nicknamed 'Bob-up-and-down', recorded by Chaucer in 'The Manciple's Tale' Prologue:

> . . . ther stant a litel toun
> Which that y-clepped is Bobbe-up-and-down,
> Under the Blee in Caunterbury weye

Nothing could better describe the switchback of Harbledown, though thankfully it has now been relieved of much of the heavy traffic that tore it in half.

Harbledown

Leave the Way at the footbridge over the Cranbourne stream and walk along the farm road following the stream and leading to the village, passing through hop fields and past big farm buildings and hop oasts.

Just before reaching the main road go by a drive on the right leading up to the almshouses, and at the beginning of the ascent you will come to the famous spring, the 'Black Prince's Well' or the 'Well of St Thomas'. The spring is surrounded by a brick kerb and half enclosed by a niche of ancient masonry partly built into the hillside, an unexpected and charming setting. The three feathers of the Prince of Wales's arms are carved over the arch of the well. In the old days the water from this font was thought to possess healing virtues, being considered to be good for the treatment of eye diseases and leprosy. It is told that the Black Prince drank here on his last journey from Canterbury to London, while another tells that the Prince was lying on his deathbed at Westminster when he craved for some water from the well at Harbledown.

The path leads up to the ten almshouses established in 1840 on the site of a leper hospital founded by Lanfranc in 1084. St Nicholas's Hospital accommodated 30 men and 30 women, but the supply of lepers soon diminished and the foundation became first a hospital for ordinary diseases and then a home for the aged. As part of his penance for his uttering the words that brought about Becket's death, Henry II in 1174 made a grant in perpetuity to this hospital of 40 marks, this sum to be deducted from money due to him from Canterbury and paid by the city annually on his behalf. Even today sums of money are still paid to the hospital by the City Treasury, thus ensuring continuance of a royal grant made over 800 years ago.

Did the name Harbledown come from 'herbal down', simple medicines extracted from herbs for the hospital patients?

The Black Prince's Well, Harbledown

Many interesting relics are preserved in the hall of this quiet retreat, one of them being a small turned money box guarded by an attached chain. According to tradition this is the actual box that the Dutchman Erasmus, when he passed this way with his friend John Colet about 1512, dropped a coin into after refusing on hygienic grounds the request of a leper inmate to kiss what was claimed to be a crystal from the shoe of Archbishop Becket.

Standing above the almshouses is the Norman Church of St Nicholas, having a wonderful view of Canterbury Cathedral. The church has much of interest, including benches on which lepers sat, and also a sloping floor which facilitated washing down the tiles after each service attended by those afflicted.

The view of the Cathedral from this point must have delighted all the pilgrims after their long and arduous journey. St Thomas's shadow has lain over the whole of this road and as we descend the hill to Canterbury our hearts are lifted as we near our goal.

Approach to Canterbury
From the Cranbourne stream the old road and NDW ascend steeply by an attractive woodland path. Halfway up this path the Way has been diverted and on the right can be seen a sunken lane of the original line. Near the top this rejoins the path and from the deep tunnelled shade of the trees we suddenly emerge upon an appalling housing estate spreading over the hillside. Golden Hill on the left is National Trust property and was presented to them to preserve a famous view of the Cathedral, but this has now unfortunately been entirely blotted out by buildings and trees.

From the top of Golden Hill the Way descends through leafy Mill Lane, soon bordered by houses and after ¼ mile/ 400m leads into London Road, formerly Watling Street. It was at this spot that travellers and pilgrims, who had followed the Downland trackway as we have done, joined the bigger company from London. Arriving at this spot on a summer's evening they would see the towers of the majestic Cathedral shining golden in the sun above the old red roofs of the city.

The NDW officially stops when it reaches the road, the A2050, but it recommences on the E side of the city some 1½ miles/2.4km away. Those who wish to take the most direct route to the city centre may do so by using the subway under Rheims Way, then continuing along a path on the far side, to a footbridge over the railway and to another path which is entered off Whitehall Bridge Road. Follow this path along the bank of the River Stour to the fourteenth-century Westgate, where you enter the city centre.

Followers of the PW on the other hand cross under Rheims Way by the subway and continue straight along London Road to the A290 Canterbury-Whitstable road, turning sharp right by the church at St Dunstan-Without-the-Westgate. We have seen that the old road never turns a sharp corner, but only here and at Winchester does it break this rule. It had to do so here because the Way had been following a course upon the N bank of the Stour, the opposite bank from that upon which Canterbury grew: a ferry or bridge had to be provided across the river and this would necessarily turn at a right-angle from a path upon the opposite bank.

The church of St Dunstan-Without-the-Westgate is principally of fifteenth-century construction. It has nothing much of interest except a tall and gracefully delicate Perpendicular font cover, a bijou Decorated chapel of 1330, and the Roper Chapel, S of the chancel. The monuments of the Roper family are in Bethersden marble – John Roper, d.1524, Edmund Roper, d.1533, and Thomas Roper, d.1597. The window in the W wall of this chancel chapel shows Dunstan, Sir Thomas More and Lanfranc, and from the top of the tower can be obtained a grand view of the city. On the opposite side of St Dunstan's Street can be seen the Roper Gateway, a red-brick Tudor building now part of a brewery – all that is left of the Ropers' suburban mansion. Margaret Roper, daughter of Sir Thomas More, Lord Chancellor of England, lived here for a time. When her father lost his head on 6 July 1535 because of his steadfast opposition to the divorce of Henry VIII from Queen

Katherine of Aragon, Margaret Roper was rowed up the Thames to below London Bridge, where a friend threw down the head from the spear upon which it was exhibited. She preserved the head in spices, and had the precious relic interred in the church of St Nicholas at Harbledown. On her death it was transferred to the family vault at St Dunstan's, where it rests in a lead casket: the box was opened in 1824 and the head seen.

St Dunstan's was one of the grandest suburbs of Canterbury, and St Dunstan's Street is the handsomest and most consistent street in the city – wide and straight to Westgate. On the S side is a splendid array of high half-timbered seventeenth-century houses – 13 gables in all – No. 71, the 'House of Agnes Hotel', being one of the best. This was described by Dickens in 1850 as the home of Agnes Wickfield, in *David Copperfield*. Dickens set many scenes of *David Copperfield* in the city, and 'The Sun' (built in 1503), now a shop near the cathedral, has a plaque listing Dickens's associations with the inn. Beyond the 'House of Agnes', and on the opposite side of the road, is the 'Falstaff', a thirteenth-century inn with some old oak panelling, and beautiful ironwork from which its sign is hung.

Continue down St Dunstan's Street, cross the bridge over the Stour and enter the lovely riverside gardens to relax and read the next chapter before beginning your walk through the city proper under Westgate, the only survivor of the six medieval gates in the city walls. It stands in splendid isolation: there is no need for a continuous wall on this side, as the narrow arm of the River Stour formed a barrier, and Westgate had its own drawbridge over it. The gateway was rebuilt in 1380, but the massive twin towers have witnessed many memorable scenes before and after that date. Henry II came this way 'barefoot and weeping' on 12 July 1174 after changing into the garb of penitence at St Dunstan's Church, to seek atonement at the shrine of St Thomas for his grim deed. In 1189 came Richard Coeur de Lion with William the Lion, King of Scotland, but in 1376 was probably the most impressive event of all – the funeral cortège of the Black Prince, eldest son of Edward III and victor of the battles of Crécy and Poitiers. The body of this national hero was brought to its resting-place in the Trinity Chapel of the Cathedral with all the splendour that medieval pomp could provide; the processions of Henry V on his way to Agincourt, Charles Stuart and Oliver Cromwell were dull by comparison.

From 1430 to 1829, the Westgate was the city prison, from which prisoners walked out only to the gallows. It is today a museum of arms and armour and a nuisance to traffic, but an indispensable treasure to Canterbury nevertheless. The general view of the city and the Cathedral from the roof of the gate is one of the most impressive of any cathedral city. (Small charge for admission, open daily except Sundays, October–March 14.00–16.00; April–September 10.00–13.00 and 14.00–17.00.)

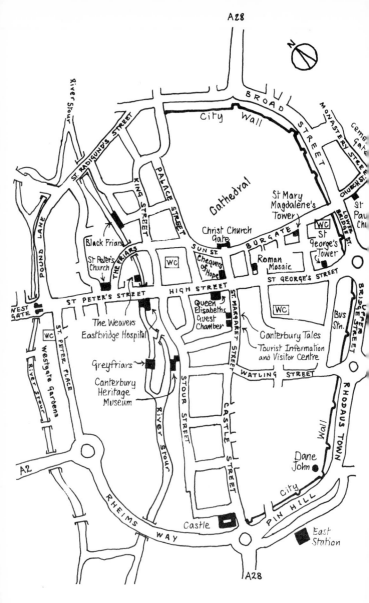

Canterbury

Canterbury is the goal of thousands of pilgrims and visitors throughout the year, as it is the chief cathedral city in the kingdom and is strategically placed between the country's principal port and its capital.

Historical Outline

Although there were extensive pre-Roman occupations on both sides of the River Stour, the Belgic tribes had, as we have seen, their stronghold at Bigbury, on the hills near Harbledown. Canterbury really came into being in the middle of the first century, when the Romans came and established Durovernum on sloping ground overlooking the Stour at a point where Watling Street – the road from Dover to London – fords the river. It was an administrative and residential centre, not a garrison town, and from it other arteries of the road system radiated to Richborough and Lympne. Roman Canterbury had the usual baths and forum, amphitheatre and large villas, much of which came to light when extensive excavations were made possible by wartime bombing. (A mosaic floor of a second/third century house, well below present ground level, can be seen off Butchery Lane.)

Nothing survives of the original Roman grid plan of streets, but the gates in the city walls still correspond to the Roman gateways. So peaceful was life in this part of Kent that walls were not needed until c.270–290, when Saxon pirates were becoming a real menace. An eastern rampart, enclosing an area of 120 acres/48ha, backing up the city wall, was subsequently followed exactly by the medieval defences.

About 590 the town became the capital of King Ethelbert, the fourth Saxon king and a heathen. His queen, Bertha, a French princess, was already a Christian when she arrived in Kent, and in her marriage agreement it had been stipulated that she should be allowed to practise her religion in her husband's kingdom. Ethelbert allocated a Roman building for her use as a Christian church, and this, St Martin's Church of Canterbury, can therefore claim to be the oldest church in England. It contains a font which is almost certainly the one where King Ethelbert was baptized by St Augustine on his eventual conversion on Whit Sunday in 597.

Under the influence of his queen, Ethelbert welcomed St Augustine and his 40 fellow missionaries from Rome when they landed at Ebbsfleet in Thanet in 597. Augustine was given Ethelbert's pagan temple, which he proceeded to dedicate to St Pancras who had a church in Rome close to the monastery from which Augustine had come. Augustine was also given land by Ethelbert, and he established a Benedictine monastery, the church of which, SS Peter & Paul, became the burial place of the kings and queens of Kent, of Augustine himself, and of the first succeeding archbishops. The extensive St Augustine's Abbey is now in ruins.

In 758, Cuthbert, having recently built a new chapel on the site of the present cathedral, directed that he should be buried therein – an interment which the monks did not dare announce until it was accomplished – and after this only one bishop was buried in the Abbey.

The city was laid waste by the Danes in the mid-9th century and again in 1011, when Archbishop Alphege was martyred after he refused to pay them a ransom for his release from captivity. The Cathedral of Christ Church was restored to its former dignity in 1023 by Canute, now a Christian, only to be destroyed by fire in 1067. It was rebuilt in 1070 by Archbishop Lanfranc, the first Norman bishop, and it is this foundation which we see today.

When Becket was murdered in 1172, it was in the cathedral that he was buried; it was to the cathedral that Henry II made his amazing pilgrimage in 1174; and it was money from pilgrims which enabled a magnificent new shrine for Becket's remains to be built by 1220, to which pilgrims flocked for the ensuing 300 years.

For the accommodation of the pilgrims, various inns and lodging-houses were established and the city grew prosperous on an immense tourist traffic. The Grey Friars, or Franciscans, established their first English foundation at Canterbury in 1224, and the Black Friars, or Dominicans, in 1237 also established a community.

In 1538, however, Henry VII issued his mock writ of summons, accusing Becket (who had been dead for 366 years) of treachery, and challenging the ghostly delinquent to appear and give an account of the deeds done in the flesh. The outcome of Becket's non-appearance at Westminster was that his shrine was despoiled and the cathedral desecrated and plundered in the Dissolution.

The cathedral was later spoiled by the Puritans in the Civil War, but despite all this, and earlier depredations, it remains a very beautiful building. Even in the severe ordeal suffered by Canterbury on the night of 31 May–1 June 1942 – when a German air raid laid waste an entire third of the old city within the walls – the cathedral suffered only superficial damage.

Many old and interesting houses and buildings disappeared in the bombing – including some in the cathedral precincts: 'Ingoldsby' Barham's birthplace; the whole of Lady Wootton's Green; the Fountain Hotel; the fine old Corn Market; the undistinguished nineteenth-century cathedral library; and also the historic St George's church – but by what seemed, and perhaps was, a miracle, the more precious monuments remained intact.

Having set the scene, we can now explore the Canterbury we all know, or feel we know – the Canterbury of narrow crooked streets and timber-framed houses projecting over the pavements, not all that different (if you disregard the plate-glass shopfronts, the advertisements, the undistinguished red-brick rebuilding) from the town familiar to the Knight, the Miller, the Reeve, the Pardoner and the Wife of Bath.

Starting at the Westgate and walking straight through the town to St George's Gate, you pass many of the principal buildings, besides getting an idea of the small scale of the town. Most visitors to Canterbury, like Chaucer's pilgrims, make straight for the cathedral, but in many ways it is best to leave this to the last. Any exploration of Canterbury will take you past it, and you are never out of sight of it for long. Canterbury is not a city to be rushed through: it is essential that one's visit should be leisurely.

It is impossible to describe here all the buildings of great antiquity and other places of interest that abound in Canterbury, but we will inevitably set out to enjoy the rich inheritance of the Pilgrims' City.

The overriding impression to the casual visitor is of a city of sharp visual contrasts and no overall unity. The main streets vary from an attractively intimate scale with buildings and frontages of different periods and styles uniting into a harmonious and picturesque streetscape to the clumsy monumentality of the widened St George's Street with St George's Tower standing forlornly among the unimaginative urban designs of twentieth-century-midland-commercial development.

The growth of motor-vehicle ownership, together with the changing conditions in social habits, have meant that the town centre has not been able to cope with the dramatic change in pace. The town has been presented with problems threatening to destroy or greatly alter its character, and the resultant effect of these pressures has been reflected in the opening up of precincts, the widening of streets and the infill of new buildings, all of which are completely out of scale and totally unsympathetic to the general streetscape of the town centre.

The enclosing city walls circle the narrow and irregular streets of an almost unchanged medieval layout which are overflowing with the daily increasing traffic. On Saturdays the main streets seize up so completely that even the dodge of forming a one-way system has ceased to be tolerable. Opposite the city walls at the Riding Gate, the new fire station with its flint walls has been blended with the ancient stonework in a way that is pleasing to the eye, but there are a few other instances where modern brickwork could have been tempered by a partial disguising to match buildings close by. In the Longmarket a modern tall building completely ruins a vista of the Cathedral from the High Street.

The old streets contain many buildings of interest, but also have many gaps and run-down houses under the threat of demolition. The City Council have cleared large areas of so-called slums, which ought to have been reconditioned, putting in their place houses and flats of depressing mediocrity. Any large sites left after demolition are used as temporary car parks, appalling and extensive vistas of tarmac occupying a considerable area of the historic core awaiting development. A multi-storey car park, grey and stark, said by some to be hideously ugly, others seeing it as beautiful, was opened in 1969. On the southern side of the city a primary distributor road built on the old moat opens up new views of the city walls for passing travellers.

It was argued that to prevent the chaos of surface car parking and to justify a policy of restricted access in the city a multi-storey car park within the city walls was necessary and this, together with published road schemes which would involve the destruction of some of Canterbury's most remarkable assets, raised many objections to the management of traffic in the city. A new multi-storey car park has been built, and a proposed 'relief road' is a sword of Damocles hanging over a wide swath of the old city S of the main street.

One third of the central area of Canterbury was laid in ruins during the war but little of historic value was destroyed. Many people moved out, and in the process of rebuilding, remains of Roman houses and streets were discovered. The red-brick architecture chosen for rebuilding the devastated areas is undistinguished, but it is not quite so characterless as in some of the rebuilt towns across the Channel in Normandy. The rebuilding set a pattern for large-scale development in the centre, and vacant sites resulted in parking facilities being provided and taken for granted very close to the shops. Modern commercial pressures had been accepted as a basis for developing a thriving shopping centre in the heart of the city, instead of preserving the city's best features and maintaining the environment.

But Canterbury hasn't survived simply as a museum piece. In addition to its traditional role as a tourist attraction it has another important function: to resist the modern commercial pressures by retaining its human scale and well-defined environment: quiet, relaxing, sharply divided from some of the less attractive features of modern city life. Although the 'comprehensive redevelopment' of the 1970s began the commemoration of the martyrdom of Canterbury, the distinctive atmosphere of small-scale old winding streets with their continuous frontages, and the overall medieval character, still essentially remain.

In 1970, on the 800th year of Becket's death, a festival took place. Numerous religious and artistic events were presented jointly by the City of Canterbury and the Dean and Chapter of Canterbury Cathedral.

These included special services, music concerts and lectures in the cathedral. A regal and royal pilgrim was Her Majesty, Queen Elizabeth, the Queen Mother, who attended the National Service on 15 July, at which the Archbishop of Canterbury gave an address.

Also held was a Son et Lumiere – 'Conflict at Canterbury' – with the physical presence of the cathedral as its background, T. S. Eliot's *Murder in the Cathedral* staged inside the building for the first time ever, while a new Becket play, *A Breach in the Wall*, by Ray Lawdler, received its world première at the Marlow Theatre.

Tour of the Town

The Westgate is built over one reach of the Stour and we enter St Peter's Street. The Church of the Holy Cross, to the right of the Westgate, was originally situated over the former gate, but was rebuilt over its present site by Archbishop Simon of Sudbury in 1380, when he rebuilt the gateway. Whereas Sudbury's gateway is in ragstone, his church is in knapped flint, but it has been heavily restored, and in 1972 was skilfully converted to the Guildhall.

At first sight, St Peter's Street appears as a modern town-planner's nightmare and a historian's delight – a higgledy-piggledy of all building styles and frontages, where windows and overhanging upper storeys jut and butt out over the narrow pavements. This is part of the fascination we expect of Canterbury, old mellow-fronted shops and ancient buildings jostling with the new.

St Peter's Church peeps out from its tucked-away site, and then we cross the main branch of the river by King's Bridge. Here, on the left, are the old Canterbury Weaver's Houses, with three gables flanking the road and five gables overhanging the water. They are undeniably picturesque, though the half-timbering may be very much restored. (Open daily: Mondays–Saturdays 9.30–17.30, Sundays 11.00–17.00.) It is one of many houses taken over by Protestant Huguenot and Walloon weavers from the Continent c.1560, who set up their looms here after the Massacre of St Bartholomew in France and the Spanish persecution in the Low Countries. Beyond the Weaver's Houses you can see the medieval town ducking-stool hanging over the river.

On the other side of the street is St Thomas's Hospital, or Eastbridge Hospital as it is now sometimes known, although its proper name is the Hospital of St Thomas the Martyr upon Eastbridge. (Open daily: Monday–Saturdays 10.00–13.00 and 14.00–17.00, Sundays 11.00–13.00 and 14.00–17.00. Admission free.) It was founded by Edward Fitz Osbold in 1175, dedicated to St Thomas Becket, and provided beds for the poor pilgrims who came to pray at the shrine of the martyr in the cathedral. Later it became a hospital, with the former chapel used as a school, and it is now partly a museum and open to the public. Part is still used as an almshouse, one of the original functions: the timber-framed almshouses are at the back.

High Street follows next and on the left is the Beaney Institute, 1897, an incongruous piece of red-brick and half-timbered Victorianism, now the Royal Museum and Public

Library. At this point a short detour needs to be made into Stour Street opposite.

An entrance under an archway in Stour Street brings you to the Poor Priest's Hospital, a group of flint buildings originally established in 1220 and rebuilt in 1373. Like all early hospitals in the city, it is built on the banks of the River Stour. The Franciscans probably lived here before they established their own friary a little further upstream, on an island in the narrow channel of the Stour. They came to Canterbury in 1224, only 15 years after St Francis had established the Order, but moved to their present site in 1267 – the first Franciscan friary in England. The Grey Friars were considerable buildings, straddling the river on two pairs of pointed arches on dumpy pillars. The remains are the most picturesque monastic remains in the city. In later years it was used by Flemish weavers, and as a prison. It is open on weekday afternoons in summer. The former hospital now houses the Canterbury Heritage – the city council's museum – where a fascinating 'time-walk' through 'the spectacle and splendour of Canterbury's story' takes you from Roman glass and Saxon gold to the wartime blitz. (Open daily throughout the year, Mondays to Saturdays, 1030–1700 and 1330–1700 on Sundays from June to the end of October).

The other riverside corner in Canterbury worth hunting for is the Black Friars. This is downstream, and the best view of it is to be had from the bridge over the Stour in The Friars. The Black Friars (Dominicans) came to Canterbury in 1237, after the Franciscans, and established their friary on land granted by Henry III. Only two of its buildings remain, the frater or refectory, on the E bank of the river, and the great hall facing it on the opposite bank.

Returning to the museum in the High Street we press on towards the cathedral, passing on the right the half-timbered and timber-framed house known as Queen Elizabeth's Guest Chamber, dated 1573, the best of its kind in the city. Instead of gables it has a parapet and some vigorous pargetting, now cheerfully painted, with moulded cupids plunging about among loaded grapevines and barrels.

Off High Street to the R is St Margaret's Street where in a medieval church is The Canterbury Tales, a vivid re-enactment of Chaucer's *Canterbury Tales*. More fun and more expensive than the Canterbury Heritage, this award-winning experience takes you with Chaucer's immortal band – the courtly Knight, the bawdy Miller, the Wife of Bath, the Nun's Priest and the Pardoner – and you can experience the sights, sounds and even smells of the fourteenth century as they recount their tales of chivalry, romance, jealousy, pride and avarice on the journey to Canterbury. (Open daily throughout the year).

The Tourist Information Centre is next door in St Margaret's Street, from where conducted tours of the city take place daily from early April to mid-November. Enquire at the TIC.

High Street becomes St George's Street at Mercery Lane which leads us left on to the Christ Church Gate entrance to the cathedral precinct. On the left are the double-overhanging beams of a pilgrims' inn, the 'Chequers of Hope'. This celebrated hostelry sheltered Chaucer: now it is part of a department store. The overhangs repeat themselves on the opposite side of the lane, and in the narrowness of the street they nearly touch overhead. The 'Chequers of Hope' once stretched back to the Buttermarket, and this and other inns in the street provided rest and refreshment for the medieval pilgrims, and shops and stalls where the pilgrims could buy healing water from Becket's Well in the cathedral crypt, medallions of St Thomas and other tokens of their pilgrimage. The overhanging fronts of the shops in the narrow lane still convey the medieval atmosphere, and souvenirs are sold to the modern tourist much as they were several centuries ago.

At the far end of the lane is the quaint little square of the Buttermarket outside the great Christ Church Gate. This magnificent and elaborate gateway was built in 1517–20 and has wooden doors dating from 1662. It is decorated with painted heraldic shields, commemorating the visit of 1500 of Prince Arthur, Henry VIII's elder brother, and is one of the most beautiful specimens of Perpendicular work in the country. The two turrets of the gate are recent additions. The originals were taken down in the eighteenth century to please people living at a distance, who said they obstructed their view of the cathedral clock! The gateway makes a fittingly splendid prelude to the cathedral.

Tour of the Cathedral

On entering Canterbury Cathedral it is advisable to sit down for a short time to allow the eyes and mind to become accustomed to their surroundings. The Cathedral Church of Christ at once casts the spell of its beautiful proportions, the vastness of the interior, the dazzling splendour of its glowing stained glass, its tomb with effigies lying in age-old peace. We arrive at the NW transept and linger at the scene of the martyrdom and the steps worn thin by the countless pilgrims before us. A slab of stone set into the E wall marks the spot near which Becket is supposed to have fallen.

Your mind is alive with visions of the past that even the milling throng of package-tour sightseers cannot blot out. You can imagine the hard face of Becket in profile gazing fixedly, still caught by the last rays of twilight filtering through the windows high up on the southern side; the choir beyond chanting; the battering of the oak door; the jangle of arms and of scabbards trailing as the four knights break in – William de Tracy, Hugh de Morville, Reginald Fitzurse and Richard le Breton; the exchange of sharp and angry insults; the blows, then Gilbert groaning, wounded, and Becket dead. The Cathedral is silent and empty, an awful and fitting terminal to the long journey.

The murder of St Thomas and the pilgrimages that followed formed only a comparatively late page in the religious history of Canterbury, for this city was the official birthplace of Christianity in England and is the chief cathedral city in the kingdom, its archbishop bearing the title of Primate of All England.

Shortly after William had captured the throne of England he called over Lanfranc, abbot of St Etienne at Caen in Normandy, to become the first Norman Archbishop of Canterbury. Lanfranc began rebuilding the cathedral in 1070, on lines almost identical to those of St Etienne, and he also reorganized the monastery of Christ Church as a priory. The building was completed in seven years – extraordinarily fast work. The nave measured 187ft/57m long, 72ft/22m wide, and 80ft/24m high, and the transepts 127ft/38m across.

The building proved to be quite inadequate for its purpose as both cathedral and priory church, and in 1096 a reconstruction of the E end was planned by Lanfranc's successor, St Anselm (1093–1109). The building was extended to nearly twice its previous size – a new choir was built, a second pair of transepts (copying an idea from a new church at Cluny, which was being built at the same time) and three chapels – Trinity Chapel, and the flanking St Andrew's and St Anselm's Chapels – all raised on a crypt. The new choir thus almost equalled Lanfranc's nave in length, being 180ft/55m long, and was 40ft/12m wide and 69ft/21m high; the E transepts are 156ft/47m across. The crypt is the largest and most elaborate in England, being 163ft/50m long and 83ft/25m wide, thus raising the choir many steps higher than the nave. The crypt has a forest of columns, their capitals carved with the best preserved Early Romanesque sculpture in the country. Not only are the shafts fluted spirally or in zigzags, or carved in a scale pattern, but some of the capitals are carved with figures, almost all of creatures fighting – a pointed-eared half-human struggles with two ferocious beasts, a wyvern fights with a dog. There is a man on horseback, animals playing musical instruments, jugglers, grotesque human heads, weird medieval animals, and, where naturalistic inspiration failed, delicately interlaced abstract patterns.

All this work of St Anselm's was begun under the direction of Prior Enulf (1096–1107) and continued on an even grander scale by Prior Conrad (1108–26). The new church was consecrated in 1130, in the presence of the Kings of England and Scotland and all the English bishops, and the earlier beatified archbishops were reburied with great solemnity in the new shrines that had been provided for them.

Archbishop Becket was murdered in 1170. In the first few days of 1171 came the first miraculous cure of a woman who appealed to Becket as a saint, and by Easter 1171 Canterbury was already a place of pilgrimage. Becket was canonized by the Pope in 1172, and in July 1174 the remorseful King Henry II crossed over from France and performed his public penance. In the autumn of that year Anselm's choir caught fire, and this disaster, coupled with the donations pouring in from the pilgrims who flocked in great numbers to Becket's miracle-working tomb in the crypt, determined that a more elaborate E end should be built as a fitting temple for the shrine of the saint.

The new shrine was built by a renowned French mason-architect William of Sens, who in 1175 began a splendid new choir and a presbytery modelled on his previous work in the Cathedral of Sens; a mixture of Roman and Gothic but modified to suit the special considerations imposed by the surviving parts of Conrad's church. (Although Gothic had been begun at Ripon and at Roche Abbey in Yorkshire about five years earlier, as a culmination of the Cistercian tradition, it was Canterbury which ensured the spread of the new style, and by 1180 at Wells it was firmly established.) Stone for the building was brought in from Caen in Normandy and landed at Fordwick, the point up to which the Stour was still navigable at that time (2 miles/3.2km NE of the Cathedral). Crippled by a fall from the scaffolding, William continued to direct the work from his bed until the E transepts were finished in 1179. He then relinquished his task to another William, usually called William the Englishman to avoid confusion, who, working to the plans of French William, completed the Trinity Chapel and the Corona, and the Crypt beneath them, by 1184. From the Corona the full length of the Cathedral is seen. It is 514ft/157m long, the fourth longest cathedral in England. Winchester, the largest, is 556ft/169m long.

Canterbury Cathedral. The Nave, looking east

The Corona, or Becket's Crown, is a circular annexe to the Trinity Chapel. Its centrepiece is St Augustine's Chair, a thirteenth-century marble tomb, constructed in three pieces for ease of transport. It is used for the enthronement of Canterbury's archbishops. Above St Anselm's Chapel is a small chamber, created by English William, in which a guard was stationed at night to watch over and protect the treasure of Becket's shrine. It served a similar purpose to that built by Anselm in the crypt, where Becket's tomb had stood earlier. The new Trinity Chapel was raised 16 steps above the level of the choir on a new and higher crypt, and was to become the Chapel of St Thomas, but it was not until 1220 that the remains of Becket were transferred with great pomp from the crypt, where they had lain for 50 years, to the new shrine. The Pilgrim Steps leading up to it are deeply indented, due to the passage of countless generations of pilgrims. The mosaic pavement is a complicated geometric pattern, c.1220, a most handsome affair of lozenges within squares, and 36 red and yellow roundels showing signs of the Zodiac, Labours of the Month, and Virtues tempting Vices.

The space once occupied by Becket's shrine is now the tomb of Prince Edward, the Black Prince (d.1376). The figure is clad in full gilded armour, the hands clasped in prayer. Above the canopy hang replicas of the Prince's gauntlets, tabard, set of armour, shield of wood, and coat of leather sewn with silk and emblazoned with the arms of France and England. (The originals, now decayed and fragile, are displayed in a glass case at the foot of the Pilgrims' Steps, at the E end of the S choir aisle.)

Immediately opposite the Black Prince's tomb is that of King Henry IV (d.1413), and his second queen, Joan of Navarre (d.1437). He is the only monarch buried in the cathedral and his tomb is one of the most ambitious alabaster monuments ever executed.

In the ambulatory around the Trinity Chapel is the Purbeck marble tomb-chest of Archbishop Walter (d.1205). The decoration in the gable, of lozenges and circles and geometric forms, matches perfectly with the mosaic pavement and chapel windows. Perhaps the Shrine of St Thomas would have looked something like this, though much more elaborate, as it dates from about the same period (i.e., 1220).

The Decorated stone screen between the choir and nave was built in 1304–5 by Prior Eastry (1284–1331). It has a contemporary iron gate, but inside is a second set of iron gates to the pulpitum, a second screen, set up about 1400. It has six remarkable figures of kings, the major surviving examples of early fifteenth-century sculpture in England, apart from those on monuments – they are Ethelbert, Edward the Confessor, Richard II, Henry IV, Henry V and Henry VI.

For over 150 years since English William's work the cathedral remained untouched, then in 1378 Archbishop Simon of Sudbury (1375–81) pulled down the Norman work which was beyond repair, and began a magnificent new nave and transepts in the English Perpendicular style to the designs of Henry Yevele, the master-mason of Edward III. They have a remarkable resemblance to those of Winchester, which was built about the same time. The nave, begun in 1391, was completed about 1405 under Prior Chillenden (1390–1421), and the transepts vaulted over – the S in 1414 and the N between 1448–68; this latter, being the deeply hallowed place where Becket had been murdered, was only touched after a great deal of hesitation. The Lady Chapel, E of the NW transept (The Martyrdom), and the corresponding extension to the SW transept (St Michael's Chapel), were both built, c.1420–8. St Michael's Chapel (also called the Warrior's Chapel) has the tomb of Stephen Langton, the leader of the barons who extracted the Magna Carta out of King John.

Meanwhile the SW tower was rebuilt, 1424–35, by Thomas Mapilton for Archbishop Chichele, but Lanfranc's NW tower stood until 1832, when it was replaced by an exact copy of Chichele's tower, a matching pair, both 157ft/48m high. The central tower, the Bell Harry Tower, is 235ft/72m high – 250ft/76m to the top of the pinnacles – and was built by John Wastell in 1485–98. It is a notable example of the Perpendicu-

lar style, with a magnificent fan-vaulted lantern ceiling, perfectly setting the seal on the cathedral. Curfew is rung nightly from Bell Harry, a bell cast in 1635, the successor to a bell called Henry, given by Prior Eastry over 300 years earlier.

Hardly any part of the cathedral remains as it was at the time of the murder. The Martyrdom was the scene of the tragedy which rendered Canterbury famous throughout Christendom. The knights entered the cathedral from the cloisters by the doorway in the NW transept and murdered Becket in the SE corner, where steps lead down to the crypt. The Murder Stone marks the spot where Becket fell: it says simply

Thomas Becket, Archbishop. Saint. Martyr.
Died here Tuesday 29th December 1170.

The pilgrimages were already in decline when Thomas Cromwell destroyed the Shrine of St Thomas in 1538 on behalf of Henry VIII, and only the surrounding pavement of Italian mosaic, worn into grooves by the toes and knees of pilgrims, remains to mark the site of the tomb. So magnificently adorned was the shrine that in 1512 Erasmus wrote that 'gold was the meanest thing to be seen'. The priory was dissolved in 1540, and the affairs of the cathedral placed under the jurisdiction of a Dean and Chapter. The cathedral suffered during the Civil War, when it was desecrated by the Puritan fanatic Richard Culmer, one of the ministers appointed to destroy objects of idolatrous worship; but it escaped the worse intentions of the German bombers in June and October of 1942.

It is impossible in this guide to do more than sketch a brief outline of the cathedral's history. Many lifetimes have been spent studying the cathedral, and many books have been written about it. Some of these have concentrated on specific aspects – the stained glass would take months to get to know

Canterbury Cathedral. The Choir, looking east

properly, and a monumental work has been written on this subject alone*. Canterbury has a fine series of tombs to its archbishops, but it is the stained glass that one should spend time looking at, particularly the 'poor man's bible' in the N Choir Aisle and the 'Miracle Windows' around the Trinity Chapel. All these windows are of mostly thirteenth-century glass, those in the Trinity Chapel depicting subjects which were miracles worked by St Thomas's shrine – advertisements for the cures which belief in the effectiveness of the shrine could bring.

The cathedral is open daily at the following times:

Sundays	07.00–19.30
Weekdays (Summer)	07.00–19.00
Weekdays (Winter)	07.00–18.15
Saturdays	07.00–17.00

although there may be restrictions in certain parts during some services. Check with the notice boards. Official guides conduct visitors around the cathedral, and no charge is made for their services. Please leave a donation in a collection box. Guidebooks and pre-recorded tapes are available for your tour, and a way-marked trail conducts you through the cathedral.

* *The Ancient Stained Glass of Canterbury Cathedral* by Bernard Rackham, 1947.

15 Canterbury to Dover 16 miles/25.6km

Between Canterbury and the populous coastal strip of Deal,
Dover, and Folkestone, is a forgotten land of downs and the
remains of great forests. The Romans built their Stone Street
and Watling Street undeviatingly across it, and traffic has
passed through it without stopping ever since. This is a pity
because the fascination of the area lies in its contrasts: from
hidden lanes and hamlets in the hinterland to the open spaces
further E, from the E Kent coalfields to areas of parkland.

The NDW between Canterbury and the coast is a somewhat
'artificial' creation, following neither historical tradition nor
the North Downs ridge, but the chosen line takes the best
route along this final stretch. We begin our last days' walk
outside the cathedral in Burgate, although the 'official' start is
beyond St Martin's Church.

The SE quarter of the City beyond Burgate and Watling
Street was the most severely bombed, and there is little of
much interest surviving. There is a massive late-medieval
timber-framed building with a double overhang, similar to the
'Chequers of Hope', stretching a long way down the street,
and then there is Butchery Lane on the right. In an alley off
this lane may be seen the mosaic Roman Pavement, together
with the remains of a hypocaust. These are by far the most
interesting of the remains discovered as a result of the
excavations after the war damage, and are shown in a large
vaulted room, together with Roman brooches and pottery.
The medieval trading tradition of Butchery Lane is carried on
by a butcher with a large blood-red bullock's head over his
shop window.

On the left-hand side of Butchery Lane are the backs of a
pedestrian shopping precinct in the New Town tradition.
Longmarket was built between 1958–61 and a route to the
Roman Pavement is signposted through it.

A few minutes' walk down Burgate is an isolated Perpendicular tower, built in 1502 – all that is left of the Church of St Mary Magdalene. The church itself was demolished in 1871, but its tower survived the blitz. It shelters a number of monuments, protected behind plate-glass windows. Prominent in the centre is the magnificent Baroque obelisk with several small boys at each corner, of the Whitfield family, dating from c.1680, placed in this position when the church was demolished. The sculpture is of Flemish influence and is typical of the style of Grinling Gibbons. A plaque on the N wall says that 'Ingoldsby' Barham was baptized here in 1788.

Another ancient tower is that of St George's Church, all that remains of the church bombed in 1942. It stands in St George's Street, in the new shopping precinct, and it was here that Canterbury's famous son, Christopher Marlowe, was baptized in 1564. Poet and playwright, he was 29 years old when murdered in a pub brawl in Deptford.

Next along Burgate, at the corner of Canterbury Lane, is a plaque marking the site of the birthplace on 6 December 1788 of Richard Harris Barham. Some of his *Ingoldsby Legends* (1840) are set in the city.

And so we come to the site of the Burgate in the old city walls. The city walls, as rebuilt in the fourteenth and fifteenth centuries, remain round the S and E boundaries of the medieval, roughly oval, city, and the most impressive length stretches N from Burgate along Broad Street to North Gate. The walls are built of flint, with projecting bastions.

Emerge outside the city walls, cross Broad Street and into Church Street St Paul's opposite. St Paul's has an Early English foundation, though most of what you see today is by Sir G. G. Scott in 1856, and typical of many of the churches in the town.

Church Street St Paul's leads into Monastery Street and the Cemetery Gate of St Augustine's Abbey.

St Augustine's Abbey
Admission: the abbey is open daily throughout the year except

Christmas, New Year and May Day. Charge for admission.

Abbey	Weekdays	Sundays
15 March–15 October	9.30–18.30	14.00–18.30
16 October–14 March	9.30–16.00	14.00–16.00
College		
Wednesdays and Thursdays only	14.00–16.00	

The Abbey and the cathedral were founded by St Augustine in 597, the cathedral to be the seat of the archbishops and the abbey to provide a burial place for them and the kings of Kent. When Augustine died in 605, the church was not completed; it was dedicated in 613 to SS Peter & Paul by St Lawrence, the second archbishop, and Augustine's body was buried within its walls. Succeeding archbishops were buried there till Cuthbert, the eleventh, was buried in the cathedral in 758. Nevertheless, the abbey maintained its importance and prestige as a place of pilgrimage.

In addition to SS Peter & Paul, there were three other churches built within the precincts of the abbey. About 50ft/ 15m to the E stood St Mary's, founded by King Edbald c.618, as a burial place for himself and later kings of Kent, and 200ft/ 60m further E was St Pancras, built early in the 7th century. To the W of SS Peter & Paul was built another church, c.1000.

This complex of Saxon churches was swept away by Abbot Scotland for a new church which he began in 1070, almost as large as the cathedral itself. This survived mostly unaltered until it was surrendered to the King's Commissioners and systematically demolished in the Dissolution in 1538, except for the Abbot's lodgings and two great gate-towers which were the entrances to the abbey precinct.

The Abbot's lodgings were adapted as a royal palace for Henry VIII, and as a staging post, along with Dartford and Rochester, between London and Dover. By the early nineteenth century everything had fallen into a state of decay, but in 1844 all that was available was bought by the Rt. Hon. A. J.

B. Beresford-Hope, who built St Augustine's College in the grounds. The destroyed abbey was excavated between 1900–27.

Tour of the Abbey and College

In Monastery Street stand two gateways to the abbey precinct. The Cemetery Gate, at the S end, opposite the end of Church Street St Paul's, was built before 1391, was heavily restored in 1839, and is now used as a house. To the N is the Great Gateway or Fyndon Gate, built by Abbot Fyndon in 1300–9, a fine piece of the Decorated period, larger than many of the similarly dated pieces in the cathedral. Elizabeth I spent a fortnight here in 1573, and the room she occupied was the one where Charles I and his Queen Henrietta Maria spent their wedding night in 1625, and where Charles II stayed on his return to England in 1660 at the Restoration.

The Great Gateway is the entrance to the college precinct. Beresford-Hope, who had bought the site of the abbey in 1844, was interested in founding a training college for missionaries. He commissioned William Butterfield as his architect; this is his first major work, and the start of a long and fruitful partnership. The two men hoped to produce a monastic environment, and all the buildings are on medieval foundations, forming an irregular quadrangle in knapped flint and stone dressings. Butterfield's design is in the Decorated style, similar to that of the Great Gateway, but far more austere. Running S from the gateway was the abbot's guest hall with the refectory above, still used as the college dining hall. Immediately S is the chapel projecting into the quadrangle. On the N side are students' cells, and on the E side is the library, standing on the foundations of the Abbot's Banqueting Hall. The college is today used by theological students preparing for ordination.

The abbey ruins are reached by a roadway through a brick arch to the left of the Great Gateway. The various levels of the abbey ruins make them hard to unravel, so we shall go first of all to the far SE corner of the site to the ruins of the Church of

St Pancras.

St Pancras is an early Saxon church of simple plan, built entirely in regularly laid Roman bricks, almost certainly by St Augustine.

Returning to the abbey church of SS Peter & Paul itself, we find that the Norman abbey is superimposed on the remains of the Saxon churches, which are shown by brick or flint outlines. The original church of SS Peter & St Paul lay under the E end of Abbot Scotland's nave, and the later Church of St Mary lay under the Norman crypt. Between the two old churches, and linking them, was Abbot Wulfric's Rotunda, built c.1056.

Wulfric's work did not last long, for it and the Saxon churches were swept away by Abbot Scotland, the first Norman abbot, to make room for his great new church. He was appointed in 1070, had visited Rome by 1073 to obtain the Pope's permission to rebuild, and when he died in 1087 the new nave had been begun: the whole church was completed by 1091. The external length of the church was 402ft/ 122m – about the size of Gloucester and Norwich cathedrals. The crypt is the earliest surviving Norman crypt in England, Winchester's being begun in 1079.

North of the church are the scattered remains of the monastic buildings. Around the cloisters there were, as usual, the chapter house and dormitory to the E, with steps in the SE corner going up to the floor-level of the great abbey church. The dormitory was a massive 193ft/59m long: a gable and two large buttresses remain. To the N of the cloisters was the refectory, a hexagonal kitchen, and off the N cloister walk are the foundations of the polygonal monks' lavatorium, where they washed before meals. To the W lay the abbot's lodging and banqueting hall, with his private chapel above.

This completes our tour of St Augustine's.

From St Augustine's, turn left along Monastery Street and then left again into Longport, the A257 road to Sandwich. Beyond the end of the precinct wall of the abbey are the

Sessions House and Prison, both built in 1808, the former in Portland Stone with two Greek Doric columns, the later in red brick with a rusticated stone entrance. Almost opposite is John Smith's Hospital, a row of almshouses built in 1657.

On the brow of the hill can be seen St Martin's Windmill, a tower mill built in 1816, but just before this a turning on the left leads us to the lych-gate of St Martin's Church.

St Martin's is undisputedly the oldest church in continuous use in England. It was built about AD 560, for not only was it the church where St Augustine and his followers first worshipped as they came over the hill from Ebbsfleet near Richborough, it was also the church which Queen Bertha, consort of the pagan King Ethelbert, was already using as a Christian oratory. The Venerable Bede describes Queen Bertha worshipping here as soon as she arrived in England in 562, and he also believed that this was the original church built during the Roman occupation. Augustine used this church as his base until he converted Ethelbert to Christianity on Whit Sunday 597: it is unlikely that the font inside the church was used for this baptism, as its 22 stones appear to have come from Caen and been fashioned by the Normans.

The generally accepted view is that the western half of the chancel formed part of Queen Bertha's original chapel, almost wholly built of Roman bricks. The church was repaired by the Normans after the ravages of the Danes, and the eastern end was added in the Early English style in the thirteenth century, and much Roman material was re-used.

The fifteenth-century windows show Augustine landing at Ebbsfleet, entering Canterbury by St Martin's Hill, and baptizing Ethelbert; another shows Queen Bertha and her maid; another Bede dying; and another English slaves in the marketplace of Rome.

Canterbury to Patrixbourne 3½ miles/5.6km

The NDW leaves Canterbury proper from the A257 on St Martin's Hill at the junction of Spring Lane, not far from St Martin's church.

Go down Spring Lane and then left into Pilgrims' Way, crossing the railway line in a cutting and going through a housing estate, past a storage depot, and then into orchard country. There is a metalled bridleway all the way into Patrixbourne, but as it is also a private road to Little Barton Farm, gates may be locked to prevent entry by unauthorized vehicles. There is a last retrospective view of the cathedral, and then the Way leads straight SE, past the end of a wood and then to a road, past Hoad Farm (parts dating from 1674) along a sunken lane and into Patrixbourne village.

Patrixbourne

Patrixbourne is a gem of a place, with half-timbered houses of hand-made bricks, Dutch gables and oast houses clustered along the Nail Bourne stream. To the S of the main village street is the large parkland of Bifrons, once the seat of the Marquess Conyngham: the house has been demolished, and only the lodge remains.

St Mary's Church, built c.1170, has some first-class Norman carving, only excelled by that at Barfreston (see later): it may have been carved by the same mason, who probably worked on Rochester Cathedral. Below the centrally placed tower, the main S Norman doorway is smothered in an elaborate riot of carving – there are five orders: top to bottom they are carved with a knot of foliage with human heads, alternating with birds and beasts; then a looped cable; then floral crosses alternating with wyverns – semi-human monsters with wings and forked tails; then an enriched chevron; and finally a roll with bands. This encircles a tympanum carved with a seated figure of Christ among angels and apocalyptic creatures. A triangular canopy above the doorway frames a niche containing the *Agnus Dei* or Lamb of God. The lamb with its halo and flag on its back can faintly be seen.

The Norman chancel arch is beautifully and unusually horseshoe-shaped: in the chancel are two aumbries or lockers, used to contain the sacred vessels, a hagioscope or squint, and a remarkable piscina – the arch of which is surrounded

by a thirteenth century triangular canopy, now mutilated.

Almost as remarkable as the stonework is some of the stained glass, Swiss – like the glass at Temple Ewell (on the A2/B2060) – and dating from between 1538 and 1670. There are no less than 18 panels, 8 in the Bifrons Chapel, the other 10 in the three Norman E windows.

The 8 panels in the Bifrons Chapel are an extraordinary and varied collection. Beginning from the E and working from top to bottom they are:

i. The Crucifixion

ii. John the Baptist on the banks of the Jordan.

iii. The story of Pyramus and Thisbe, familiar to us in *A Midsummer Night's Dream* – Pyramus gorgeously dressed in crimson, with a sword thrust through his body, Thisbe throwing up her hands to heaven, and a lioness and her cub looking on.

iv. The adoration of the Shepherds.

v. Peter Gisler, a distinguished Swiss soldier, on pilgrimage to Jerusalem.

vi. The raising of Lazarus from the dead.

vii. A Swiss standard-bearer in rich armour of silver and gold, with a white feather in a black cap. The man with pack-mules is on the St Gothard Pass.

viii. The tragic death of St Meinrad in the ninth century.

The three Norman lancet windows are each divided into panels and show Bible scenes. They are, from top to bottom, *a) North lancet:*

i. Christ in Gethsemane, with Peter carrying a gold-hilted sword, and in the background the towered city of Lucerne at the foot of snow-clad mountains.

ii. A Crucifixion scene, with the Madonna in a blue mantle and Mary Magdalene crouching at the foot of the cross; Michael is trampling on the dragon.

iii. Samson holding the jaw-bone with which he slew the Philistines.

South door, Chuch of St Mary, Patrixbourne

b) Central lancet:

i. A knight, 1579.

ii. A Roman soldier in rich armour carrying a tilting spear. He has a crimson cloak and stands under a Roman arch.

iii. The adoration of the Magi, with small pictures of the adoration of the Shepherds and the Annunciation in the top corners.

iv. St John the Evangelist and Elizabeth of Hungary, by Martin Moser of Lucerne.

c) South lancet:

i. A knight in armour.

ii. Another Gethsemane scene, with Christ in agony and the disciples sleeping.

iii. Samson slaying the lion. This picture is an exact copy of a woodcut by Albrecht Dürer, and shows Nurenberg in the background – Dürer's native city.

There are large and small figures of knights, monks, angels, and saints, most of them in vivid clothing. They are the work of Peter Brock of Altdorf and Martin Moser of Lucerne, two of the best Swiss painters of the sixteenth century.

Bekesbourne

Almost contiguous with Patrixbourne is Bekesbourne, which has connections with four people famous in their own time.

The remains of a Tudor palace, built in 1552 but destroyed in the Civil War, was the hiding place of Archbishop Cranmer, who came here on the death of Edward VI. After he ceased to be head of the church he spent a few critical months here awaiting arrest and martyrdom.

Bekesbourne was the birthplace in 1677 of Stephen Hales, who was second only to William Harvey (whose statue we can see in Folkestone) in the founding of the science of physiology. He invented ventilating machines and processes for distilling sea-water.

Here also lived, and lies buried, Dr Beke, who spent many years in Abyssinia, mapping 70,000 square miles/181,300sq km, fixing the latitude of scores of stations, and recording a dozen native languages. He crossed the eastern edge of the high table-land of East Africa and the rivers of the Indian Ocean, and, although he did not discover the source of the Nile in the Abyssinian mountains, he pointed out to Speke the way into the Nile basin.

At the Howlett's estate 1 mile/1.6km N of the village, the millionaire John Aspinall has a zoo park. Mr Aspinall specialises in collecting tigers and gorillas, but the zoo has been the cause of local concern: in the four years 1976–1980 some 20 animals escaped.

Patrixbourne to Bishopsbourne 1 mile/1.6km

Beyond Patrixbourne's church you go S around a field and then on a bridleway along the edge of a wood, climbing up to the top of a cutting which takes the A2 to bypass Bridge; and after a short way you cross a private road to Highland Court, a large mansion on the left, built in 1904 for Count Zabrowski, the racing motorist of Chitty-Chitty-Bang-Bang fame. The house is now a hospital.

Bridge is a dour main-road village with little of much interest. Its grotesque church of St Peter was built by Scott in 1859–61. If you want to divert from the Way, it is best to continue a little further to Bishopsbourne. From the Highland Court hospital, keep on the bridleway alongside the bypass for a short way and then go across the field, alongside a wood, to where the Bishopsbourne road – Coldharbour Lane – crosses Barham Downs. Bishopsbourne is down in the Nail Bourne valley, flanked on both sides by Georgian mansions in large parks.

Bishopsbourne

Bishopsbourne is little more than a cluster of houses by a small green, leading to the long church of St Mary's, with its strongly buttressed but unimpressive Perpendicular W tower. The church is interesting for its glass – the tower window of 1874 is by William Morris & Co, the main figures of Faith, Hope and Charity being by Burne-Jones. The window in the

S chancel chapel of St Catherine's has fine Dutch and Flemish glass of the sixteenth and seventeenth centuries: one panel shows the building of the Tower of Babylon and another is a meticulously detailed Massacre of the Innocents. There are Flemish pictures in this window of Samson and Delilah; a lovely medallion of the Prodigal Son, and in the tracery there are six small Flemish scenes.

The four chancel windows have angels in medallions encircled in foliage, kneeling on one knee with outstretched arms, and holding in each hand a golden crown. A small window high up above the pulpit has rich fragments showing the Madonna and St Barbara, who is wearing a wreath and holding a tower.

The E window is blazoned with the arms of Richard Hooker (1553–1600) who was rector here in 1595. Hooker was the celebrated Elizabethan divine, and defender of the Established Church against both Catholicism and Puritanism. Much of his magnum opus *Of the Laws of Ecclesiastical Polity* was written here, Book 5 published in 1597 and being partly instrumental in moderating the views of the Elizabethan church. There is a bust of Hooker on the S chancel wall, a typical scholar's monument, with his bust dressed in a mortarboard and doctor's robes, between pilasters made of piled-up books, with cherubs; there is also a statuette of him beside the pulpit.

Hooker's rectory has disappeared; E of the church is a late-Georgian successor (now called Oswalds): it was Joseph Conrad's home from 1920 until his death in 1924.

Downstream of Bishopsbourne is Bourne Park, a stately house beyond a reedy lake. No exact date is known, but it was built by Elizabeth Archer for her young son, Sir Hewitt Archer, who died in 1726. It has a big hipped roof on a white dentilled cornice, with dormers and symmetrical chimney-stacks. Plum- and vermilion-coloured bricks are enriched with stone for the string-course, keystones and quoins.

Upstream is Charlton Park, a large, long, low, ochre-painted

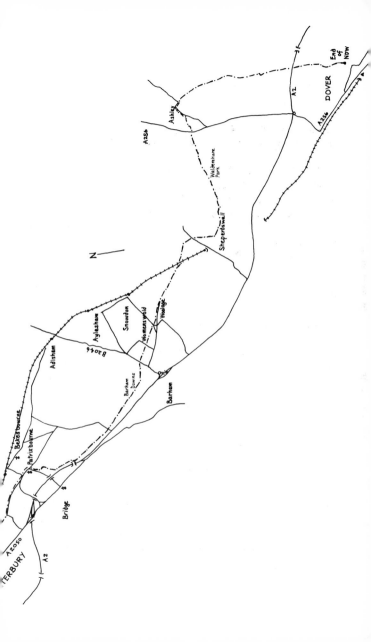

CANTERBURY

A2050

A2

Bridge

Patrixbourne

Bekesbourne

Adisham

B2046

Aylesham

Snowdon

Womenswold

Woolage

Barham

Barham Downs

Shepherdswell

Waldershare Park

A256

Ashley

A2

A256

DOVER

End of NDW

N

Georgian house which hides a Tudor mansion house under its skin. The Georgian additions were made about 1790 by John Foote, a close friend of the Prince Regent: the huge ballroom upstairs was built specially for George, who used to relax there with amateur dramatics after the rigours of reviewing his troops on the wind-swept Barham Downs nearby.

Bishopsbourne to Womenswold 3 miles/4.8km
From the Bishopsbourne road the NDW continues as a bridleway SE above and parallel to the A2, across the fields following orange-painted guideposts for 2 miles/3.2km, to the site of Barham Mill. This was a fine, big, black smock-mill, built in 1834 by John Holman of Canterbury. It was still in working order in 1965, but it was tragically burnt down in 1970 when attempts were being made to restore it.

From the site of the windmill the bridleway strikes E past Upper Digges Farm on your L and a cemetery on your R to reach the B2046 Adisham Road to Aylesham, a 1920s village of acres of orange-roofed semis 1 mile/1.6km N, built for miners of Snowdown Colliery nearby.

Across the B2046 the bridleway leads to Womenswold, emerging from a farmyard just N of the church. There are several old red-brick cottages, some dated 1737, 1745 and 1752, and some are thatched. St Margaret's Church stands on a mound in the middle of the village, its nave and chancel under one roof making it look long and inadequately balanced by the little flint W tower. The tower and chancel are Early English, the nave probably Norman – see how the flints are coursed.

Three handsome hanging monuments grace the N wall of the nave. Two are by Sir Robert Taylor – one to Thomas Marsh (d.1659), Lt. Colonel of the Militia of the Cinque Ports, an expansive obelisk of multi-coloured marble with his bust in relief; and the other of John Marsh (d.1752) with his bust in the round. There is also a monument to Elizabeth Nethersole (d.1737) with Corinthian side-columns, two small naked boys with their heads in the clouds, and a skull beneath.

Womenswold to Waldershare Park 5 miles/8km

From Womenswold the Way continues in the same direction as before to a road, then through a corner of a wood to another road, and N to Woolage Village, another colliery village.

At the village the Way goes down alongside a field opposite the post office, crosses a stile into the far end of the recreation ground, and turns R to join the road to the E of the village. It leaves the road at a corner to take a track (bridleway) alongside a wood up to Three Barrows Down. The tumuli can be seen in the wood on the hilltop at 339ft/103m. The trackway ends at a railway bridge where a road is carried over the cutting. Cross the bridge and immediately take the right fork on the Eythorne road in the same direction as before. Just after Long Lane Farm and Cottage, a path strikes S, cutting out a corner at the next crossroads, and you meet another road beside another railway line, not this time the Dover-Canterbury line but a mineral branch line serving Elvington (Tilmanstone) colliery. To the S is Shepherdswell village.

Shepherdswell is also called 'Sibertswold', perhaps in some way connected with the Saxon king: it was Sibert who started Westminster Abbey. St Andrew's Church, built 1863, is undistinguished.

Far more interesting, and well worth a detour, is the simple late-Norman Church of St Nicholas at Barfreston (also spelt Barfrestone), 1 mile/1.6km N. St Nicholas was built in flint and stone on a hillock in the centre of this little village about 1170–80, and is said to have been a thank-offering by a nobleman who nearly lost his life while hunting in the forest. Consisting of a nave and chancel, it is a very small church – it is only 43ft/13m long, its nave 16ft/4.8m wide and chancel 13ft/4m wide. The walls are 33 inches/0.8m thick. There is no tower or turret: the bell hangs from a yew tree in the churchyard. There is nothing in Kent to touch the richness and exuberance of stone carving in this little church, so small and so heavily decorated that it is more like a reliquary than a

building.

The masterpiece of the church is the S doorway, which confronts you with an overwhelming display of carving, illustrating the medieval world in a microcosm. A bench beside the gate enables you to sit down in comfort to take it all in. On the tympanum above the door is Christ in Glory, surrounded by legendary and symbolic beasts. Above him, on the second roll, in high relief, is a seated bishop, thought to be Thomas Becket: if this is so, it may be as old as the oldest known figure of the archbishop, that in the church of Godmersham. There are major and minor shafts to the doorway, the capitals carved with animals fighting and men on horseback charging one another. The voussoirs give three orders: the inner order is a thin roll with leaves, but the middle order is a thicker roll for a dozen sunken medallions carved with figures showing the bestiaries from which the Middle Ages took their garbled ideas of natural history, making comparisons between man and animals – a hare drinks a toast to a partridge; a monkey rides a goat, with a rabbit over his shoulder; a bear or dog plays a harp; an ass gives water to a stork; two dogs drink from a pot; and there are other fantasies. The outermost order, immediately inside the dripstone, shows scenes from life on the manor estate – perhaps that of Adam de Port, who held the Barfreston estates at that time. Whether by accident or design, the topmost figure is the villein on whom the whole system ultimately depended; among the other figures are the minstrel, the cellarer and the steward.

The subjects seem to be basically the signs of the Zodiac and the labours of the month on the outer row of medallions, but there are warriors at the bottom of each side, and Samson one up on the right.

The blocked-up N door is also carved, but far less elaborately. Around the exterior there are 76 corbels carved with animal and human heads, and these alone would be outstanding anywhere. There are also some mass-clocks scratched on

South door, Church of St Nicholas, Barfreston

the columns of the S door. The church is closed but the interior is something of an anticlimax.

On the northern outskirts of Shepherdswell, the Way crosses the railway at a level crossing and goes up a track and then due S across fields, past a timber stable, across a footpath and then down another track to come out by the village school. The triangular village green and pub lie just to the right, but we cross the road and continue SE past the churchyard, and then across the fields E to another section of disused mineral railway to Coldred Court and the tiny Church of St Pancras, isolated from Coldred village ½ mile/800m to the SW. This Saxon-Norman type church is one of the two Kent churches dedicated to this saint – we have seen the other at Canterbury – and stands on a large (3 acres/1.2ha) earthwork, forming a ruin on the N and W sides of the churchyard.

From the crossroads beside Coldred church, the Way goes NE through Waldershare Park, 540 acres/218ha of fields and woods, famous for its beeches, Spanish chestnuts and fine avenue of limes.

As you leave the woodland behind at the Coldred crossroads you can see across the fields to your right on the edge of a large wood in the Park, a gargantuan plum-coloured brick Palladian Belvedere, erected by Sir Robert Furnese, who seems to have suffered from a touch of megalomania. The Belvedere is a square tower, roughly twice as high as it is square, built in 1725–7 at a total cost of £1703 7s 4d. There are large Venetian windows in Gibbs surrounds on the N and S sides, and round-headed Ionic windows on the E and W, and a balustrade in carved Portland stone runs round the top.

The path goes straight across two large fields, through the growing crops, heading for the NW corner of the wood, and then the house comes into view. The large, brick, Queen Anne mansion was built for Sir Henry Furnese, son of a Sandwich merchant who made his fortune in London. Furnese bought the estate in 1705 and died in 1712, having all but completed his new house, which was built after a design of Inigo Jones in the reign of William III. The house was gutted in 1913, but subsequently refitted. The main front of the house, with giant Corinthian columns, faces the garden to the SW, but we can only see the W front as we come across the Park. Formerly the seat of the Earl of Guildford, it is now divided into flats.

After passing the mansion, the Way follows a drive E and NE then at a fork in the drive goes across a field into the churchyard of the isolated Church of All Saints. The flint church was almost entirely rebuilt in 1886 and as such it has nothing much to offer, but it is now disused and liable to fall into decay. This would be a scandal, because it is the monuments which one comes to see, and they should be preserved. The church key can be obtained from the vicarage next door.

The monuments are housed in identical-looking red-brick

The Belvedere in Waldershare Park, from Coldred

chapels, one on each side of the chancel. The S chapel was built c.1697 first in English bond, then in Flemish bond, and the N chapel was built in c.1712.

The S chapel contains a huge tomb with two colossal figures of the Hon. Peregrine Bertie and his wife Susan, 4th daughter and co-heir of Sir Edward Monins (d.1663). It was their heirs and trustees who sold the estate to Sir Henry Furnese in 1705. Sir Edward Monins himself (d.1602) lies in the N chapel, as does Susan Bertie (d.1697). His monument is a black and white architectural tablet, an open pediment on Corinthian columns; hers is a tomb-chest behind original iron railings, with reclining figure.

The N chapel contains the masterpiece of Thomas Green of Camberwell, a massive three-tiered edifice to Sir Henry Furnese (d.1712). It almost touches the roof of the chapel and leaves no room for anything else. It uses four kinds of veined marble. The main base tier has diagonal angle plinths on which sit life-size mourning females, and the next stage has cartouches (tablets with ornate frames) of arms with little boys

Waldershare House

standing at each corner. At the top urns are balanced on colossal volutes (spiral scroll, one of the component parts of an Ionic column), with cherubs' heads fixed to the bulging curves of each volute. The whole is a spirited composition, the allegorical figures of grief at the bottom and joy at the top. It is so overwhelming in this small church that one cannot fully appreciate how very fine it is.

Waldershare Park to Dover 4½ miles/7.2km

Having crossed the A256 Dover-Sandwich road, the Way goes S of Minacre Farm to a road which leads you into Ashley village. Where the village street makes a sharp bend left to East Studdal, you go straight ahead, on a path going SE over a hill and to the Roman Road just N of Maydensole Farm.

The Way joins the Roman Road from Richborough and Dover and follows it due S for 3 miles/4.8km to the outskirts of Dover. Just S of the crossroads at Maydensole the Way leaves the road by forking L on a RUPP and goes E of Cane Wood to cross another road, and then through the small hamlet of Pineham. The Roman Road then becomes a good track, still a RUPP, heading up the gentle slope of the Downs for a good 1 mile/1.6km to a height of about 400ft/122m, crossing the new A2 Dover Bypass.

The track drops down suddenly into Dover, with a view of the castle and harbour ahead and the clocktower of the Duke of York's Royal Military School to the L. The track follows the side of a dry valley, becoming a metalled lane, dropping steeply down 200ft/61m, across a railway line and alongside Charlton Cemetery, to end at Old Charlton Road on the outskirts of Dover.

This is the end of the Canterbury Loop section of the North Downs Way. To visit the castle, go straight across Old Charlton Road and up the steps opposite, to take a sunken path between two other cemeteries, which turns S to emerge beside the main gates of Connaught Park. Turn into the park, which is charmingly situated on the hillside with delightful views over the town and the Western Heights. Follow the main path up past the aviaries and turn right along the woodland walk, overlooking the lawns, flower beds, and tennis courts. The path runs along the level with a view of the castle ahead, and you emerge from the park where Connaught Road meets the A258 Castle Hill Road. Dover Castle rises majestically ahead, and you can enter it by the Constable's Gate.

Bibliography

Author	Title	Publisher
Hilaire Belloc	The Old Road	Constable 1904
R. H. Goodsall	The Ancient Road to Canterbury	Constable 1960
Henry Fearon	The Pilgrimage to Canterbury	Associated Newspapers
Donald Maxwell	The Pilgrims' Way in Kent	Kent Messenger 1932
D. J. Hall	English Medieval Pilgrimages	Routledge & Kegan Paul 1966
Sean Jennett	The Pilgrims' Way	Cassell 1971
Ronald Hamilton	Summer Pilgrimage	P. & G. Wells Winchester 1973
Mark Chapman	Walking on the North and South Downs	Robert Hale 1985
Keith Chesterton	A London Countryway	Constable 1981
J. H. N. Mason	A Guide to the Weald Way	Constable 1984
D. J. Allen and P. R. Imrie	Discovering the North Downs Way	Shire 1980 (Aylesbury)
H. D. Westacott and M. Richards	The North Downs Way	Penguin 1983
John Hawell	Walk the North Downs	Bartholomew 1987
Denis Herbstein	The North Downs Way	H.M.S.O. 1982
Alan Charles	Exploring the Pilgrims' Way	Countryside Books (Newbury) 1990
Neil Curtis	National Trail Guide – North Downs Way	Countryside Commission/ Ordnance Survey/ Arum Press 1992

Index